BECOMING THE NEWS

BECOMING THE NEWS

HOW ORDINARY PEOPLE RESPOND TO THE MEDIA SPOTLIGHT

RUTH PALMER

Columbia University Press
New York

Columbia University Press
Publishers Since 1893
New York   Chichester, West Sussex
cup.columbia.edu
Copyright © 2018 Columbia University Press

Library of Congress Cataloging-in-Publication Data

Names: Palmer, Ruth, 1979 January 16–
Title: Becoming the news : how ordinary people respond to the media
spotlight / Ruth Palmer.
Description: New York : Columbia University Press, 2017. | Includes
bibliographical references and index.
Identifiers: LCCN 2017011442 (print) | LCCN 2017027153 (ebook) |
ISBN 9780231544764 (electronic) | ISBN 9780231183147 (cloth : alk. paper) |
ISBN 9780231183154 (pbk.)
Subjects: LCSH: Reporters and reporting. | Attribution of news. |
Journalists—Interviews. | Journalism—Objectivity.
Classification: LCC PN4871 (ebook) | LCC PN4871 .P36 2017 (print) |
DDC 070.4/3—dc23
LC record available at https://lccn.loc.gov/2017011442

Columbia University Press books are printed on permanent
and durable acid-free paper.
Printed in the United States of America

Cover design: Noah Arlow

FOR MY PARENTS,
ANN AND CHARLES PALMER

CONTENTS

PREFACE

As a college student I had a summer job delivering electric fans to the poor in Austin, Texas. I believed in what I was doing: fans in that dripping heat could save lives. The fan drive was run by a nonprofit and, thanks to a scrappy public relations person, it had received a fair amount of media coverage. I was happy to hear the project plugged on the radio because it brought in donations and volunteers, but I also found it thrilling. I remember sitting up straight when the PR guy said a local disc jockey had invited one of us down to the station. All my friends would hear me! Sure, I'd be nervous, but I'd be famous! The executive director took the gig. Fame slipped away.

My turn finally came when I was told a reporter from the *Daily Texan*, the University of Texas student newspaper, wanted to do a story on us, and could she join me on one of my deliveries the next day? This was it. Not the journalistic big leagues, but you had to start somewhere. I wasn't a UT student, but I knew a lot of folks who were, and a lot of people—neighbors, former teachers, my parents' friends—who picked up that paper on campus. I felt nervous and excited. I practiced being articulate about the cause.

I felt both jittery and disappointed when I met the reporters. They looked like regular college students. But there were two: a reporter and a photographer. That felt special. Someone suggested that, instead of handing the fan to the person who answered the door, I might go inside and set it up. I didn't normally do that, but okay. The photographer took pictures and the reporter asked a few questions. It was over very quickly. I remember thinking I hadn't completely blown it but that somehow the whole thing had not gone quite the way I had anticipated; like I had expected to be the director of the scene but wound up just a minor player.

Then I waited. Finally, a neighbor brought a bunch of copies for my parents, who "must be very proud." They were. But I stared at the front page with a mix of horror and fascination. There I was, face enormous in mealy newsprint, neck divided cruelly by the fold. Thick arms, thin lips, pursed in concentration. So this was what I really looked like. I knew that must be me, but I didn't recognize myself. And the quotes—the quotes were the worst part. Yes, I had sort of said those things. The gist was there, but the grammar was off. I sounded weird. Not like me. Somehow the article got everything and missed it all at once. People would think I was an idiot.

They didn't. They posted the article at work. Friends called with congratulations. My parents' pile of newspapers grew. I felt both sheepish and proud. Between the praise and my inability to pinpoint exact errors, I didn't feel I could complain or ask for a correction.

Copies of that article are still stashed somewhere in my parents' house, probably the attic. It would be hard to find it now. That was the year 2000. In some ways, "making the news" has changed since then. In many ways, it is the same.

ACKNOWLEDGMENTS

Thank you to the eighty-three people who shared their stories with me for this study. Your generosity inspired me throughout this process and I continue to learn from you.

Thank you to Columbia University Press, especially Philip Leventhal, my editor, and the anonymous reviewers for their time and helpful feedback.

I'm grateful to my professors at Columbia who supported this project from the beginning. Many thanks to Todd Gitlin, whose own work inspired this study, for his tireless guidance and for helping me believe it could be a book. I am indebted to Michael Schudson for invaluable advice on this project when it was in its infancy, and as I moved it to adulthood. My deepest gratitude to Andie Tucher for guidance intellectual, literary, and personal, and for crucial feedback at key moments. Many thanks to Robbie McClintock for modeling a life of inquiry and teaching.

A special thanks to Frank Moretti, a close mentor and friend throughout my time at Columbia. He died before this book was finished, but his influence is everywhere in it.

Thanks to my friends and colleagues from Columbia Journalism School's PhD in Communications Program. I especially want to single out Danielle Haas and Rasmus Kleis Nielsen, who gave invaluable feedback at every stage of this project. Many thanks as well to C. W. Anderson, Soomin Seo, and Katherine Fink. They all read sections of this work and were exceptionally generous with feedback, encouragement, and companionship.

Thanks, too, to Sarah Stonbely, Katherine Brown, Lucas Graves, Kirsten Lundberg, Annie Rudd, Julia Sonnevend, Ri Pierce-Grove, Laura Forlano, Zohar Kadmon Sella, Colin Agur, and Ben Peters for contributing in ways direct and indirect with their ideas and friendship. Thanks to the Mellon Interdisciplinary Fellows Program at Columbia's Interdisciplinary Center for Innovative Theory and Empirics (INCITE) for critical funds, work space, and community.

I am deeply grateful to my colleagues at IE University in Segovia and Madrid for giving me space, ideas, and just enough pressure to see this project through, especially Vincent Doyle, for research Wednesdays and sanity; Juana Abanto, María José Ferrari, Javier González, Pamela Rolfe, David Álvarez, Diana Gómez, Nuria Santana, and Mónica Bartolomé, for ongoing intellectual and personal encouragement; Begoña González Cuesta, Luisa Barón, Miguel Ángel Gabaldón, and Iôna de Macedo, for gracious leadership and logistical, moral, and financial support.

For perspective, companionship, and good cheer, thanks to my close friends Julia Walker, Emily Alexander-Wilmeth, Steve Eichinger, and Jenny Rhodes in New York; Colleen McMillon, Beth Schmierer, Laura Guijarro, and Almudena González del Valle in Madrid; Emily Yamada in Seattle; and Mollie Webb in St. Louis.

And thank you to the Palmer clan—Ann, Charles, Stephen, Ann S., Benjamin, and Henry—for their love and support, and my education.

BECOMING THE NEWS

1

VICTIMS OF THE PRESS?

Like the credulous widow who wakes up one day to find the charming young man and all her savings gone, so the consenting subject of a piece of nonfiction writing learns—when the article or book appears—his hard lesson.

—JANET MALCOLM, *THE JOURNALIST AND THE MURDERER*

It's fun to be in the news!

—MARCEL

It's like a death.

—BETH

The phenomenon of appearing in a news story is, in purely quantitative terms, extremely common. Thousands of ordinary Americans wind up in print and broadcast news every year, as witnesses, experts, criminals, victims, heroes, community representatives, and freaks. Qualitatively speaking, going through the process of *becoming* a news subject is complicated and can be profound. It often involves a series of socially and psychologically significant events, starting with proximity to meaningful, even life-altering, occurrences. Witnessing a crime, surviving an accident, and saving a life would all be heady experiences even if they went unreported. Once they are identified as newsworthy, however, subjects must navigate complex interpersonal exchanges with journalists. They then have the strange experience of seeing themselves represented in a public medium before a large audience. Ultimately, they must manage the hard-to-anticipate effects of that publicity. As a whole, riding the wave of news subjecthood can affect how people see and understand journalism, but also how they think about their own identities, reputations, and place in the world. This book is about what that feels like.

Given the essential role ordinary people play as subjects in the products and processes of journalism, it is odd that their perspectives have not been the focus of systematic study before. From the audience's point of view, ordinary people named and featured in the news are a constant presence. They are essential translators of information about the world. Without them, it would be hard for us to understand what happened on that college campus, on that battlefield, or in that street half a world away. And yet, despite their hypervisibility in the product, we usually know little about the ordinary folks we see in the news. They blend so seamlessly into news products that we often take them for granted. People of great interest today are completely washed under in the churn of the news cycle tomorrow. Only rarely, something may catch our attention—perhaps someone caught in a vulnerable moment—and make us wonder what went on behind the scenes. Is it right for journalists to swoop in and press a bereaved mother for a quote? What was she thinking? Did they do justice to her story? Did she regret it later?

For reporters, human subjects are essential for getting the job done. Despite the many changes the industry has seen in recent years, talking to eyewitnesses and interviewing subjects remain some of the core tasks of reporting. There are no signs that is changing. Online publication and cutthroat competition ratchet up pressures on journalists to provide fresh content, which means they must continually recast the product with real-life characters. Those characters provide essential information to reporters, who usually show up after events have already occurred, cannot be experts in everything, and are not supposed to speculate about citizens' opinions or include their own. Even when putting people in a news story might not be technically necessary—in, say, a story on economic trends—they clearly make stories more digestible for audiences. Remove the unemployed person and the business owner, and that job numbers story would be flaccid, confusing, and dull. And yet, for all they interact with news subjects continually, journalists often know little about whether their own subjects felt a news story did them justice, or whether that coverage had any subsequent effects on their lives.

When I was a Ph.D. student studying the sociology of journalism, I was also struck by the absence of journalism subjects' perspectives in the academic literature. We knew a lot about how journalists worked and about news products; somewhat less about news audiences; and almost nothing about the views and opinions of the many ordinary citizens who interacted with journalists and saw their own stories reported in the news. Just as they are in journalism itself, news subjects are absolutely central to journalism studies; it was their own *voices* that were strangely absent. So my colleagues and I debated what constituted an ethical relationship between journalists and their subjects and analyzed how different events and social groups were portrayed in news products. We critiqued the shortcomings in how people were represented in those products; we were indignant on their behalf. In other words, we talked a lot *about* the citizens represented in the news, but we never talked *to* them. Why had they agreed to speak to reporters in the first place? What did they think of the journalists who interviewed them—and what did it feel like to be interviewed? Just how common was it for subjects to feel a "shock of nonrecognition" when they saw themselves in the news?[1] Did they feel news coverage helped them or hurt them in the end?

I decided to find out. From 2009 to 2011 I interviewed eighty-three people who had appeared in newspapers in the New York City area or a mid-sized city in the western United States that I call West City. Not celebrities or public figures, participants were all private citizens who had popped up in the news for different reasons, some quoted as people-on-the-street or consulted as experts, others featured in stories on trends, issues, or events. We met to discuss in-depth their whole experience "making the news" and what that experience meant to them. They described the events and issues that brought them to the attention of reporters in the first place, their interactions with journalists, their assessments of the resulting news coverage, and any effects it had on their lives. In this book I chronicle their stories and outline the main patterns that emerged in how they made sense of their experiences interacting with journalists and seeing themselves represented in the news.

In some important ways news subjects' perspectives are different from those of other members of the public. They interact more closely with journalists than most citizens do on a daily basis. Since their own names, words, and images are on display in the resulting news stories, they are also more personally implicated in those stories than members of the public usually are. Understanding how people experience and understand journalistic processes from this unique vantage point is interesting for its own sake. Their experiences with news production are often very meaningful to subjects themselves and have practical and ethical implications for journalists and those who study them.

But as nonjournalists who get a brief, intimate look at how the news gets made, ordinary news subjects can also provide rich qualitative data about public opinion of the press. Those insights would be interesting even at a less turbulent moment in journalism's history, but this is a particularly compelling time to study how citizens think and feel about journalism. I conducted this study before the U.S. presidential election of 2016. For over a decade, digital tools, tight competition, and increasingly fragmented audiences had already been changing the way news was constructed and consumed. The authority of mainstream media was already widely perceived as under threat. The presidential campaign of 2016 and its outcome provide further evidence of those trends. Public opinion of the mainstream news media is now at an all-time low—and it was low before.[2] Anti–mainstream media rhetoric in the campaign clearly resonated with wide swaths of the American public. All these factors raise the stakes for understanding how the American public thinks about and relates to mainstream journalism. News subjects' stories about what appearing in the news meant to them are a window into what journalism means to people more broadly—what they value about it, and how they believe it can help or hurt people like themselves.

WHAT "MAKING THE NEWS" MEANS TO NEWS SUBJECTS

My central argument in this book is that ordinary news subjects' experiences, varied as they are, follow a consistent pattern: subjects gradually give up control over their stories to journalists, only to be held accountable by the public for how they are represented in the news. Unlike public figures, who have resources that can help them influence journalists, ordinary folks who become the focus of mainstream news attention usually have little power in their relationships to journalists and media outlets. That does not mean that all journalists take unethical advantage of that inequality, nor that all subjects have negative experiences when they are named in news stories. But their relative lack of clout does affect ordinary news subjects' choices throughout the news production process, and how they make sense of their experiences overall.

I argue that even in today's digital environment, appearing in the mainstream news is still an important way citizens can communicate with a broader community about events and issues. Journalists can provide credibility, status, and a guaranteed large audience that many citizens do not feel they can get any other way. However, to access those benefits, subjects must relinquish control to journalists over how their stories are told to the public. That is a big risk, since news stories have a great deal of credibility with their audiences: whether subjects themselves feel the news coverage is accurate or not, they will have to deal with the consequences of many people believing it. If news coverage portrays them as socially deviant or otherwise morally unfit, the ensuing stigma can be profound and enduring. And yet for many potential subjects, cooperating with journalists is still a bargain worth striking. The benefits of addressing, or simply displaying oneself to, a large news audience can be so great that many subjects conclude they are worth the risks of being misrepresented or having to deal with negative repercussions.

From news subjects' point of view, the news production process begins with their association with a trigger event or issue, the nature of which influences everything that comes afterward in the process. In some cases (plane crashes, terrorist attacks, family tragedies) the trigger completely overshadows the subsequent coverage in the subject's life. In many cases, however, subjects have goals they hope to accomplish by speaking to reporters about the trigger. Most potential news subjects are aware—at least on an intellectual level—that when they agree to speak to journalists they are giving up control over how they will be represented in the product. In that sense, at least, they have agency and are not victims.

And yet at the interview stage many subjects find that their efforts to control their own stories begin to flounder. They rely on oral and behavioral cues from journalists to anticipate how those journalists plan to frame the story, and they adjust their own behavior accordingly. But even the most media-savvy subjects usually realize at this stage that they have limited influence over how reporters will ultimately represent them.

For many subjects, the moment of truth is, of course, the moment when they confront the coverage. Here two important themes emerge. First, subjects judge the accuracy of that coverage on a different scale from journalism professionals. For subjects, what matters is whether errors and other facets of their representation adversely affect their goals and reputations. Subjects can be quick to dismiss even seemingly grave errors of fact if they appear to be nondamaging. Second, errors or no, seeing oneself in the news is a singularly odd business, often more emotional than rational. Interviewees described a range of emotions—titillation, embarrassment, and existential angst, among others. Those feelings were usually linked to their growing realization that a convincing version of themselves, generated by someone else, was circulating in public, beyond their control.

Repercussions of appearing in a news story can range from the mundane, such as receiving congratulatory messages, to the existential, such as the questioning of one's very identity. Of these, increased status was one of the most common effects, even when the depiction of subjects was not celebratory or even particularly flattering. On the other hand, the subjects who suffered most were those depicted for wrongdoing, or in a light that led audiences to question their moral worth. In those cases, interviewees described in detail what it felt like to be truly stigmatized. Today, the speed and reach of online media often exacerbate the impact of stigma, status, and other repercussions that news subjects must manage.

The core narrative of this book, then, in some ways challenges the conventional view that the authority of mainstream news media is in wholesale decline. Certainly, social media tools now allow everyone to publish material. Competition has grown, audiences have self-segregated, and no journalist today has the reach or authority of a Walter Cronkite. The election of 2016 now seems like a continuation, if not a culmination, of all these trends. But I found that the mainstream news media remains a significant and, in some ways, unique pathway for private citizens to relate to the broader public. The rare combination of credibility, status, and prominence that being mentioned in mainstream news affords is all the more valuable (and potentially damaging) to many individuals today because it can help them stand out from the crowd in a teeming media landscape. While some organizations and individuals may feel they can achieve all this on their own via social media, my interviewees generally did not believe they could. From their perspective, journalists remained powerful gatekeepers because they had the authority and resources to bestow many benefits and frame individuals' stories in ways that could have long-term repercussions for them.

Interviewees interlaced their stories about becoming news subjects with comments about the news media more broadly. Many made sense of their recent firsthand experience by describing it in relation to what they embraced as the conventional wisdom about the news media, or ideas they had developed about it as consumers: the journalist who interviewed them was, or was not, like those they had seen on television. Between interviewees' particular stories and their comments about journalism in general, an underlying narrative emerged about how they felt the news media related to citizens like themselves. That narrative usually predated their experiences as news subjects, but those firsthand experiences—whether they had ultimately been positive or not—brought the larger narrative into sharper focus, for them and for me. Simply put, interviewees felt that there was something uneven in the way the news media related to the people; that journalists had a disproportionate amount of power in their relationship to citizens and would bear few repercussions should something go wrong. That reporters did not always take unethical advantage of that power was a welcome discovery for some interviewees, but it was not nearly as salient to them as the overwhelming feeling that they always *could*.

The idea that the news media hulks over the citizenry, at times providing individuals with special opportunities, but with the power to do great damage to them as well, felt true to interviewees on a deep level. They felt like David, to journalism's Goliath. That narrative is strikingly at odds with how journalists and journalism institutions normally characterize their relationship to the public. In that view, members of the news media work and fight on behalf of the people. *They* are David, facing down the powers-that-be in the name of the citizens. In the conclusion to this book, I take up these two competing narratives once more and explore what they can teach us about widespread distrust of mainstream journalism today.

AN OLD- AND NEW-MEDIA PHENOMENON

To understand why appearing in the news continues to be so significant to people, even at a time when managing mediated representations of ourselves is our daily bread, it helps to tease out four fundamental features that distinguish being mentioned in the news from other forms of mediated public display. While other types of public representation share one or more of these features, few if any have them all. The combination matters a great deal in our overflowing media environment because it makes mainstream news stories, and those who appear in them, stand out from the crowd when doing so is a blood sport.

First, unlike news *sources*, who may speak only "on background" to journalists and never see their names in the resulting story (more on the difference below), subjects, by definition, *appear in a news story*, usually by name. That means news subjects always have something personal on the line because their names, images, or descriptions will be put on display in the product, whether they directly interact with journalists or not. As a result, news subjects must deal with the material, emotional, and psychological effects of seeing themselves and being seen in the resulting news story.

Second, setting aside op-eds or other citizen submissions (which were not included in this study), contemporary mainstream news subjects *do not write their own stories* but instead provide material that is then filtered through a series of decisions made by reporters and editors. Submitting to representation by someone else distinguishes news subjecthood from many forms of self-publication now available to individuals using digital tools. Scholars now generally accept that the news does not hold up a plain mirror to the world but rather a kind of funhouse mirror.[3] News subjects experience the funhouse mirror firsthand as their images, comments, and stories are mediated, often heavily, by journalists and journalistic processes.

At the same time, being plucked from the crowd for full journalistic treatment *takes place before a large audience*, the third feature that defines this experience. While self-publishing online dangles the alluring possibility of fame before us, a news appearance promises it, albeit in modest form. For many of my interviewees, their news appearance was the moment in their lives when they had been noticed by the most people.

Subjects imagined that those large audiences not only saw the coverage but also believed it. Based on their subsequent interactions with people who had seen them in the news, this usually proved to be true. This is the final factor that defines news subjecthood: being represented by a journalist in a mainstream news product means being represented *in a product that makes authoritative truth claims*. Even if those truth claims do not hold equal weight with everyone in the audience, this is not the same as being tweeted about, mentioned in an obscure blog, or depicted in another genre that does not have the imprimatur of an institutionalized news source. Subjects' reputations and opportunities are likely to be influenced by the coverage, whether subjects themselves feel it is accurate or not, because it appears in a genre and outlet that many in the audience are likely to believe.

Interviewees in this study used language like "I made the paper!" that may well sound distinctly old-fashioned to academics focused on more recent trends. In fact, one of the central findings of this study is that news subjecthood, even today, is both an old- and a new-media phenomenon. It teaches us as much about continuity in journalism as it does about change.[4] For many study participants, the most salient aspects of appearing in the news were not tied to digital innovations and continue to operate relatively unchanged from earlier eras: the publicity virtually assured by a mainstream news appearance, the uncanniness of seeing oneself in the news, the status or stigma bestowed—all these undoubtedly predate the internet and are central themes in the pages to come.

However, like many other forms of public display today, a news appearance is also a digital affair, and digital publication often magnifies these features. It increases potential audiences geographically and temporally. The legitimacy and status that can come from appearing in a mainstream news story are especially valuable currency in an environment where anyone can publish anything about oneself. Digitization also introduces new features, such as searchability, that can increase some of the benefits and risks of a news mention. Today, embarrassing or even reputation destroying articles no longer rot in the attic.

Another, less obvious trend that undoubtedly affects what it is like to be a news subject today has to do with how news content has changed over the years. Ordinary people have played a role in American news since the earliest American newspapers. Of course that role has changed a great deal over time, and a complete overview is beyond the scope of this book.[5] However, to understand what it means to be a news subject today, it helps to be aware that American journalism has become more interpretive over the past century or so. Scholars looking at changing trends in the form and content of news have identified a gradual shift toward longer, more explanatory newspaper formats and articles, and toward greater interpretation, or "mediation," by journalists in TV news.[6] By the 1990s the many small, event-centered snippets that characterized reporting a century before had gradually been replaced by longer stories that gave more extensive explanations for why things happened. They presented ordinary people not just by name (say, John Doe bit a dog yesterday), but rather as representatives of trends and demographic groups (perhaps: John Doe, a 58-year-old undocumented immigrant, bit the dog of his employer yesterday. It was the latest in a series of crimes committed by undocumented immigrants in the downtown area, etc.).[7]

The implications of these changing trends for potential and actual news subjects are profound. Today, a news subject will likely be cast as a representative of a given group and have his or her personal story explained in relation to broader trends. One imagines John Doe's experiences seeing himself represented in the two examples above would probably differ. In the former, he may contest the technical accuracy of the facts in the article. In the latter, however, he is playing a role in a larger saga of which he may not even be aware. It may well clash with his own interpretation of his experience. In other words, the space for journalistic interpretation and, therefore, what I refer to as "subjective errors"—omissions and other editorial choices that are not *technically* inaccurate—is obviously greater. As I discuss in chapter 5, these were, in fact, the kinds of errors that most bothered my interviewees when they saw how journalists had told their stories.

WHAT IS THE DIFFERENCE BETWEEN A SUBJECT AND SOURCE?

Journalism scholars have studied news sources extensively but news subjects far less. Why is that, and what exactly is the difference? The two categories overlap, but they are not identical. Technically, the difference hinges on whether the person is named in the news product. News sources are people who provide information to journalists but who may or may not be named in the published story. News subjects are people who are represented in the product but who do not necessarily speak directly to journalists.[8] By that definition, sources who speak "on background" to journalists and never appear by name in a published story are not subjects. Meanwhile, an accused criminal who does not speak to journalists but is nonetheless named in the news is a subject, not a source. I was primarily interested in

understanding how people react to the way they, themselves, were represented in the news and how that affected their lives. Since that is the crux
of the difference between source and subject, subject is the more accurate
term for this study.

But the difference also holds a key to explaining why the ordinary
people whose perspectives I explore in this book have not received more
academic attention. Scholars who study journalism usually analyze either
how journalists do their work or the content of the news. All other aspects
of the news ecosystem, including audiences, have simply received less attention. One consequence of the "newsroom centricity" of journalism
scholarship is that when scholars do focus on audiences and other aspects
of journalism, they tend to see them from the perspective of reporters and
editors.[9] The term "source," for example, is the term used by journalists.
The word emphasizes their essential role as fonts—sources—of information for reporters.

To journalism scholars, studying the role of sources in journalistic
work is essential because they play such a fundamental role in influencing
which stories journalists report and how they report them. Since sources
are usually looked at narrowly as people who provide information to journalists, most of what goes on in their lives before and after journalists show
up on the scene does not get studied at all. Instead, most research focuses
on which sources journalists use most, and to what degree those sources
influence journalists' choices about how to report the news. Since public
figures and spokespeople for the government and other big institutions
are the sources on whom journalists most rely, most academic studies
about sources likewise end up being about powerful public figures or their
representatives.[10] Scholarship on journalism thus ends up reproducing one
of the trends it most criticizes in journalism itself: it dedicates a disproportionate amount of space to the same old powerful sources, while voices
of ordinary citizens remain muted at best.

ARE NEWS SUBJECTS VICTIMS OF THE PRESS?

As noted above, when news subjects (as opposed to sources) are the focus
of research, scholars usually talk *about* them rather than *to* them. For example, one could argue that in many content analyses of news coverage

ordinary citizens actually play a starring role: they are the ones being counted and codified. But those studies almost never involve asking subjects themselves to give their input on how they have been represented, or to reflect on the processes that got them in the news in the first place—these are analyses of news *content*, after all. So scholars critique subjects' representations on their behalf. As a result, news subjects are implicitly cast as passive figures in the news process, if not outright victims.

The victim theme becomes more explicit, however, in studies of reporter-subject interactions. There, no one has done more to promote the idea that journalists habitually mislead their prey than *New Yorker* journalist Janet Malcolm, with her now-classic book *The Journalist and the Murderer*.[11] Still assigned frequently in journalism courses, the book tells the story of a convicted murderer deliberately misled by a journalist who was pretending to be his friend. Malcolm casts the murderer as the journalist's victim and, by extension, as a representative of all journalism subjects. Many journalism professionals know her oft-quoted opening lines about the journalist's role by heart: "Every journalist who is not too stupid or too full of himself to notice what is going on knows what he does is morally indefensible. He is a kind of confidence man, preying on people's vanity, ignorance, or loneliness, gaining their trust and betraying them without remorse."[12]

Tellingly, the second part of her opening salvo (the epigraph of this chapter), which is about consequences for subjects, is almost always left out.[13] Not all journalists and scholars agree with Malcolm's provocative claims, but they have been extremely influential. Scholars studying how journalists should and do relate to their subjects frequently take Malcolm's opening lines as their starting point and often find evidence to support her conclusions as they analyze professional texts, interview journalists, and even observe journalists in the newsroom.[14] Out of all the studies discussed here, subjects' own perspectives are most obviously relevant in these discussions about how journalists relate to subjects, and yet here, too, subjects themselves are almost never consulted.

In the rare cases when subjects have been asked their opinions, surprising tensions emerge between what scholars are looking for and what subjects actually say. As I discuss further in chapter 5, over the years, scholars have periodically surveyed news subjects in order to study journalistic accuracy. When subjects are asked to count and classify the errors in the stories in which they themselves are named, they do identify many errors.

And yet they rarely judge errors as truly severe, and many subjects who appeared in *inaccurate* stories still say they are not just willing but "eager" to appear in the news again in the future.[15] This does not seem like victim behavior. If many people are eager to be in the news again *despite the inaccuracies*, there must be something they get from the experience, some reward that matters more to them than whether journalists got all the facts straight.

To get a sense of what more in-depth, less newsroom-centric study of news subjects might yield, we can find some interesting examples in studies not of the news but of other media genres such as reality TV, and daytime TV talk shows. Scholars have used qualitative methods to explore not just whether subjects appearing in those genres felt they were accurately represented but what their motives were, and what their involvement with the programs meant to them overall.[16] Those scholars emphasize participants' experiences and perspectives as worthy of study in their own right, on their own terms. Subjects emerge as complex individuals whose agendas often conflict with those of producers, and who sometimes feel ill-used but also sometimes benefit from the experience. In other words, subjects have agency and are not easily characterized as mere victims. Similar studies of journalism subjects can help us move beyond the limited understanding of their role that a newsroom-centric approach provides.

WHAT STUDYING SUBJECTS CAN TELL US ABOUT JOURNALISM

ON JOURNALISTIC WORK

News subjects' experiences are fascinating and worth attention in their own right, but they can also provide interesting insights about journalism. Since the perspectives of ordinary people who become the focus of media attention have been broadly ignored in studies of journalistic work, almost anything they can say about their encounter with news production could potentially shed new light on those processes. Their perspectives on their interactions with reporters and photographers, for example, can inform ongoing practical and, especially, ethical concerns for journalists. What really are subjects' motives for speaking to journalists? How do they experience being questioned by reporters? Do they feel exploited or ill-used by journalists, and if so, when and why? The next three chapters explore these questions.

Subjects' interpersonal encounters with journalists are little altered by recent digital innovations, but subjects' insights about them take on new significance in these dynamic times for journalism. Scholars in recent years have talked a lot about journalistic "boundary work," referring to the debates and rhetorical tools journalists use to try to define and defend their profession from possible incursions from without.[17] In a digital environment, competition for legacy journalism has surged, a trend best captured by the oft-heard comment that "everyone's a journalist now." Journalistic boundary work has correspondingly crescendoed to a fever pitch. Debates about what constitutes an appropriate professional relationship between journalists and their subjects are central to journalistic boundary work, so they have, unsurprisingly, flourished in recent years as well.[18]

For example, websites *Gawker* and the *Daily Beast* claim to produce news but apply different criteria for newsworthiness from many legacy news institutions. Both have come under fire recently for publishing stories critics say compromise subjects' privacy but lack "real" news value. One of those cases culminated in a lawsuit, brought by one disgruntled subject and funded by another, that ultimately drove *Gawker* into bankruptcy and provoked still further debate about subjects' privacy.[19] Subjects' own perspectives about their interactions with journalists and journalistic processes thus add another dimension to these discussions, at a time when they are key sites of negotiation over how the field wants to define and position itself.

Subjects' reactions to how they are represented in the news product and the after-effects of news coverage on their lives can also inform ongoing ethical debates. I address those topics in chapters 5–8. While some aspects of news subjects' experiences are little changed by digital publication and circulation, the effects of appearing in a news story are, and often dramatically so. Deciding how to balance private citizens' rights to security and privacy against the public's right to know is an ongoing ethical challenge for journalists. The calculation today should be different from in the past because the ramifications of being named in a news story are different. News stories today adhere to subjects in web searches, can lead to cyber-harassment, and leave digital trails that are hard to erase. My findings about how news articles reverberate in the lives of news subjects in today's digital world can help inform those discussions.

ON NEWS AUDIENCES

Ordinary news subjects are also members of the general public that journalism presumably serves, so their insights can contribute to what we know about how readers and viewers receive the news, and what they make of it. In recent years, technical affordances have made it possible for audiences to create, share, and comment on news products online, sparking widespread discussion about the changing role of "the people formerly known as the audience."[20] As a result, some scholars have been heralding an "audience turn" in journalism studies—a growing interest in how ordinary people think about, feel about, and engage with journalism institutions, processes, and products.[21] As audiences flock to other sources and distrust of mainstream media escalates, it no longer seems sufficient to take the audience into account only implicitly, or pay homage to the public only in the abstract.[22]

The questions news subjects help us answer about audiences are not the traditional ones normally asked of them, about which news stories they read or watch. Examining journalism through subject's eyes more closely resembles the flip side of studying the "industrial construction" of audiences, or how producers of media think about their consumers.[23] Instead, we analyze how consumers think about producers. Interviews with news subjects thus uncover richly textured data on "lay theories" or "folk theories" about how journalism works and flesh out our understanding of public opinion of the press.[24]

While frequent surveys appear to have sewn up questions about how Americans feel about the press—not good—they leave many questions unanswered. Probing deeper issues, such as how citizens believe journalistic processes do and should work and what it really means to trust journalists, requires innovative qualitative methods.[25] One approach used in the social sciences to explore how people think about big, seemingly abstract institutions, concepts, and issues is to ask people to discuss concrete "episodes" in their lives in which those more abstract phenomena played a role.[26] My interviews with news subjects apply this method. Their anecdotes and commentary about particular journalists and news stories revealed a great deal about their general expectations and understandings of how (and how well) journalism functions. Those impressions are interlaced throughout the book and become the focus of the concluding chapter.

VICTIMS OF THE AUDIENCE?

News subjects can give us insights into news audiences in general, but their perspective is also unique. They are able to describe what it is like to *be consumed* as part of the news product and thus have an audience of their own, at a time of digital publication and frictionless online circulation. This leads me to a final point about what this phenomenon can tell us about journalism today. News subjects are key to making the news as we know it possible. As such, news producers and consumers are morally implicated in how they are treated in the process, just as we are morally implicated in the treatment of those who play key roles in other goods we produce and consume. If the process is inherently exploitative or victimizing, as the journalism studies literature tends to assume—or even if subjects just feel that way—we have a problem.

As we shall see, that is not always the case. News subjects often find the experience gratifying, even if the product is imperfect or their goals are only partially met. As my interviewee Marcel summed it up, under many circumstances it *can* be "fun to be in the news."[27] But one category of subjects raises serious concerns. One reason ordinary people wind up in the news is that they have deviated from the norm positively or negatively— our criminals, heroes, and oddballs. It would be nice if we always felt empathy for the individuals we see in the news, or at least gave them the benefit of the doubt. After all, we know that what we are seeing is not their complete story, and that news can be sensational, distorted, or just plain wrong. However, when we are faced with what appears to be social deviance in the news, we often feel more judgmental than empathetic. Online reader comments posted on news stories provide stark evidence of that tendency. Those comments can quickly devolve into ad hominem attacks and other forms of online and offline harassment of the people named in the articles.

That the news media play a role in publicly shaming and even terrorizing individuals is not new.[28] Today, however, audiences can join in via social media and actively participate by initiating, escalating, and sharing scandals, in extreme cases resembling a cyber mob.[29] The whole saga is archived online by default and tied to unfortunate subjects' names by search engines. While in the past, shaming by the news media could certainly damage a reputation, today that damage can be far easier to achieve and more enduring. All told, being named in a stigmatizing news article can be so traumatic that subjects may well conclude, as my interviewee Beth did, that making the news is "like a death."[30]

That our own role in news shaming can be so rabid and merciless is striking because, when we are asked to address journalist-subject relations in the abstract, often our sympathies tend toward the subject—these are "victims of the press," remember? Talking with news subjects can raise awareness about how ordinary citizens contribute to the creation of the news, but also how their lives can be affected by this process to which audiences actively contribute.

STUDYING NEWS SUBJECTS

I detail my methodology in a note on method at the end of this book, but a few remarks are in order here. Since the phenomenon of news subjecthood had been so little studied, it made little sense to use quantitative approaches to test existing theories in order to draw statistically generalizable conclusions. Those theories did not exist. It was clear that in-depth interviews were the best approach. Following what sociologist Kristin Luker calls the "logic of discovery," my goal was to identify patterns and categories relevant to the experience of news subjecthood—to provide a generative study for more focused future research of this vast terrain.[31]

Following a grounded theory-based approach, I proceeded inductively.[32] I began by contacting potential participants after seeing them mentioned by name in one of four newspapers: the *New York Times*, the *New York Daily News*, the *New York Post*, and the single daily newspaper that serves West City. When I reached out to them I did not know if they had been happy with their news coverage, or even if they had seen it; all I knew was what I had seen in the published story.

Because I did not know what categories and variables would prove most relevant to understanding subjects' experiences, initially I spoke to people of all ages and backgrounds who had played as many different roles, in as many different kinds of stories, as possible. My sampling became more purposive as I collected and analyzed data, and theories began to emerge. As it became clear that the type of news story and the subject's role in it were some of the most important variables in determining how subjects experienced news production processes, I increasingly prioritized including as much variety as possible in those areas. I spoke to a wide range of people who had played many different roles in many different kinds of news stories, until patterns came into focus that were consistently repeating in subsequent interviews—a stage sometimes called "theoretical saturation."

The final sample thus includes subjects who appeared in the news as people-on-the-street, experts, survivors, heroes, witnesses, criminals, activists, and subjects of human interest stories of all kinds. Some participants were quoted only once in one news outlet. Others were involved in ongoing stories. All participants had been mentioned in newspapers, but many had also appeared (usually for the same story) in other media, including television and radio. In those cases, we discussed their involvement with those other media as well. While I deliberately excluded public figures like government officials, prominent business leaders, and celebrities because being in the news was a commonplace for them, I did include small business owners, civic activists, and performers who were not household names; in other words, people for whom being named in the paper was still out-of-the-ordinary but not necessarily entirely novel. Other subjects had been in the news only once or twice before, if at all. In the pages that follow, all names are pseudonyms. I have concealed and, in some cases, slightly altered identifying details.

As I analyzed my data, I found myself returning repeatedly to James W. Carey's well-known ritual and transmission views of communication.[33] They play an important role in the coming chapters, especially when I explore subjects' reasons for wanting to appear in the news (chapter 2), and how subjects' reference groups responded to their moment in the spotlight (chapter 7). Along the way it also became clear that the phenomenon of news subjecthood encompasses interpersonal interactions (with reporters) as well a variety of psychological and social processes that fall outside journalism studies' usual purview. To understand them, I turn to several scholars and theorists whose work has been used to understand other mediated processes but who are not commonly used to understand journalism in particular. For example, to analyze the interview stage and the potentially stigmatizing effects of appearing in a news article, I use some of the less familiar texts of interaction sociologist Erving Goffman.[34] To un-ravel the more aesthetic and existential aspects of seeing oneself in the news, I turn to Roland Barthes's and Susan Sontag's work on photography, as well as Sigmund Freud's famous essay on "The 'Uncanny.'"[35]

While I was doing my fieldwork, interviewees and other scholars often asked if I would be talking to journalists as well, to "get their side of the story." Otherwise, they argued, I was essentially taking subjects' word for what happened. That is true: I am certain the reporters of some of the stories discussed here would dispute the claims made by their subjects. Still, the answer is "no," for two reasons. First, journalism scholars and journalists themselves do a lot of writing about how journalists think and work, in contrast to news subjects who are rarely given a voice at all. I felt my time would be better spent including more perspectives from news subjects than speaking to journalists. Second, this project explores subjec-tive experience. Its aim is not to verify in any objective sense what "actu-ally" happened in any of the scenarios described. For example, the relevant question is not whether a subject actually *was* deceived or betrayed by a reporter, but whether he or she *felt* betrayed, and why.

The focus of this study is also not on how different social groups—specific minority groups, for example—are treated differently by journalistic pro-cesses. No doubt they are. There is no reason to believe that pervasive systems of oppression fail to influence the processes and patterns I describe. I do highlight social differences occasionally when interviewees called attention to them, but these important issues warrant more focused study, and I hope they will get it.

That said, this study does provide the basis for cautious inferences about how marginalized groups might experience news production. Since I did not choose my interviewees to reflect any particular demographic, education level, ideological bent, or political affiliation, in the end they included people of all races and socioeconomic backgrounds, but the ma-jority were middle-class whites, with a high school education or above, between the ages of 26 and 55, living in urban or suburban areas. They were what sociologist Ann Swidler refers to as "mainstream," even "proto-typical" Americans.[36] In other words, they did not belong to the minority or marginalized groups we know to be most systematically underrepre-sented, misrepresented, and misunderstood by American mainstream institutions and structures. Quite the opposite, in fact: they were, in many ways, the default audience for whom many of these news products were made. As such, if my interviewees felt disadvantaged in their interactions with the news media—which they sometimes did—we can logically infer that members of more marginalized groups would likely feel even more so.

PLAN OF THE BOOK

My interviewees' stories varied in many ways, but one of the most consistent patterns I identified was the basic chronology of events. This book is designed to follow that chronology. When given the opportunity to talk to journalists, most subjects have reasons and objectives for doing so, which they weigh against the perceived risks of giving an interview (chapter 2). During the interviews that follow, subjects have an opportunity to present a version of the story they want to convey, but their limited experience and limited information about how journalists plan to frame their stories often complicate their efforts (chapters 3 and 4). When they finally see the coverage, subjects apply complex criteria to assess its accuracy while digesting more intangible feelings about being represented in this particular public forum (chapters 5 and 6). Then, whether they are happy with their representation or not, they must weather the public's response to it, which may boost their status or mark them as stigmatized (chapter 7). Subjects today must also contend with what it means to have their stories published online, easily shareable and likely searchable for many years to come (chapter 8).

For all their interactions may be the beating heart of journalistic production, reporters and their subjects do not understand each other particularly well. They play vital but essentially opposite roles in the production of news, and as such their differing agendas and perspectives make understanding difficult. Journalists ultimately control how subjects are represented and feel ownership over the articles and newscasts they produce. Subjects supply raw material for those articles and newscasts, disproportionately deal with the consequences of how they are represented in them, and never stop feeling that it is *their* stories being told.

That journalists and their subjects should have different perspectives and priorities is not necessarily a bad thing, but it can put them at odds when it comes to determining what is ethical and fair in reporting on the lives of ordinary citizens. In chapter 9, "Lessons for Subjects and Journalists," I summarize my main findings as a set of five key differences between how journalists and ordinary news subjects view the news process. I find that journalists and subjects fundamentally differ over (1) whether journalists or subjects are the rightful owners of news stories, (2) whether journalists primarily hold power to account or hold positions of power themselves, (3) whether it is appropriate for journalists to seek out subjects to fill in the blanks of prewritten stories, (4) what constitutes fair reporting of controversies, and (5) just how important the repercussions of news stories really are. Ultimately, I find that journalists are primarily concerned about following *processes* that will allow them to produce stories that are technically accurate and balanced, while subjects tend to be far more concerned with the *outcomes* of those stories—whether they capture subjects' experiences in ways that ring true to them overall, and whether the repercussions of those stories seem fair.

In the final analysis, many of my interviewees had good experiences interacting with journalists and were happy with the outcomes of those interactions. Almost all of them said they would cooperate with journalists again in the future. Even those who were *not* happy with the resulting news coverage said they would risk it again, in hopes of a better outcome. And yet whether they personally had positive or negative experiences making the news, interviewees tended to embrace a deeper narrative about the way journalism relates to ordinary people—the David and Goliath narrative mentioned above. According to that "deep story," on one side of a divide stand powerful people with access to a huge audience and resources to control how other people are represented to that audience.[37] On the other side stand citizens who do not have those resources themselves but instead depend on the powerful people and institutions who stand opposite them in order to address the masses.

That narrative—one of inequality and the constant *potential* for abuse, even if it is not abusive every time—permeated our conversations and flows as an undercurrent through this book. In the final pages I explore how that narrative may contribute to the long-welling distrust of the mainstream media that has gripped the country, and what it can teach us about how to rebuild that trust.

⸺ ∞ ⸺

It is hardly surprising that conclusions drawn from news subjects' insights and ideas about news processes should differ from those based on close study of the newsroom. My interviewees were seeing these processes from a completely different position, as journalism outsiders given a peek inside the news production process. The difference between how journalism scholars and news subjects use the phrase "make the news" captures the difference in their perspectives on news production well. Academic books about how journalists produce the news have titles like *Making News*, *Manufacturing the News*, and, more recently, *Making News at the New York Times*.[38] As those titles illustrate, from an academic perspective, journalists make the news. They apply methods, routines, resources, and values to construct it out of the stuff of the world. For a subject, to "make the news" is to be chosen by powerful gatekeepers for inclusion in an exclusive public forum. This is "making the news" like one might "make it" in Hollywood. It signifies a rare achievement in the face of adversity and overwhelming odds.

2

WHAT'S IN IT FOR THEM?

Weighing the Pros and Cons of Becoming a News Subject

ALEGRA: I was pregnant at the time and my baby didn't survive because
of it, so we felt that if we could at least get this out to one pregnant
mom and she alerts her gynecologist, you know, earlier than I did, and
is saved, then it's helpful.

For public figures and celebrities, engaging with the news media is
clearly part of the job; when we see them in the news we only rarely
question their motives. Private citizens, on the other hand, usually
do not *need* to speak to the press, and sometimes their motives for doing
so can seem downright inscrutable. Absent clear explanations for what
they are doing on our TV or in our newspaper, it can be tempting to chalk
it up to naïveté or self-interest: See that grieving mother surrounded by
microphones, getting grilled by reporters? Poor thing. Big mistake. She's
so upset. She must not understand what she is getting into. Or worse:
Maybe she's an attention seeker. In that case, she deserves what she gets.

Unflattering assumptions about news subjects' motives are common in
the literature as well. Both journalists and journalism scholars tend to
portray ordinary folks who wind up in the news as either short-sighted
and naïve for letting journalists take advantage of them or, worse, blinded
by self-interest and narcissism.[1] They rarely acknowledge that private citizens might have good reasons to speak to reporters—reasons that might

be practically and morally defensible, and quite possibly worth all the risks.

Subjects like Alegra challenge reductive assumptions about what drives subjects to engage with the news media.[2] Her decision to speak to the press was shaped by complex circumstances, as they often are. She had contracted a serious medical condition, which turned out to be far more dangerous for pregnant mothers than had been previously understood. She awoke from a coma to find she had lost her unborn baby. She was also surprised to find herself a local celebrity. While she was still unconscious, her mother-in-law had contacted reporters so they could alert the public about the dangers of the condition, and they had been following the story with great interest.

Right away journalists started calling to request interviews with Alegra herself. No fan of the spotlight, and still recovering from the trauma of losing her child, she considered turning down the requests, but she knew her story could help others avoid the same fate. If her illness had been caught earlier, her baby could have been saved. She agreed to give several national print and TV interviews, including one with the *New York Times*, after friends and family advised her that it would be a good way to get the word out. Reporters and camera crews came into her home, disrupting her physical therapy schedule and family life. One TV station pushed to see a picture of the baby she had lost, right up until the moment the story aired. All in all, the process was more upsetting and inconvenient than glamorous or fun, but she felt in the end it was worth it. She knew she might have helped a mom—even just one.

In this chapter I explore the hopes and fears interviewees said they took into account when reporters approached them and asked them to participate in a news story. The decision to speak to reporters is not a simple cost-benefit analysis—it is much messier and less rational than that.[3] It is also important to remember that my interviewees were speaking about their decisions with the clarity of hindsight. But that said, I asked them to try to explain the thought processes behind their decisions to speak to reporters, and many were able to articulate them in detail. Understanding their reasoning—or, better said, the way they explained their own reasoning back to themselves and articulated it when asked—is the first step toward comprehending how they experienced the subsequent stages in the news production process and what "making the news" ultimately meant to them.

Below I present a typology of the main motives and drawbacks they said played a role in their decisions. Many, like Alegra, had specific goals they hoped to achieve with news coverage, and nearly all their motives were related to the large size of the audience they associated with a news appearance. They were attracted to what they perceived as a rare opportunity to communicate with so many people at once. Meanwhile, the hard-to-predict repercussions that a news appearance might have on their objectives, reputations, and loved ones were by far their most common concerns.

Some of subjects' reasons for speaking to reporters had little to do with the content of the specific story in which they were asked to participate. Sometimes appearing in the news is just plain fun. But many were like Alegra: their decisions to speak to the press were inextricably tied to the events and circumstances that had led reporters to contact them in the first place — in their words, to "what the story was about." Thus I begin below with a brief discussion of these trigger events and issues. Triggers came first chronologically in subjects' encounters with the news process, usually preceding even the arrival of reporters. More important, however, they shaped subjects' interpretations of all subsequent stages in the news process, starting with whether and why they wanted to speak to reporters in the first place.

HOW TRIGGERS SHAPE WHAT IT MEANS TO MAKE THE NEWS

Stop anyone on the street and ask them if they want to be in a news story and you will likely hear some version of "Depends what it's about." The answer is so commonsensical it may surprise only journalism scholars. In our race to dissect how journalists construct the news, we sometimes downplay the role of real-life occurrences in that process.[4] Interviewees in this study, on the other hand, tended to reverse that emphasis. They did not think of their own contributions primarily as elements in a construction but first and foremost as grounded in real-life events, issues, or topics: a plane crash, unemployment, or climate change. We can think of these occurrences as triggers because, from subjects' point of view, they were what set the news production process in motion. Their own firsthand knowledge or insight about the trigger was the reason reporters had sought them out in the first place.

For complex stories there might be multiple triggers, and different people involved in the news process can have different ideas about what exactly the trigger is. Is the real trigger broad unemployment trends or a specific round of layoffs? As I discuss in later chapters, differences of opinion about triggers and how to frame them can lead to misunderstandings and conflicts between subjects and reporters. But the key point now is that subjects' entire experience with the news process will be inflected by what they believe the story to be about. Baldly put, one's experience being named in the news will be fundamentally different if it is for raping a child, saving a child, or losing a child.[5] I spoke with people who had lived through all three, and while many factors differed in their accounts, it was hard not to conclude that the most important one, the factor that most determined how their sagas "making the news" played out, was the trigger that set the whole process in motion.

Ruby's experience illustrates well how triggers can influence a subject's reasons for wanting—or not wanting—to speak to the press. She had been caught in the crossfire of a gang-related shooting near her home in Harlem. One minute she was walking home from the store with a bag of potatoes, and the next thing she knew, she was lying in the street with blood pouring from her leg. As she lay in the hospital, a *Daily News* reporter snuck past security to ask her some questions. She explained to me why she agreed to let him interview her:

RUBY: [forcefully, with indignation] Because it was a random gang shooting! And here I'm going to the store at three in the afternoon, and then I'm shot! And this has disrupted my life. And I'm thinking [NYC mayor] Bloomberg is downtown telling everybody the city is safe and he's building these stadiums and doing all of this stuff and it's not safe to walk the streets and I've lived in New York—this June it'll be forty-nine years—and I never felt afraid here before. But I'm constantly listening to him telling how safe it is. Being here in Harlem all these years, it was never a problem up in Harlem, until in the last year and a half.

Q: So you felt like people should know about this.

RUBY: Yes![6]

As Ruby forcefully explained, the shooting itself was not incidental but absolutely *central* to her decision to speak to the press. She interpreted the crime in the context of her ongoing life experience and broader social trends she felt strongly about. She interpreted the opportunity to speak to the press in that context as well: by speaking to a reporter about her own experience, she could call the public's and the mayor's attention to serious safety concerns in her neighborhood.

Like Ruby, many news subjects have already had a meaningful—sometimes intense—experience with the trigger by the time the reporter gets involved. In extreme cases, the trigger may be so overwhelming or traumatic that it temporarily eclipses everything else in a subject's life. Sometimes I struggled to get interviewees to talk about their interactions with the news media at all because they only wanted to talk about the trigger.

That was the case for several interviewees who had survived the plane crash in 2009 that came to be known as the "Miracle on the Hudson." A commercial jet had emergency-landed in New York City's Hudson River, and all on board had miraculously survived. The event was heavily covered by international media, and the survivors were besieged by reporters eager for firsthand accounts. One survivor, Albert, gamely answered my questions about reporters and news coverage, but when I asked him for his final thoughts he said, "Being in Flight 1549 outweighs being in the newspaper by a thousandfold."[7] Lesson learned: the crash not only loomed far larger in his memory than any news coverage of it ever could, it colored *everything* that came after it. The various survivors of the crash that I interviewed all had different reactions to the media attention, but on this key point they were unanimous: the dominant feature of all their experiences was having faced certain death and survived.

That subjects already have a relationship to the trigger by the time they are approached by reporters is most obvious when the trigger is a breaking news event like a plane crash or a crime. But even when citizens are stopped by reporters on the street to comment briefly on, say, a city council decision, they are being asked their opinion because presumably they have been, or will be, affected in some way. Subjects of human interest and trend stories are likewise contacted by reporters because they have some kind of expertise or experience with the issues in question, and subjects of profiles are mostly being asked to talk about themselves. In other words, almost by definition news subjects have a connection to what they are being interviewed about, so there is going to be baggage there. As I discuss below, whether interviewees considered speaking to reporters an opportunity they could not pass up, a risk worth taking, or just plain fun, the trigger and their relationship to it played an important role.

As deeply involved or highly invested in trigger events as subjects often are, they may not have much control over how those events play out. Some triggers, like surviving a plane crash or getting shot at random in the street, seem designed to prove how little control people have over the events in their own lives. And yet, looked at as the start of the news production process, subjects' engagement with the trigger prior to the arrival of journalists is the moment when they have the most control over their own version of the story. As soon as reporters show up with an intent to cover the trigger, some of the subject's control is already lost. Now the decision is whether to participate in a journalist's retelling of the story.

MOTIVES AND GOALS: WHY SUBJECTS WANT TO BE IN THE NEWS

Like many choices, the decision to speak to reporters is often as fueled by emotion and intuition as by tidy reasoning. Many variables come into play. Some interviewees recalled being so addled or elated by the trigger that they did not carefully think through their decisions to speak to reporters. Others said their feelings about the trigger *were* their reasons for wanting or not wanting to give interviews and left it at that. Some had mere moments to consider reporters' propositions; others had weeks or even longer to think them over and even consult their reference groups. But across these many variations, patterns emerged among the main pros and cons interviewees said they considered in the process. In this section I discuss the most-cited pros.

All of the pros discussed here are, at least to a degree, trigger-dependent. On the surface, sometimes subjects' reasoning may seem to have little to do with the specific story being reported. A number of interviewees told me that "being in the news is fun," which certainly seems to be a comment on the news process itself, not the underlying events being reported in a particular case. But a negative trigger can counteract that feeling completely. Being in the news is *not* fun when you have blood pouring from your leg or you euthanized your husband. But the first five categories below are what we could call trigger-determined goals, insofar as they are largely shaped by the underlying events and issues. The next two categories describe less trigger-defined reasons that subjects saw appearing in the news as an attractive opportunity. As is often the case, these categories are useful analytically, but in real life they overlap and intersect.

INFORMING THE PUBLIC

By far the most common reason interviewees said they agreed to speak to reporters was to comment publicly on an issue or topic. For some it was as simple as that: they liked the idea of expressing their opinion to a large audience. They felt they had a worthwhile contribution to make, usually because they had experience with the issue at hand or had studied it extensively. Other interviewees went a step further: they cared about the issue and hoped to use the opportunity to educate the public, combat misperceptions, mobilize public action, pressure power, or some combination thereof.

The experts and community activists I spoke to exemplify this category. They had dedicated a fair amount of time and energy—in some cases their whole lives—to a particular topic, so they felt well suited to address the public about it. Some spoke of it as an obligation or mission.

University professor Bella, for example, was contacted by several reporters, including one at the *New York Times*, to comment on a new video game related to her area of study. Her field hardly ever gets press attention, so she saw it as a great chance to influence public perception about the issue. She is literally one of the world's foremost authorities on the topic and cares passionately about it, so who better? As she explained:

> BELLA: I do strongly feel it's part of my calling and my mission to shape perception of [this subject]. . . . I've begun more and more to see that actually I have a job to do in whatever time is left, in helping people see this [topic] better, because it's been crusted over with misconceptions for centuries.[8]

Political and community activists expressed a similar drive. Norma, for example, was a Tea Party leader in her small town. She had never been political before, but in a short time she had embraced the movement and felt eager to educate the public about it. She seized the chance to cooperate with a *New York Times* reporter who had contacted her because, she said, "I think there's a lot of misconceptions about the Tea Party. And I was hoping that we could set some of that straight."[9]

Subjects who hoped to educate the public and correct misperceptions, like Norma and Bella, saw speaking to reporters as a rare opportunity because they felt they had no other way to address such a large audience. Even activists and educators who had been frenetically campaigning for their causes via other means said the mainstream media was a unique tool in terms of reach. Professors and specialists in many fields can probably relate: not everyone is eager to tune into one's blog about mitochondria or the *Iliad*, even though they obviously *should*. Those efforts can feel like preaching to the choir anyway. By contrast, a news article in even a small local paper goes out to masses of exactly the kinds of people who are hard to reach otherwise: those who are not already invested or well versed in the topic.

Some interviewees said they wanted to address a large audience for multiple overlapping reasons, including to educate the public about a social cause, and to pressure people in power to address it. Daniel, for example, hoped to call the public's and politicians' attention to specific policies he passionately felt were wrong and needed to be changed. A substance abuse counselor for at-risk youth in the Bronx, he jumped at the chance to explain to a *Daily News* reporter what his job had been and why his forced departure would have profound negative consequences for the community:

> DANIEL: The only reason I agreed to do that story was to bring light to the whole situation. To show people that they're lettin' people go that's good for these kids. In the South Bronx you gotta stand up, you gotta keep these guys on board. Mayor Bloomberg, Governor: we need help. Please help us! I wanted that to be the topic. Please help us.[10]

WITNESSING

Witnessing is closely related to awareness raising. The main difference for analytical purposes is the trigger: here the trigger is an event, not an issue.

In this category I include people who had been involved in crimes, ill-nesses, and accidents, and others who testified to reporters about family members or acquaintances who had been involved in such events. They were the types of news subjects whose motives can seem the most baffling when we see them in the news, because they are often visibly shaken or clearly suffering from loss or trauma. Understandably, some interviewees said that their ability to reason through the ramifications of speaking to the press was probably dulled by shock. But by the time they sat down to our interview, many were able to articulate their motives for telling re-porters about what they had seen.

Many said they wanted to bear witness for the same reasons people wanted to speak out about ongoing issues: to educate the public, correct misperceptions, and pressure for change. Several witnesses of crimes and other traumatic events, like Ruby the gunshot survivor, were quite eager to share their stories. They felt their experiences could help shed light on more widespread injustices, institutional failures, or troubling social trends they believed people should know about. As Ruby said, she had lived for forty-nine years in Harlem and *never* had crime been this bad; hopefully by telling her own story she could call the public's and policy makers' attention to escalating gang activity in the neighborhood.

In that same vein, I found that survivors of family tragedies—perhaps the category of subjects whose motives seem the most difficult to under-stand of all—actually had fairly simple reasons for speaking to the press: they hoped their stories could inform others, call attention to injus-tices, and spare further suffering. Alegra, the pregnant mother whose quote opened this chapter, is a perfect example of that. So is Lucy. She was initially hesitant to speak to reporters about her father's death. He had been given a diseased organ in a transplant operation and the error ulti-mately killed him. But she later concluded, "I'm so eager to share the story because I feel that it will help other people. . . . And I feel that prob-ably this could save lives."[11] Before her loss she had not realized that such errors could occur. She had taken no steps to study up so she could ad-vocate for a safe transplant for her father. Her story—and his—could help others avoid a similar tragedy.

I also spoke to several witnesses of deadly or life-threatening events in-volving strangers. The victims may have been unknown to them, but they still talked about feeling obligated to speak out about what they had seen. In some cases they were the only witnesses to the events, and they felt strongly that the truth should be known and documented for its own sake, and for the sake of the unfortunate people involved. Bradley described that feeling. He was one of only two people in a position to see what had really happened when a small airplane crashed near his local airport. He had taken his young son sledding at the airfield, when the plane suddenly plummeted to the ground, killing everyone on board. He was still disturbed by what he had seen when we spoke about it, but he explained that he had decided to speak to reporters after overhearing someone else give an inaccurate account to the police:

> BRADLEY: It wasn't like I wanted to be on the news. I heard this woman saying, "It sounded like it had engine trouble, it sounded like it was trying to land." And everything she was saying wasn't true. So one of the only reasons I was talking [to reporters] was like, let's get the story straight. That was the bottom line. . . . I mean, me and this other guy were the only ones that really, truly saw it beginning to end.[12]

Some family members of victims expressed a similar impulse. Although shocked and upset, they felt they knew their loved ones better than anyone else, so they should be the ones to tell the world about them. In a striking example of that, Liana spoke to a reporter at the police station about her teenage brother, who had been stabbed to death in a street fight just hours before. She explained that since her brother was a young black man, she worried people would assume he was a thug or a gang member. She was uniquely positioned to witness to his upstanding character before negative assumptions shaped the story:

> LIANA: I just felt that had they spoken to someone else they would've given them wrong information about my brother or about the incident. I felt it's better to be the front line and say, not what happened, but "this is the kind of person my brother was and the life he lived."[13]

Some witnesses, however, acknowledged less altruistic impulses. They described feeling a thrill at knowing they were the only people who had information others wanted, like the charge of knowing a piece of gossip others would be eager to hear. Deanne, for example, saw a woman attempt suicide with a small child in her arms. Even while she was giving press interviews she felt a creeping sense of discomfort—like she was helping to exploit a woman's private problems. At the same time, being one of the only witnesses was strangely titillating:

> DEANNE: So there was still part of me that was simultaneously repulsed by [talking to the press] but also kind of—yeah. I do think I was kind of drawn in to the whole thing. Like, yeah, this is a big story. I don't really know how to explain it, but it was again, "Okay, wow, you're right: I am an eyewitness. Like, I was one of the only two people who saw this happen." . . . And so, yes, there was a little bit of excitement, like, "Whoa, you wanna talk to me?" . . . And then there was still also that, "Oh, but maybe I shouldn't." Because, to be honest, my heart was heavy. So it was a weird feeling of, "My heart is really heavy. Having seen this." But there was a little bit of, I would even say, euphoria. Like, "Oh my god, you wanna talk to me? "Great!" It's kinda weird as I think about it, but both of those things existed for me.[14]

Cynics might argue that even selfless-seeming subjects were probably motivated—at least in part—by a thrill at knowing something otherwise unknown, or a desire for attention they would never admit. While that may be true in some cases, many people in this category were speaking about painful events that clearly still caused them pain when we spoke. Some, like Bradley, had not even seen the news coverage. In those subjects' cases, if publicity and attention had played a role at all, they were certainly not their primary motives.

PUBLICITY

On the other hand, publicity clearly *was* the primary motive for some subjects. They saw speaking to the press as an opportunity to promote a business, organization, event, or other personal venture. Publicity and awareness-raising overlap a great deal: people may start a business for the public good or want to drum up attendance at an event as an extension of their educational mission. But in general I use "publicity" to refer to those goals aimed at increasing turnout, profit, or name recognition. Even when their venture was not the main focus of an article, some interviewees said they had hoped to use the opportunity to get in a quick plug aimed at potential participants or clients. But having one's business *featured* in an article, as long as the topic was not controversial and did not cast the business in a very negative light, was like winning the lottery, publicity-wise.

Shannon won that lottery. She was on a date when she happened to meet an employee of the West City paper. After chatting briefly about the small business she owns, he asked if she might be interested in talking to a reporter about her work for a feature story:

> SHANNON: I did it because I knew that it would benefit my business a little bit, in the sense that it was prestigious. You know, to be featured, and to be able to kinda tell my story a little bit. So really, I'm a pretty private person, but ... I thought, "That's a really great piece of press for my business." You know, with all the competition here ... for my business, that was really the sole thing.[15]

Subjects like Shannon used speaking to reporters as an opportunity to engage in old-fashioned public relations. They could trumpet specific features of their business, bolster name recognition for their brand, and pump up their status since getting chosen to appear in the paper differentiated them from the competition. Sophie, who spoke to a reporter about an immigration rally she was organizing, summarized this perspective well. Under the right circumstances, she observed, "News is the cheapest, freest way of advertising."[16]

HELP WANTED!

A number of interviewees said they did not know exactly *what* they were looking for when they agreed to appear in the news—that was the whole point. They had a problem they were unsure how to fix but figured someone in the audience might rise to the occasion with a solution. It was a bit like crowdsourcing a dilemma but with a much broader reach than most citizens could hope to access via social media or other means at their disposal. I interviewed husband-and-wife team Jon and Jane in the ground-floor apartment where they run a small business, and they exemplify this category. The New York City Department of Buildings was threatening to shut them down owing to a zoning violation, a harrowing saga that had begun several months before. As Jane explained, "We were feeling—we are still feeling—rather desperate and in a really bad way, and pretty much with a good potential to be completely financially ruined, so it was pretty exasperating."[17]

Even with a lawyer's help, Jon and Jane were unsure how to protect their interests, so they called their plight to the attention of a customer, who happened to be a reporter for the *New York Times*. Within hours, one of his colleagues was interviewing them for a feature they hoped would unearth some kind of solution or assistance. I asked them to explain their intentions:

> JON: It was just generally, "Hopefully this will help." And I think, from reading a lot of other stories about similar things, just getting another one out there is good. Right?
>
> JANE: Yeah. No, we didn't have any specific agenda. . . .
>
> JON: Y'know, we're in this position, and we're all alone, and we're looking for—
>
> JANE: Help!
>
> JON: Help.

Other interviewees knew exactly what they needed but were looking for a person to provide it. I spoke with several unemployed people who were quoted or featured in articles about economic trends and related issues. All hoped their article, because it would be seen by so many, might lead to work or some other opportunity; being named in the paper was like having a "job wanted" ad placed in the paper on their behalf. Jessica, for example, was featured in the *New York Post* for holding up an eye-catching sign at a demonstration about the economy. She had the opportunity to explain her views on unemployment, and, more important, to let the world know she was looking for a job. As she said, "Being laid off, you just need to tell anybody and everybody."[18]

REPUTATION MANAGEMENT

Speaking to the press can also be a way to avert or address damage to one's reputation. As Jon explained, in addition to putting out a general cry for help, a news article about how his business was being unfairly persecuted by authorities could help preserve a hard-won reputation among his clients:

JON: I hated the idea of [city officials] coming here, closing us down, and us disappearing, and everybody wondering, "Where have they gone?" So I think it was a way of getting the message out to our customers and telling them, "We have this thing, and it's not our fault." . . . Y'know, I have a reputation that we've built over twenty-something years of being really honest and straightforward, available and all this stuff.

Jon and Jane saw their news appearance as a chance to head off potential reputational harm, but speaking to reporters can also be a chance to correct damage already done. Chris, for example, contacted the West City paper to request a follow-up article after his name was severely tarnished in the original. He had been accused of raping a minor at a party, a story that was reported in many local media outlets. His name and picture were everywhere. Enemies gloated, friends disappeared, and Chris spent a month in jail. Then the girl admitted she had made the story up.

At first Chris hesitated to contact the media for a follow-up article. He was eager to put the whole episode behind him. But with encouragement from his mother and lawyer he decided to try to correct the public record, for himself and his family. He explained, "[The follow-up coverage] clears my name and wipes off the slate. It tells the whole world that you're an innocent man."[19] As I discuss in chapter 8, the persistence of articles online today can complicate efforts to wipe the slate clean. But Chris saw his follow-up article as an essential first step.

SOCIAL PRESSURES: ENCOURAGEMENT FROM REFERENCE GROUPS

Even though Chris knew an article could help clear his name, he said he probably would not have contacted the paper if his mother and lawyer had not insisted. Like him, many subjects said they were encouraged—or pushed—by friends, family, or colleagues to speak to reporters. Some, like Wendy, said input from their reference groups was not the sole reason they ended up cooperating with reporters but that it did help them make up their minds. As Wendy explained, a friend's request was one of several factors in her decision to speak to the press about her opposition to a controversial art installation in West City:

WENDY: I wasn't gonna leave Gail high and dry. . . . This is something I believe passionately about and I can tell that if I don't do it, no one will. And I was terribly uncomfortable throughout the whole thing, but Gail needs someone to talk to the press? I will go talk to the press.[20]

When the pressure to speak to the press comes from colleagues and bosses it can be particularly tough to refuse. For example, Keith, a New York City cop who got full-blown hero treatment for intervening in a terrorist plot, was essentially muzzled about any significant details by the NYPD public relations department.[21] When it came to posing at press conferences and making innocuous comments, however, there was no question of refusing. A chief ordered him to attend a press conference within hours of the incident. Soon he was surrounded by his superiors and shaking hands with the mayor, all under the strobe light of news cameras. It was, literally, a command performance.

Social pressure is less trigger-dependent than the previous categories in the sense that, given the opportunity, subjects consult with their reference groups almost no matter what the news coverage is about. However, the precise form the pressure takes is heavily influenced by the underlying trigger. If Keith had been asked to speak to a reporter about the irrigation business he runs on the side, he would not have been ordered to do so by his boss, but he might have consulted his wife.

SOCIAL AND EMOTIONAL REWARDS

When she was told her state agency had sent out a press release about her latest project, Annie told me, "I was kind of excited. I said, well, this'll be kinda neat. I'll get to be in the newspaper!"[22] Many interviewees said they got a kick out of the prospect of "making the paper," though the main source of the thrill seemed to vary. For some, being interviewed by reporters was especially exciting. But the most common reason subjects seemed to find making the news fun was that they associated it with fame and attention. Many people referred to it as their "fifteen minutes of fame," and some actively sought that sensation.

Marcel, for example, was stopped by a reporter on a subway platform and asked to comment on proposed fare hikes. He explained:

MARCEL: It's fun to be on the news. Like, I feel, it's fun to have random people who watch the news say, like, "Oh! I saw you on the news!." . . . Like I said, it does seem kind of exciting to be on the news. Like, "Oh! They're gonna ask me—what's gonna happen? I get to say something." And then my name will come up [on the screen], so I'll be famous.[23]

Subjects who said they had been excited about fame and attention were usually more thrilled about getting in the news at all than about getting in the news for a particular type of story, but the trigger still mattered. Appearing in the news seemed to be most uncomplicatedly fun when interviewees had little invested in the coverage, as was often the case in person-on-the-street interviews like Marcel's. Meanwhile, subjects associated with controversial triggers or crimes were understandably not eager for fame at all.

Personality also clearly mattered when it came to some peoples' attraction to the spotlight. Some interviewees explicitly described themselves as attention cravers. Chuck, for instance, explained that he had jumped at the chance to speak to reporters about an arson case in his neighborhood partly because he was just the kind of guy who enjoyed press attention:

CHUCK: There's no question that there is exhibitionism involved. I mean, it's a rush to get in the paper, to get on TV. . . . Psychologically I'm more inclined to prefer it rather than not. If there's a reporter standing there I'll probably, one way or the other, make an indication that I want to talk to him. . . . I think there are a lot of people who would run from [talking to a reporter], and I would run toward it.[24]

Some interviewees, like Chuck, openly acknowledged that they were motivated by exhibitionism or a desire for fame, but I suspect it factored into more peoples' decisions than were willing to admit it. Several noted that *other* people approached by reporters for the same story seemed turned on by the prospect of making the paper but attributed nobler goals to themselves. Others seemed ambivalent about their own desire to make it into the product. Helen, for example, was one of several college students quoted for a *New York Times* article on college social life. At the reporter's request, she took him to a university bar so he could get the local feel. Her description beautifully illustrates the mixed feelings some subjects felt about their own attraction to the spotlight:

HELEN: I remember [the reporter] went to the bar, and once he said, "I'm a *New York Times* reporter," girls were just flocking to him trying to be interviewed. And they were saying the most outlandish statements. . . . And then the girls got up on a table and started dancing for the photographer. . . . Everyone was like, "Oh my god, we're gonna be in the *New York Times*! This is so cool!" And they just told him whatever he wanted to hear, basically.

Q: Well, did you want to be in the article?

HELEN: I remember during the night I looked at my friend Kelly who was also in it, and I was like, "Darn it, we're not even gonna be in it." Because I don't know—I guess I did wanna be in it.[25]

RISKS AND REPERCUSSIONS: WHY SUBJECTS HESITATE TO BE IN THE NEWS

Interviewees ultimately found the reasons discussed above compelling enough to agree to press interviews, but that does not mean they failed to recognize the risks involved. Most said they had been aware, at least in theory, that speaking to the press could backfire in various ways, and that they had weighed the cons against the pros before making their decision. In this section I explore the misgivings about participating in a news story that interviewees said most concerned them. As was true for the advantages discussed in the previous section, the categories here often overlap, and many subjects cited more than one. And, just as many of the benefits subjects sought from appearing in the news were inextricably tied to the trigger events and issues, many of their concerns could be traced back to what the news story was about.

POTENTIAL NEGATIVE EFFECTS ON PRIVACY, REPUTATION, GOALS, AND PEOPLE

The most common reason interviewees said they hesitated to speak to reporters—by far—was that it seemed risky. When I asked them to explain what they meant, they had different ideas about what, exactly, was risky about it. Some, especially when the topic was controversial or socially unacceptable, said the trigger itself was inherently risky. Crimes, feuds, lawsuits, and polemical political issues felt like hot topics that could easily cause problems for subjects if linked to their names in the news. Other interviewees said they immediately sensed that speaking to reporters meant giving up control over their stories—a feeling that did not emerge for some other subjects until later in the news production process. But whatever the perceived source of the risk, subjects' main concern was ultimately the same: that the published story would have negative repercussions on their goals, their reputations, or their daily lives. In other words, they were not primarily worried that the coverage would represent them inaccurately or negatively—although that was often a concern. Rather their main fear was that the coverage, accurate or not, would have negative *effects*.

The feared repercussions differed by case. Some subjects worried for their safety or privacy. Emma, who had made the news for euthanizing her critically ill husband, said she feared harassment because of the nature of the trigger and the public's strong feelings about it. I asked if she was eager to speak to reporters, and she replied:

EMMA: It's a very mixed feeling. On the one hand it's the desire to tell my story, and on the other hand it's, "What am I going to stir up by doing this?" And, are people going to . . . vandalize my house, [starting to chuckle] write "murderer" across my garage or whatever.[26]

Many subjects said they had worried that appearing in a news story about a particular trigger or under specific circumstances could damage their reputations—to them a news appearance represented the opposite of the reputation repair described above. I explore what it feels like to appear in a stigmatizing article at length in chapters 7 and 8, but for now the essential point is that people were aware of that possibility and feared it. For example, I interviewed Sophie in the mobile home she shares with her husband and two young children. She had been quoted in the local paper because she had helped organize a rally about immigration reform. In the lead-up to the rally, she had turned down a last-minute opportunity to do a TV news interview, partly because of concerns for her reputation:

SOPHIE: I have two kids that run around, one that likes to be naked most of the time. And I honestly did not want to be on the news perceived as some redneck. You know, it was with no notice, so the kids had trashed the house. You know, there was no way for me to get the house as clean as I'd like it because it was going to have video cameras and all that sort of thing, and I didn't want to be immortalized in such a way. . . . I didn't want to be identified with moms with unruly kids, living out in the country, chickens running around on the porch, you know?

Other subjects worried that a news appearance could undermine specific projects or goals, like legal proceedings or business plans. And many were apprehensive about negative effects on other people, including family members and other players in the news story. Deanne worried for the woman whose suicide attempt she had witnessed: perhaps news coverage of the event would hurt a woman who was clearly suffering already. And Barbara, one of several Tea Party leaders interviewed by a reporter for the *New York Times*, explained that she had grudgingly gotten used to giving press interviews, but concerns about her family dogged her:

BARBARA: I kinda think I'd rather not have any press—'cause it does sometimes hurt your feelings or your children's feelings, or your spouse's. So you do wanna help guard people. But any time you wanna make a difference, you do have to work with the fourth estate.[27]

SOCIAL PRESSURES: DISCOURAGEMENT FROM REFERENCE GROUPS

Just as some subjects were encouraged by their reference groups to speak to reporters, others, like Tea Party leader Barbara, got the opposite advice. She explained, "Our people thought, 'Don't talk to [the reporter]! Don't give him any ammunition.' And one of our cofounders flat out told me we should never interact with media. Never." Their reference groups mostly expressed concerns similar to subjects' own, about negative repercussions for their security, reputation, or goals.

Subjects seemed most likely to heed warnings against speaking to the press when the story at hand had legal or professional implications. Several said they had already given at least one interview before their legal counsel jumped in to tell them to *stop* before they damaged their cause. Jon and Jane, for example, had gone out of their way to contact the

New York Times about their impending eviction, with the blessing of their initial legal counsel. Then a referral to a specialist lawyer quickly put an end to their media campaign:

> JANE: It was the fancy specialist zoning lawyer that they referred us to who has been very negative about [media coverage], ever since the beginning. Totally negative about it. . . .
>
> JON: Yeah. Because we're paying this lawyer a lot of money, we feel like we better do what he says, otherwise, why are we paying him all this money? So he said, "Don't talk to politicians, don't talk to press."

SPOTLIGHT AVERSION

Bathing in the spotlight may be a major draw for some, but it is a big drawback for others. Interviewees who dreaded fame and attention—like those who said they longed for it—usually attributed it to their own personalities, describing themselves as "self-conscious," "camera shy," or spotlight averse. Albert, one of the "Miracle on the Hudson" survivors, chose not to speak to the media until the anniversary of the event a year later. He contrasted his own reaction to the press attention with that of other passengers:

> ALBERT: I knew right away I didn't want to [talk to the press]. They came over to me right away and I was like, "No thanks, no thanks." And I walked away and I avoided it. And there were some other people who were eager to get to them. I saw that, you know? Other passengers. There's a couple people that were the face of the reporting. And they went on *Oprah*. They went on *Ellen*. They went on all those things and they had a great time. . . . I'm not into it. I like my own quiet life.

Spotlight aversion is not as closely tied to triggers as the previous two categories, but there is no question that the two can be linked. Albert explained that, when he attended the anniversary party one year after the plane crash, he found himself so elated that he overcame his reticence and spoke to reporters. His experiences suggest that even subjects who dislike the idea of media attention under most circumstances, and especially following traumatic events, might just overcome their resistance when conditions and triggers are more favorable.

INCONVENIENCE OR INTRUSION

Albert's last comment, that he likes his "own quiet life," suggests another downside to participating in news coverage. Activities associated with it can intrude on daily life. Speaking to the press can take time and energy, demands that can seem especially onerous in the wake of traumatic trigger events. In a stark illustration of that, Liana gave one interview about her brother's murder but declined subsequent requests. She and her family, she explained, "felt one interview was enough and we just had other things on our mind that needed more immediate attention. For example, his burial."[28] Her comment is a good reminder that life does not grind to a halt for subjects to give interviews, and often other demands on their time and attention simply matter to them more.

Money was another issue. Paying subjects is frowned upon at most mainstream news organizations, although it is not completely unheard of to compensate them for expenses. But none of the interviewees in this study had received any kind of compensation, and the costs of taking off work or traveling to interviews can add up. Ivan, a shopkeeper who rescued a child from an accident near his home in the Bronx, bitterly attested to that. He said every time he closed up shop to give an interview he took a financial hit, so he just stopped doing it. As it turns out, being a hero can quickly get expensive.[29]

TOUGH CHOICES AND MISSED OPPORTUNITIES

In many of the quotes above we can see subjects weighing pros and cons against one another: Is telling my story worth risking my safety? Is publicity for my business more important than my privacy? How does raising awareness for a political cause stack up against my family's welfare? In general, the more invested subjects were in the trigger, especially if that trigger was controversial, the more they felt they needed compelling reasons to give interviews; the risks were simply too great to agree lightly.

Colleen, for example, said she really struggled with whether to speak to a *New York Times* reporter about the new private school where she was an administrator. She was aware that schools in general sometimes got harsh treatment in the paper, and her school was designed to serve a specific niche population—more controversial still. She knew she would have to field adversarial questions, and that the coverage might ultimately be negative. In the final analysis, however, Colleen concluded that the potential benefits outweighed the considerable risks for her, the investors, and the future of the fledgling school. When I asked her why she wanted to do the article, she explained:

> COLLEEN: Well, because we are a new private school. The potential for some good exposure, and to generate interest and additional applications to the school, since we just opened, seemed to be worth the risk. Because I do know and had been told by various people that [press coverage] can go either way. That you can go in, all good intentions, laying out a thing that you would like to have displayed to the world and it may not turn out that way. . . . So I went back and forth about whether or not to do it—whether we don't need that, we can't take the risk—but ultimately came down on the side of the potential benefits outweighing the potential risk. And I know there are people sweatin' bullets because sometimes they do hatchet jobs on the schools. I know that. But this could help us. This could really put us on the map.[30]

When they were highly invested in triggers, sometimes subjects felt the potential benefits of speaking about them were so great that they outweighed even serious risks to their own well-being or goals. Several subjects who generally preferred to avoid the spotlight or felt self-conscious about being associated with a particular issue said those more personal concerns paled alongside the potential good they felt they could do by speaking out. They were willing to sacrifice personal comfort for what they saw as a public benefit. And a number of subjects involved in public conflicts said they concluded that the risk of *not* speaking to the press, thereby letting the opposing party control the debate, outweighed the risk of speaking to them. Michelle, for example, came to that decision about her controversial lawsuit against a religious group. She told me:

MICHELLE: I knew [speaking to the press] wasn't something I wanted to do. But I also was kind of caught between a rock and a hard place because I didn't want them just telling their story and it all being one-sided, and us not getting to say anything about it. . . . I thought there had to be some balance. I didn't think it would be advantageous to me whatsoever for them to talk and me to just be like, "No comment."[31]

I interviewed a few people who had not had the opportunity to speak to reporters but found themselves named in news stories anyway. Tellingly, they said they wished they *had* spoken to reporters to at least try to set the record straight or defend themselves. That was the case for Paul, who was visiting friends in West City when he and his girlfriend were attacked by a homeless person on the street. In the skirmish that followed, Paul sustained a grisly but non-life-threatening injury. The news coverage, including a brief article in the local paper that contained several errors, was apparently taken straight from the official police report. Paul and his friends were never contacted by reporters. His reflections on that point were revealing:

Q: Well, at any point did you think, "Gee, I would kind of like to talk to them [reporters] about this?"
PAUL: Yeah, I mean at this point, as time has gone on, I could live without it. But initially, yeah. You know, like I said, I had noticed a couple inaccuracies, and I'd rather they had more of an eyewitness account to what happened . . . just for the sake of accuracy. You know, if my name's gonna be on something, I'd rather it be like 100 percent true than, you know, 90 percent true.[32]

Like Paul, Beth wished she had been given the chance to correct the record in the press. Her plea deal for a white-collar crime she had committed forbade her from speaking to the media, but she said it was enraging to not be able to give her side of the story after being eviscerated in a major paper. She realized speaking to the press would likely have just perpetuated the story—and yet the compulsion to defend herself was almost overpowering. She said, "So much of me wanted to say, 'Look, this is a bunch of crap.' Or just some rebuttal, or my part of the story, or something that was gonna fix it!"[33]

Beth and Paul could not know what would have happened if they had spoken to reporters, but they, like the vast majority of interviewees, had concluded that speaking to the press was often better than not. If a story with their name in it was going to be publicly circulated, they concluded that it would be better to at least try to shape that story—even though completely controlling the message was out of the question—than to just sit back and watch it unfold.

PUBLIC ADDRESS AND PUBLIC DISPLAY: SUBJECTS' GOALS IN RITUAL AND TRANSMISSION TERMS

As the examples in this chapter illustrate, it is reductive to assume all news subjects want attention or have no idea what they are getting into when they agree to interviews with journalists. Many interviewees did consider various pros and cons before talking to reporters about a particular trigger, but under the specific circumstances in which they found themselves, they ultimately concluded that it was in their best interests to cooperate. They mostly realized that doing so was a risk—that they were giving up control over their stories, and that the published version might have negative repercussions. And yet the opportunity to address a specific message or simply display themselves in the news product seemed worth that risk.

A number of factors make a news appearance an attractive opportunity for a private citizen. I address the status and legitimacy the news media can bestow in later chapters. But when interviewees reflected back on their initial decisions to speak to reporters, the large size of the news audience was the element they emphasized most. Today, public figures and other powerful subjects, such as celebrities and government spokespeople, can undoubtedly parlay the same resources that have long helped them influence journalists, such as access to exclusive information and teams of PR professionals, into more direct communication with their audiences via social media.[34] By contrast, many private citizens still have no guaranteed way to communicate with the masses other than to engage with the mass media if and when the opportunity comes their way.

Looking over subjects' various motives for speaking to reporters, two broad categories emerge: public address and public display. These align well with James W. Carey's well-known transmission and ritual views of communication.[35] According to Carey, when we define communication and the news media in particular using a transmission model, we focus on how they disseminate specific information and messages to the people. That is usually our default definition of communication. Interviewees whose primary goal was to address the public hoped to transmit specific information to a large audience, whether as an end in itself or to effect change. In those cases, the information subjects wanted to communicate was often directly related to the trigger: they wanted people to know about their political cause, or violence in their neighborhood, or their brother's death, and what those specific events indicated about other, broader issues.

But Carey argues that there is a ritual dimension to much communication as well, which we often overlook. When we focus on this ritual dimension, we do not emphasize the new information being conveyed, but rather how shared norms and worldviews are upheld and reinforced through, for example, the routine act of reading the dramatic but often similar stories in a newspaper. Interviewees who were eager to appear in the news for its own sake, regardless of what the story was about, jumped at the opportunity to display themselves before the public, with all the status, fame, and fun that such a display affords. That kind of display usually had little to do with what information was being transmitted and more to do with the ritual of being seen by many people. As I discuss in chapter 7, a news appearance has a powerful ritual significance: that a subject is important enough to be singled out for mass attention. Little wonder many people find it fun. In those ritual-oriented cases, subjects' personalities played an especially big role: some people love the spotlight, and a news appearance can be gratifying to them for that reason alone.

The various downsides interviewees said they took into account when they decided whether to speak to reporters can also be seen in terms of transmission and ritual. Spotlight aversion is often more related to appearing in the news at all than appearing in a particular story, so we can classify it as a ritual concern. Here, again, subjects' personalities mattered a great deal. For people who do not like attention, appearing before a large audience can be unappealing if not outright terrifying. Meanwhile, subjects' concerns about potential negative repercussions of news stories on their goals, reputations, and families were often more transmission-oriented since they were more closely tied to the specific content being conveyed in a given story, and concerns about how that content might resonate with the public.

Looked at in these terms, when it comes to subjects' motives for wanting or not wanting to participate in the news, transmission concerns tend to trump ritual concerns. Even subjects who enjoy attention in general and would get a kick out of a news appearance about something innocuous will probably not jump at the chance to talk to reporters about their own bad behavior and may find it a complicated bargain for a story about their lawsuit or controversial political views. Meanwhile, subjects who loathe attention may overcome that aversion to communicate an important message to the public: The grieving mother we see in the news is probably not basking in attention. She may well hate it on a good day, and even more right now. But listen to what she is saying. Her child was a good kid. Or someone did not do their job. Or laws need to be changed. Or talk to your doctor about this *now*. That is why she is there, and that is what she wants us to know.

As I discuss in the next two chapters, even when subjects enter into an interaction with reporters with a clear idea about the message they hope to transmit, they often find that the circumstances and conversational demands of the journalistic interview—not to mention reporters' behavior—complicate their efforts to get that message across. The interaction is often a tricky one for subjects to navigate, with no guarantees that their goals will be met. They may still be recovering from shock, or care passionately about the topic under discussion, or have trouble articulating their ideas when faced with packs of aggressive reporters wielding unfamiliar equipment. It turns out that understanding the risks of becoming a news subject in the abstract is a far cry from regulating one's behavior accordingly throughout the interview process.

3

THE INTERVIEW STAGE PART 1

Encountering Journalists

E thical questions about how journalists should interact with their subjects, especially with so-called naïve subjects who have little experience with the media, are the one aspect of news subjecthood that has received a lot of critical attention. The questions raised are of practical interest to reporters, but they are also just plain interesting. They go right to the core of what it means to behave honestly in any interpersonal encounter, and they ask to what extent reporters can ethically apply different standards when they conduct interviews.

Clear answers are hard to come by, even among seasoned reporters. How can reporters extract useful information from subjects without manipulating them too much? And—especially contentious—how forthcoming and honest must journalists be with their subjects about what they intend to write? That question is central to *The Journalist and the Murderer*, Janet Malcolm's classic treatise on the journalist-subject relationship.[1] Malcolm's provocative conclusion that all journalists are essentially con artists who seduce and betray their subjects still sparks heated debate among journalism scholars and practitioners. But since journalism subjects themselves are rarely asked their opinions, we are missing a key piece of the puzzle: we know little about whether they actually *feel* conned, or how they perceive their interactions with journalists at all.[2]

Absent their input, reductive and unflattering portraits of subjects emerge, much as they do when we speculate about subjects' motives.

Unsuspecting subjects, we are told, are intoxicated by journalists' rapt attention and skillful conversation. They foolishly share their most intimate thoughts and damaging stories. Like a bad hangover, the sickening consequences become clear only the next day, when they see the published story.[3]

But is that really true? *Always?* How do subjects themselves actually think and feel about what goes on in their interviews with journalists? I argued in the previous chapter that, more so than we might assume, potential subjects do consider pros and cons when approached by reporters. When they agree to give interviews, often they realize they are giving up control over how their stories will be told to the public, but the potential benefits are worth the risks to them. So the question now becomes: does something happen during the interview to derail their goals, or to con subjects into behaving in ways they normally would not, and certainly *should* not in interviews with journalists? Is there really something about journalistic interviews—something that differentiates them from other encounters—that reduces reasonable people to babbling fools?

The answer is yes—to a degree. Encounters with journalists are both similar and different from other, more familiar kinds of interactions, which can make them tricky for subjects to navigate. In this and the next chapter I explore how interviewees described their interactions with journalists, and analyze those interactions through the lens of Erving Goffman's concepts of face-work and framing. The interview stage warrants two chapters because it was very important to interviewees themselves. For some, interactions with reporters made more of an impression than the resulting news coverage. For many, the interview stage stood out as their only opportunity to try to influence how journalists would go on to tell their stories.

I begin in this chapter by dissecting how two competing sets of conversational norms can influence subjects' decisions to speak to reporters. I go on to explore how the logistics of the interview and subjects' impressions of journalists influenced how they felt and behaved while the interviews were actually taking place. In chapter 4 I focus on the substance of the discussion that took place during the interviews, especially on how subjects and journalists forged agreements and navigated disagreements over how the raw material under discussion should be presented in the news product later.

COMPETING SETS OF INTERACTIONAL NORMS: GOFFMAN'S CEREMONIAL ORDER AND JOURNALISTIC WORK

To understand how journalistic interviews differ from other interpersonal encounters, it is helpful to understand first how they are similar. Sociologist Erving Goffman, whose work on interpersonal interaction has been used in a number of important studies of media, provides a helpful theoretical framework for that task.[4] According to Goffman, all interpersonal encounters have basic social norms associated with them, two of which are "face-work" and the display of involvement in conversation.[5] He argues that all participants in an interpersonal encounter are socially obligated to present a "face" appropriate to the situation. A face is a performance of the self that we adopt and display—not unlike a mask—based on our understanding of what is acceptable in a given social situation. We constantly engage in face-work, or little adjustments of our faces, to maintain our good standing, to keep the interaction flowing smoothly, and to ensure that our fellow interactors are comfortable.

For Goffman, this is sacred stuff: maintaining face and helping others do so—for our own faces depend, in part, on how well we help others maintain theirs—constitute a moral obligation. In fact, deliberately damaging another's face, or even just failing to respond to our partner's cues for what is appropriate in an interaction, constitutes a violation of what Goffman calls the "ceremonial order." That term, with its religious connotations, refers to the smooth flow of an encounter, with all participants retaining a base level of dignity. Imagine telling your professor or boss that she has spinach in her teeth during a meeting, and you have a pretty good sense of what rocking the ceremonial boat feels like. She loses face. You lose face. The whole encounter is suddenly uncomfortable, and strenuous face-work must be done to set it aright again.

The precise face-work required to uphold the ceremonial order differs, depending on the situation and the players. In conversation-heavy interactions, including interviews, an important part of face-work is displaying the right degree of involvement. The appearance of "spontaneous" involvement—which is the ideal state—actually requires great skill. We constantly express our involvement by nodding, or disagreeing, or looking puzzled. Sometimes we express more interest in the conversation than we feel in order to keep the encounter flowing and our faces intact. However, a delicate balance is required here: if we express *too* much interest when we feel none, we are judged insincere and our behavior misleading, because our partners cannot accurately read our cues and do the appropriate face-work to re-engage us. We are faulty interactors, which, to Goffman, are essentially faulty people. We have fallen down on our moral duty to uphold the ceremonial order.

The good news here is that letting our eyes wander around the room if our conversation partner is a bore can be exactly the right thing to do: it sends honest signals that they need to make adjustments to keep us interested. At the same time, the best conversationalists, the people you most want at your party, are exceptionally good at spontaneously involving others, often by seeming positively enraptured themselves. As they know, there is probably no more effective way to keep us enthralled than a listener who asks us questions and appears fascinated by everything we have to say. As my interviewee Billy observed, "The best way to flirt with somebody is to get them to talk about themselves."[6]

Billy had appeared in a long profile in the West City paper, and he was talking about the reporter who had interviewed him. Indeed, the first way interviews with journalists tend to differ from normal conversational encounters is simply that journalists are often particularly skilled conversational interactors. As Pulitzer Prize winner David Halberstam puts it, "reporters by dint of their training have a considerable amount of charm and grace and the ability to get people to talk—to project a kind of pseudo-intimacy."[7] Journalism textbooks advise reporters to prepare questions that will engage the interviewee; to always project interest; to volunteer their own thoughts and feelings as necessary—all to make the person feel comfortable and "induce the source to speak freely."[8]

Should a source seem reticent, Melvin Mencher's guide to news reporting goes a step further, suggesting what he calls "role-playing." As he puts it, "Role-playing is generally successful if the reporter acts out a role appropriate to the subject and situation. . . . Reporters can adopt the role of friend, confidant and companion when sources appear to need encouragement before they will talk."[9] Now in its twelfth edition, Mencher's book is one of the most widely used journalism textbooks in the United States. This is not fringe advice.

And yet we can start to see here how a journalist's highly developed conversation skills might tip an interaction into a moral gray area. Yes, journalists are skilled at getting people to talk, but how skilled is too skilled? Are projecting pseudo-intimacy and role-playing just extensions of the normal face-work necessary to maintain the ceremonial order, or do they cross a line into "faulty interaction" because they are too insincere? Just reading Mencher's description, many nonjournalists would probably argue the latter. While feigning interest in a conversation may sometimes be acceptable to avoid hurting someone's feelings and help everyone involved maintain face, expressing *too* much inauthentic emotion seems morally suspect.

The advice offered by journalism textbooks may appear to contravene what we normally think of as moral behavior in conversation; however, textbooks offer this kind of advice, and journalists may adopt these behaviors because, for journalists, the interview is *primarily* an instrumental interaction. This is the second way that interviews with journalists differ from many other conversational encounters. Veteran journalist Isabel Wilkerson's description of her own technique to get her sources "to feel comfortable enough to tell [her] anything" illustrates this beautifully:

> But what I mainly try to do is to be a great audience. I egg them on; I nod; I look straight into their eyes; I laugh at their jokes, whether I think they're funny or not; I get serious when they're serious. I kind of echo whatever emotion they seem to be sending to me. I do whatever it takes to get them talking. I call these more guided conversations than interviews. . . . What's much more important is that there is an interaction that gets me what I want.[10]

From the journalist's point of view, the key is that "there is an interaction that gets me what I want." The exigencies of normal conversation described by Goffman do not disappear, but an additional layer of demands on the encounter is introduced on the journalist's side. A professional journalist's livelihood, and her professional face, depend not just on her maintaining her basic dignity in the encounter, as is always the case, but on her obtaining information from it.

In other words, journalists must navigate two sets of conversational norms during interviews. First, they must follow those norms that govern all spoken interaction, which are necessary to maintain Goffman's ceremonial order; otherwise they risk immediately alienating their interlocutors. Second, they must apply norms associated with the instrumental aspect of the encounter, in which information is being extracted from the subject for a news article. Debates about what degree of insincerity is acceptable in interviews are essentially debates over which of these sets of conversational norms should prevail: the ceremonial/human or the instrumental/professional.

As I argued in the previous chapter, many news subjects also go into interviews with goals in mind. For them, too, the interaction is at least somewhat instrumental. But we can still make an important distinction between the professional extractor-of-information and the amateur pusher-of-it. Unlike journalists, for whom two competing sets of norms are clearly at work in the interview, ordinary news subjects are more likely to be guided by those of normal conversational encounters. They may be completely unfamiliar with "empathic listening," role-playing, and other techniques used by reporters to get them to open up.[11] Differences in preparation and perspective like these should raise red flags because even the most well-intended communication between people of contrasting backgrounds and value systems can lead to one party misinterpreting their interlocutor's level of sincerity and saying things he or she later regrets.[12] News subjects confronted with apparently sympathetic reporters certainly seem poised to fall into that trap.

So is that actually the case? How do these dueling sets of interactional norms affect how subjects experience interviews? How do they assess and respond to journalists' face-work? Below I turn to my interviewees for answers, beginning with how they described their initial encounters with reporters, and how those reporters' behavior affected their own decisions to cooperate.

THE CEREMONIAL ORDER AS REASON ENOUGH (OR NOT) TO AGREE TO AN INTERVIEW

If we look at the first moments of an encounter between a journalist and a potential subject through Goffman's lens, the logical question is not why a subject would agree to an interview, but how he could justify refusing. Goffman argues that as soon as one person has initiated an encounter, all involved become morally obligated to help one another maintain face. Refusing to speak to a journalist who has requested an interview would be akin to refusing to shake a proffered hand. And yet, as any journalist will attest, people can and do refuse all the time.

Since I sought out people who had appeared in the paper, not those who had turned down the opportunity, I do not have much data to explain how people justify turning down reporters. The risks and concerns I discussed in the previous chapter probably contribute. But the instrumental nature of the encounter itself could also help potential subjects justify cutting off interactions with journalists. It may be comparable to our feeling fine about slamming the door on a salesman as soon as we find out why he rang our bell: we recognize that the encounter is primarily intended to extract something from us, so we flout the ceremonial order in a way we would not if we thought our interlocutor's motives were less self-interested.

Since most interviewees did agree to speak to reporters, however, they provide rich data on the role face-work can play in getting subjects to agree to talk to reporters. All my study participants said reporters introduced themselves as such, and they understood from the outset that the encounter was intended to get information from them for a news story. In other words, at least on this most basic level they were not conned into an interaction they fundamentally misunderstood. But few felt that just helping out a reporter—in other words, just helping the reporter save face— was reason enough to give an interview. More often, subjects said wanting to help journalists was an *additional* reason they decided to give an interview, on top of the more trigger-related goals discussed in the previous chapter.

Alegra, for example, said as much. Recall from the last chapter that she spoke to reporters about losing her unborn baby after she became ill. The condition was especially dangerous for pregnant mothers, but few had come forward with their stories, so Alegra's case was of great interest to reporters. Alegra did not like being the center of attention under normal circumstances. She had been seriously ill and lost a child; these were not normal circumstances. And yet, when I asked her if she felt certain right away that she wanted to speak to a newspaper reporter when he called, she responded:

ALEGRA: Yeah, I'm not the person to say "no" either. I don't like saying "no" to people. So yeah, I said "yes" automatically. But I'm not going into this like, "Ooh, yay! I'm getting the spotlight on me," y'know? I really don't like that at all. But, like I said, I don't like saying "no" either, and I do wanna get the awareness out there.[13]

I discussed Alegra's main reason for wanting to speak to reporters in the previous chapter: she wanted to alert pregnant women to the dangers of the illness. As she says above, she wanted "to get the awareness out there." She hoped her experience would spare others the same loss. But she acknowledges here that the social demands of the initial encounter played a big role as well: she agreed automatically because she simply does not like "saying 'no' to people." Her experience highlights the pressure some people feel to uphold the ceremonial order, even under circumstances that would seem to justify their refusing.

Alegra was one of few interviewees who explicitly identified not wanting to turn reporters down as one of her motivations, but the nature of face-work is such that we are often unaware of it. That suggests that not wanting to refuse reporters simply because it is hard to refuse engaging with any socially skilled interactor may well be a factor in subjects' agreeing to interviews more often than they realize.

Some interviewees seemed to associate a kind of glamour, mystique, or status with journalism in general. For them, getting attention from any professional reporter was appealingly novel or outright flattering. But I also found that, contrary to Janet Malcolm's surprising claim that subjects' willingness to talk has nothing to do with the skill and behavior of the journalist, subjects' inclination to engage with reporters had a lot to do with who those reporters were and how they conducted themselves.[14] In some cases, individual reporters' reputations preceded them. For example, Leyla was contacted by a veteran *New York Times* reporter who covered her field. She explained that, "In my world getting an email from [reporter] is like getting an email from some really famous actor. [Reporter] is a big deal for me."[15] She promptly agreed to be interviewed.

And the appeal of getting attention from reporters can be especially strong when they behave in particular ways. Maggie, for example, described her encounter with a young reporter at a meeting for mature women on the job market:

MAGGIE: At our breaks she started walking around and talking to different people. And she singled me out. And the funny thing that got it going with me is that she was asking everybody their age and when I said my age, she said, "Oh my god, you certainly don't look—!" and gave me all these compliments, and everybody likes to hear that, and I said, "Oh, thank you." That's what started it. She was very, very easy to work with, y'know. You liked her.[16]

Maggie did not want to say "no" to a friendly young reporter anyway, but the flattery did not hurt. Many subjects described being approached by reporters who seemed, if not as ready with the compliments as the reporter in Maggie's case, friendly, sympathetic, and professional. Subjects who had been involved in traumatic or alarming events especially appreciated reporters who seemed sensitive to what they had been through. Those who combined sympathy with a kind of neediness for cooperation were especially hard to refuse, as Liana's case illustrates. She spoke to only one reporter at the police precinct mere hours after learning of her brother's death. She explained why she selected that reporter in particular:

LIANA: I spoke to [the reporter] because she seemed very kind and very sympathetic about the situation. It wasn't like an older person that was very cocky and very arrogant that just needed information to put out there for their story. The way she approached me, and the fact that she seemed, sympathetic about the situation—so I said, well okay, I would do her this one favor. And not only that, she looked very young, an aspiring reporter, and I didn't wanna crush her dreams of having a big story under her name. Those reasons really said to me I'm gonna try my best to assist her as much as I can.[17]

Not only was the reporter sympathetic and kind, she seemed young and like she could really use Liana's help. Whether they were doing it instinctively or intentionally, in Maggie's and Liana's cases the reporters were playing up Goffman's conversational norms: they were friendly, were sympathetic, and projected a subtle but persistent need for the subject's assistance. Their professional face, in fact, depended on the subject's cooperation. That a subject like Liana can feel compelled to help out a reporter even immediately after learning of a loved one's death suggests just how strong and persistent the exigencies of face-to-face interaction with an effective interlocutor can be.

In other cases, reporters applied skillful face-work but *also* made explicit arguments for why subjects should agree to be interviewed. In fact, often they invoked the trigger-related goals discussed in the previous chapter: this was subjects' chance to address the public, to debunk myths, and so forth. Sloan, for example, spent weeks as a juror on a high-profile police abuse case in New York.[18] When the jury finally came to a verdict he was eager to put the whole thing behind him; he had gotten shingles from the stress and just wanted to get home. So it unnerved him when a young reporter from the *New York Times* knocked on his door within twenty minutes of his homecoming. Her appearance and manner did not seem very professional, and Sloan was on the brink of refusing to talk, when she thrust a cell phone into his hand and he found himself speaking to a senior reporter back in the newsroom.

This guy was clearly an old pro. He was sympathetic, explained exactly what he was looking for, and why Sloan should give it to him: here was Sloan's opportunity to explain to the public how the jury had come to its decision in a trial of great public interest. Otherwise, how would citizens know this key piece of the judicial puzzle? Sloan found himself discussing the case. As his experience illustrates, a particular reporter's ability to simultaneously play up the demands of spoken interaction and tap into trigger-related reasons a subject might want to speak to the public anyway can be a compelling combination.

A number of subjects said they found themselves agreeing to interviews not because the reporter was sympathetic or convincing but for the opposite reason. Reporters appeared in a flurry, were pushy and demanding, and subjects, a bit stunned at the apparent urgency of the encounter, found themselves complying almost before they knew what was happening. Carmen described that scenario. Her mother contacted the *New York Daily News* after 22-year-old Carmen was attacked in an attempted robbery. The local precinct detectives had brushed off her complaints, so the reporter jumped at the chance to pursue a story about police neglect. With little preamble, he appeared with a photographer at Carmen's home, where she was recovering from surgery to repair her jaw, broken in the attack:

CARMEN: I just woke up. They showed up like, 10, 15 minutes after [the phone call]. So they come to the house, with his photographer, and I was kinda like, "Hold on!" [indicating that they were very pushy and persistent]. 'Cause they were like [in a rushed, pushy voice], "Oh! So what happened?!!" I'm like, "I'm trying to tell you what I feel about what happened! I can't give you any more information." So of course he was all pushy. He wants information so he's gonna be really pushy. Like aggressive. . . . So basically I told him what happened.[19]

Some subjects who found reporters inappropriately pushy used that as an excuse to refuse to speak with them, as Sloan was about to do when the first reporter knocked on his door. But many, like Carmen, found it easier to agree than to refuse. Journalists in these cases were engaged in a kind of aggressive face-work in which they took advantage of conversational norms that made it unlikely subjects would refuse to speak to them—even if they were outright rude. They overtly privileged the instrumental aspect of the interaction over social niceties, while unprepared subjects found themselves clinging to the latter. In such cases, subjects' personalities and prior experience also seemed to play a role. Some said they were not accustomed to interacting with aggressive interlocutors and simply did not know how to decline. Carmen, a soft-spoken young woman, felt quite bowled over by the reporter and photographer who appeared in her home. When I asked her if she felt she could refuse to pose for certain pictures— they were eager to get a close-up of her wired jaw, which made her uncomfortable—she responded, "No. I felt pressured. What they wanted was what they wanted. And they were gonna get it from me. It was bad."

Even interviewees with more assertive personalities found it hard to refuse aggressive reporters when they were still recovering from the shock of trigger events. Deanne, for example, had a strong negative reaction to a TV reporter who interviewed her about a suicide attempt she witnessed. The reporter seemed phony and out to sensationalize the incident. And yet, before she knew it, the camera was on and she was being interviewed:

DEANNE: So I saw the reporter and her crew. I think she had a little posse of three people with her. But the minute I said, "Yeah, I was here. Yeah, I saw what happened," I didn't expect that immediately she was gonna say, "Harry, turn on the lights," and I was gonna have a microphone in my face. There was just no transition. She never said, "Would you be willing to discuss it?" It was just, "Boom. We're in it." And this is probably part of the "people person" in me somewhere, where I certainly could've just said, "Oh. I'm not comfortable with this. I don't know how I feel"—but y'know . . . we've already started, so I guess it's weird to walk away after we've already started and the camera's on me. I mean, I've already kind of tacitly agreed to give her this interview, so I don't wanna be rude. But again, this was all [snaps fingers] within seconds. Really quickly. I just really tried to end it as quickly as possible.[20]

While Deanne knew that, technically, she could have stopped the interview, "the people person" in her—essentially the well-socialized interactor of whom Goffman speaks— felt compelled to cooperate. The camera, crew, and microphone also played a role, which other interviewees mentioned as well. They found the equipment itself intimidating, all the more so because it came with equipment operators. A single reporter became a "posse," and walking away felt even harder to do.

As the examples above illustrate, in most cases journalists' behavior when requesting interviews did take advantage of social norms guiding most interactions, whether in a subtle or a more aggressive way. But it would be a stretch to say categorically that they did so to an unethical degree—at least, most interviewees did not think so. Some of them definitely felt pushed, in extreme cases like Carmen's quite forcefully so, but none felt conned into giving an interview. Only a small number of even those subjects who felt pressured said they regretted it later. Sloan, the juror, and Deanne, the witness, both felt, looking back, like there was little to be gained from speaking publicly about the issues in question. With more time and space to consider the proposition, they felt they would have come to that conclusion. And yet, given the behavior of reporters, it was easier to acquiesce than to refuse.

A TALE OF TWO FRAMES: ENCOUNTER FRAMES AND STORY FRAMES

If interviewees did not feel unfairly seduced into participating in the news process, is there anything that took place *during* their interviews with journalists that could constitute a kind of con? Once more, Goffman provides a helpful conceptual framework.

Recall that performing appropriate face-work depends not only on who the interlocutors are but also on the situation. According to Goffman, interactors continually define and reaffirm what the situation really is—what he calls the "frame" of the encounter—by performing feedback cues.[21] The frame of a conversation may be, for example, a friendly chat, a heated quarrel, or a formal interview. We can change the frame by changing our cues; however, understanding the frame of the encounter as it moves through various registers is essential because we need to adjust our behavior accordingly. We respond differently if we think our conversation partner is joking or in earnest, just as we shift gears when a friendly chat becomes an interview.

Today, the more well-known definition of the term "framing" is actually a modification of Goffman's original concept. Journalism scholars have repurposed the term to refer to the process whereby journalists make decisions about what to include in a news story, and how to include it. But insofar as an encounter between a journalist and a subject already has a frame by Goffman's definition—that of an interview—the news construction process is really one of reframing that interview for public consumption. It follows that the "true" frame of the journalistic interview itself is that whatever happens in that frame *does not stay in that frame.* Unless special arrangements have been made between the subject and the reporter, whatever the subject says or does during the interview will be put through a deliberate process of reframing in order to make it a standardized piece of news.

I established earlier that this is an instrumental encounter intended to extract information for a news story. All we are adding now is that that material will not just be copy-pasted into a news product but picked over, pruned, and repackaged. For clarity's sake, from now on I will refer to the frame of the encounter as the "encounter frame" and the frame of the news story as the "story frame."

Even if subjects know in the abstract that whatever happens in the encounter frame is fair game for repackaging in the story frame, it is not necessarily easy to manage that in practice. Goffman suggests that, even for savvy subjects, the exigencies of a face-to-face conversation will lead almost inevitably to the subject's performing in a way that will not work as well out of context, a paradox he tellingly dubs "informant's folly": "when an individual knowingly provides a report for purposes of relay, he falls into the assumption that he can interlard his comments not only with directional cues which will go unreported, but also with off-the-record asides of various kinds. . . . We embroider our discourse with multiple voices (or "registers"), and some of these, being wholly responsive to the site in which the discourse actually occurs, are doomed to be out of place if witnessed away from their original setting."[22]

In other words, behavior appropriate to an interpersonal encounter can seem weird and inappropriate when reframed in another setting, such as the news product. People who appear routinely in the news often receive media relations training precisely because behaving in a face-to-face encounter in ways that will work well in the news product can feel completely unnatural. How could it be otherwise, since it requires prioritizing a nonpresent audience over the one in the room, and saying only things that will somehow survive the reframing process intact? For instance, ignoring a question and responding with your own preconceived, bullet-pointed message, an old media relations trick, is completely at odds with the norms guiding most interpersonal interactions. And yet it makes perfect sense given the oddities of the journalistic interview: subjects avoid saying things in the immediate encounter that they do not want repackaged for public consumption and ensure that the only quotes from which journalists can choose are those that best convey their own preferred messages.

But if journalistic encounters can look and feel deceptively like normal interpersonal encounters—to such a degree that professional news subjects must receive special training in order to resist behaving as though they were—where does this leave less experienced news subjects in an interview? How do they understand and manage an interview once it is underway?

Interviewees in this study interacted with reporters under many different circumstances, including prescheduled formal interviews; spontaneous on-the-scene conversations; discussions via phone, email, and social media; meetings in bars, cafes, or homes; and long days on the job with reporters observing their every move. As discussed in the first half of this chapter, none of them felt deceived into giving interviews. They understood the first principle of the journalistic interview frame: that they were speaking to reporters to provide them with information they could use for a news story. But understanding that in an abstract way and recalling it throughout the encounter are different, and subjects varied in how well they felt they were able to manage the latter.

On one end of the spectrum, several less experienced subjects said they were unsure about when the interview even began and ended. That kind of confusion over the basic demarcations of the journalistic encounter was quite rare among interviewees and usually occurred only in special situations—for example, when subjects had been surrounded or shadowed by reporters in informal settings—that made the boundaries of the encounter frame especially fuzzy. Eve, a Miracle-on-the-Hudson survivor, experienced that at the anniversary celebration of the event. The party was held back on the Hudson, this time on a boat, with sponsors and reporters milling around:

> EVE: I was talking to a reporter, and then he ended the interview on camera. And so I was still kind of chitchatting with him saying, "[redacted]" and I didn't realize that there was a reporter behind us, and he wrote that down, and it was in the [newspaper] the next day. [Laughter] I was like, "Oh, for God's sake, of all the things to quote me as saying!"[23]

The boundaries of the interview frame also blurred for some subjects when all or part of the interview took place via digital tools. For example, two interviewees had agreed to participate in a series of articles for the *Daily News* about a group of friends starting a special exercise regimen. The reporter occasionally emailed them to check on their progress, and they were surprised to find their emailed responses extracted in the paper.

On the other end of the spectrum, interviewees with a lot of experience talking to the media tended to be the most wary during interviews. Recognizing the vulnerability of their position, they tried to maximize their chances of conveying their messages while minimizing any potential damage that might result, no matter how the reporter decided to use their words. Gail, a longtime arts and neighborhood activist in West City, described how that felt:

> GAIL: It's this very painstaking, thoughtful conversation you have to have with the reporter, because you may talk with him for an hour, and they write three words, or five words, and put in their own context. So, you're really vulnerable when you're talking to the media. When you're talking to a reporter, that's the whole thing that's going through your mind. It's like, "if I say this, how is it going to be interpreted?"[24]

Even media savvy subjects like Gail find interviews challenging. She said she often emerged from them worried she had said too much. No wonder: subjects must respond to the immediate demands of the encounter, while also trying to present a face that will translate well when squeezed into a story frame that may or may not be fully developed, and about which they usually know little.

Journalists, too, must respond to the demands of two frames. But, as I discuss below, they are usually better positioned to do so effectively. In the remainder of this chapter I explore how subjects navigated the encounter frame, with its sometimes competing demands. I focus in turn on how triggers, the logistics of the interview itself, and the behavior of journalists influenced their efforts to maintain face while they were being interviewed.

AFTERSHOCK, AFTERGLOW, AND NERVES: HOW TRIGGERS AFFECT FACE-WORK

Triggers affect how subjects behave in journalistic encounters in two distinct but overlapping ways. First, events and issues that become newsworthy are often exceptional, dangerous, or controversial. Exposure to them can have emotional and physical effects on those involved. Naturally, a heightened emotional state or physical pain can affect subjects' ability to control themselves as they normally would in a conversation. For example, when Eve left the emergency room after her plane crash-landed in the Hudson River, she was immediately swarmed by reporters and found herself saying things she probably would not have, had she not been so stunned. She recalled, "I sometimes had a hard time just even focusing on what they were asking me. There were some questions that were very personal, and some of them I answered just because I was a little bit in shock still."

The trigger can also overwhelm subjects in a positive way. Albert, another crash survivor, had refused to speak to reporters in the immediate aftermath of the accident. But he was so elated (and possibly tipsy) at the one-year anniversary celebration—Grey Goose vodka sponsored the event—that he found himself giving in, and even enjoying it. He recalled, "I was like, 'Eh, whatever. One-year anniversary. I'm excited. I'm celebrating my life. It's been great.' So I just let it happen."[25] In the midst of that euphoria he, a resolute media cynic, made not one but two ecstatic mini-speeches to eager reporters. So the aftershock—or afterglow—of triggers can influence subjects' willingness to cooperate with reporters and how they feel when speaking to them.

Second, it can be hard for subjects to maintain their composure during interviews if they are highly invested in the outcome—that is, if they care a lot about the story being reported in a particular way, and its having particular effects. As we saw in the previous chapter, based on their relationship to a given trigger, subjects develop goals and objectives for what they want to get out of a news story—to raise awareness for a cause, publicize a venture, and so forth. Interviewees who were not highly invested in how a particular trigger was going to be repackaged for the public usually felt relatively relaxed during interviews. People stopped for a quick quote on the street, for example, simply had little at stake in how the news story turned out. But when the stakes were high, and subjects highly aware of it, the little voice that usually whispered to them to guard their faces in public sometimes rose to a distracting volume that actually made it harder to do so.

Colleen, for example, described the process leading up to her article's publication as "excruciating." An administrator at a new private school featured in an article in the *New York Times*, she was deeply invested in the school coming across well but knew that its whole philosophy was controversial. She felt "very apprehensive" throughout the interview process and hyper-aware of every tiny detail in the interview:

> COLLEEN: I probably think too much, but going through my mind is, "Okay, I already answered that. Are you coming back to it to see if I say the same thing? Or would you like clarity?" So I've even got this little thing going on in my head because I'm just really being careful.[26]

Journalists themselves are not immune to trigger-related strain when conducting interviews. Famous on-air examples of broadcast journalists succumbing to their emotions do come to mind (to wit, Walter Cronkite visibly shaken by the news of John F. Kennedy's death; CNN's Anderson Cooper, weekly). However, the structure of the news production process is such that journalists often arrive after major events have transpired and approach issues as outsiders. Moreover, reporters are trained to remain as neutral as possible, and often their professional faces depend on it. To top it all, journalists' part of their interaction with subjects is often edited out of the final product anyway: interview questions rarely appear in written newspaper articles, and only sometimes in broadcast news.

Combining these factors, it is hard not to conclude that under most conditions subjects are more likely than journalists to be strongly affected during interviews by their proximity to triggers, potentially in ways that later seep into the coverage. Deanne, the interviewee who felt taken off-guard by a team of television journalists after she witnessed a suicide attempt, made that point when she described watching the newscast later:

DEANNE: My hair's a mess, I've got no makeup, I've got this little kid. I'm a little bit scattered, and I'm obviously very emotional. My voice is shaking. It was all just so off-the-cuff, I didn't know what the question was gonna be, and—I guess, her questions took me aback.

Q: And you feel like that came across?

DEANNE: Yeah. I did.

ENVIRONMENT, EQUIPMENT, AND CROWDS: HOW THE LOGISTICS OF THE ENCOUNTER AFFECT FACE-WORK

Just as subjects' investment in the trigger in question can affect their ability to remain calm and composed in an interview, the logistics of interviews can also influence their face-work. This is no great claim: the physical circumstances of any encounter play a role in how interactors behave. Technical difficulties or distractions often disrupt the flow of encounters, but normally both actors simply do compensatory face-work and move on. But the structure of journalistic encounters can be particularly unforgiving in this regard because much of the contextual material that can help make sense of how subjects were behaving in the moment will be completely edited out during the reframing process. Susan, for example, felt her quotes in an article about wildlife in a local park sounded pretty inane.[27] She explained that she had not been at her best in the conversation because she was standing by a lake in the park, speaking to a journalist by phone. Between a poor cell-phone connection—they kept getting cut off—and a blustery wind, she struggled to convey her views coherently during the interview. But of course, none of the contextual factors were included in the resulting article—only her already choppy quotes, chopped still further.

Journalistic encounters may also overlap with other interactions in ways that affect the subject's face-work. In situ, the ways the different layers of the encounter intersect are evident to all involved, but taken out of context, the subject's behavior can seem stilted or odd.

If other people are listening in on the interview, for example, suddenly subjects must concern themselves with *three* different audiences: the reporter, the observing crowd, and the eventual news audience. Dudley, a welding student who was interviewed about an accident at his technical school, found the challenge of performing face-work appropriate for three different publics such a strain he ended up presenting a babbling hybrid that failed on all accounts:

> DUDLEY: I was very conscious about how I was speaking. Because I'm used to carrying myself one way at school, versus . . . not. When I'm at school, I'm not very articulate. Lotta slang, lotta cursing. And so it was weird because I was like, "Oh no, I don't wanna blow my cover in front of all my friends that I can actually speak English." And on the other hand, I do wanna articulate what I saw so it's somewhat understandable. So I ended up just sounding like an idiot. I was making sure, "Use big words, Dudley, use big words. Oh, wait, no—but that's too big!" So I was rushing really fast and I was trying to get my point across. Meanwhile, I was also listening to what my one friend, Harrison, behind me is screaming, "You made it. Oh! Listen to you Dudley, oh, you're an expert! Yadayadada." So I was distracted by him, I was telling him to shut up, I was trying to talk to the camera. . . . Yeah, it was a mess! And finally he just stopped recording. I was yelling at everybody, I was like, "Great. I sound like a fucking idiot."[28]

Although the cameraman did not use the footage, Dudley immediately had a similarly scattered exchange with a *New York Post* reporter and was quoted saying something he felt made him sound uneducated and inarticulate. He had said it largely for the benefit of his school friends who were watching the interview, not the general public. Between the chaotic surroundings and his need to choose which face to present, he felt like he ended up performing a phony version of himself. He explained, "It was very rushed. I was using some fucked up accent that isn't natural. I don't know where it came from . . . I misrepresented myself. That's not how I speak [normally]."

As I mentioned earlier in this chapter, journalistic interviews sometimes involve special equipment, and for some subjects that was the biggest distraction of all. In theory, notepads, cameras, and recording equipment can be helpful to subjects because they are reminders that the conversation, however friendly and casual, is an interview that will be repurposed for a different audience later. In practice, however, that awareness can lead subjects to underperform.

For instance, Jay, a ferry boat captain, said being followed by TV cameras was distracting not just for him but for his passengers, which in turn distracted him more. Above all, it made him feel uncharacteristically self-conscious and nervous. When I asked him what the TV interviews were like, he responded:

JAY: Nerve-wracking. . . . All the passengers were looking, like, "Oh, what's going on? What's going on?" And I'm trying to talk to them and drive, but when they're on your face, and the camera's right here, and they're like, "Yeah, don't worry about the camera." How do you not? This huge piece of equipment? . . . I'm like, "Oh my God, is my hair OK?" I never cared about that before![29]

Emma said she felt comfortable with the reporter who visited her home for an in-depth profile about how she had cared for her critically ill husband before his death. By contrast, the presence of the photographer felt strangely invasive:

Q: What was it like having the photographer here?
EMMA: Well he was quite nice. It was a little weird because it definitely had a sense of—I can't think of the word I want, but just—invasion. Much more so [than talking to the reporter] . . . I'm not really sure why I had that feeling. But, you know, as he would snap pictures—it's sort of like I didn't have as much control, maybe. In a conversation I can kind of control what information came out, but with a photograph it's just, "there it is!" you know?[30]

Emma had realized when she spoke to the reporter that she would have little control over how the encounter would be reframed later, but at least she could decide which bits and pieces of her story she told, and how. The photographer, on the other hand, came into her home and took what he wanted. It was disconcerting to feel that the one part of the process over which she had had a bit more control—the presentation of her story in the interview stage—was slipping out of her hands.

Subjects who had been invited for interviews at television and radio stations described a similar but even more extreme sense of having lost control over the encounter. The setting, equipment, and norms of behavior were unfamiliar to them, so they found themselves taking direction from journalists on the latter's home turf. Sometimes the interviews were carried live, adding another layer of anxiety to many subjects' performances. Kim illustrates this well because she was interviewed for both TV and print and was able to compare the two experiences. A young woman from Long Island, she did a number of press interviews at the request of the New York Department of Labor because she was one of the first users of an unemployment program it sponsored. I asked her to compare her TV interview to a normal conversation, to which she responded:

> KIM: I wouldn't say it was conversational because the reporter was telling me, "Don't look at the camera. Look at me. Look at my eyes, don't look around." I think it was a little bit of a distraction because when we first started the interview I was swaying in my chair little bit and not realizing I was doing it. And he told me, "You've just gotta sit still. And don't look at the camera." . . . And I think it was the fact that I knew this was gonna be seen all over Manhattan.[31]

Between trying not to move or look at the camera and knowing whatever she did would be seen by many thousands of people, Kim understandably found it hard to relax. The reporter, by contrast, not only knew the drill, he instructed her on camera-appropriate face-work. By comparison, the interview she did with a print reporter felt much less stressful and more like a conversation between equals:

> KIM: So it was more personalized because the two of us were standing there having a conversation together and he was writing down everything that he had found out. I didn't have a camera in front of me so it wasn't like I was being thrown on the spot. . . .
> Q: So it felt more like a regular conversation?
> KIM: Yeah. Yeah.

As these examples suggest, just as triggers may affect journalists' behavior in interviews but are likely to affect subjects more, the material objects involved in journalistic encounters probably place amateur news subjects in a relatively more vulnerable position. Inexperienced subjects, especially, may be unaccustomed to filtering out the kinds of distractions that can negatively affect face-work, including hyperawareness of a large, absent audience, unfamiliar equipment, and the demands of live or camera-ready behavior. Meanwhile, this is just another day on the job for professional reporters, whose performance in the interaction may well be edited out of the product anyway.

GROUPS, GUTS, AND FAKERY:
HOW JOURNALISTS AFFECT FACE-WORK

Journalists' behavior during interviews also made a strong impression. Even the presence of a silently observing journalist can influence how subjects feel and behave, as Thomas, an actor whose rehearsals were visited by a reporter, pointed out. He said even though the reporter was unobtrusive, he still felt a bit self-conscious just having him in the room, "Because there's someone there. You're 'on.' You know you're being watched and it's gonna potentially be out there for public consumption."[32] As Thomas's comment suggests, a reporter's body, like a camera, can be a helpful reminder of the eventual news audience, but it can also be disconcerting. Some subjects who were observed at their jobs for long periods of time felt they were gradually able to forget about reporters, but, at least at first, everyone felt self-conscious, if not outright uncomfortable. And, of course, journalists rarely remain silent in encounters. As I discuss below, interviewees described various reactions to journalists, ranging from overwhelmed, to warm, to outright disgusted.

"LIKE SHARKS ATTACKING": JOURNALISTS IN GROUPS

Reporters made an especially strong impression on subjects who had been involved in major events, or whose stories appeared in national publications that spawned interest from many others. In those cases, subjects' lives were consumed for days or even weeks by fending off or engaging an onslaught of journalists. While not everyone had a miserable experience, they all said it was overwhelming. Several said they were bewildered at how reporters had tracked them down, either at home or by phone; how quickly they did so; and how insistent they could be.

Jay, the ferryboat captain who rescued plane crash survivors from the Hudson River, described facing a wall of reporters and flashing cameras when he got back to the dock immediately afterward. I asked him what the reporters were like and he said:

> JAY: Like sharks attacking. Like [imitating voices of pushing reporters], "No, I had him next!" Or "I had him next!" . . . then you had like three people around you with ten different microphones, and this one's asking a question, and that one, and they're all trying to feed off of each other. And it was just kind of overwhelming. Because I still had no idea—it didn't sink in what was really going on.

As Jay points out, the aggressive scrum of reporters felt all the more overwhelming because they closed in on him before he had fully digested what had happened. Eve, a crash survivor mentioned earlier, concurred. As she left the hospital a few hours after being pulled from freezing waters, and still recovering from the shock of it all, she faced a crowd of eager journalists. She took the time to speak to them and even found some of them sympathetic and concerned. But overall, she said, "It was a little bit scary. It's quite confrontational, actually. They want information, and they are in your face to get it, and so I found it a little bit daunting."

Some subjects said that the questions began to feel so repetitive, and the need to constantly perform in interviews so tiresome, they were eager to return to their normal lives when the attention died down. Others felt telling the same story multiple times actually had some benefits. They improved with practice or, as Tanya concluded, "it was therapeutic to talk about it and get it out."[33] But maintaining one's face when tag-teamed by reporters can be hard. Keith, a New York City cop who made national news for helping to foil a terrorist plot, found being pursued by reporters for days afterward nearly as surreal as the trigger event. There were droves of them, and they were incredibly persistent. When I asked him what he thought of the reporters he replied, "The media? Hounds. Hounds. Relentless.

Like, you'd tell 'em, 'I can't say anything.' And then . . . they would keep trying. That's what they do. They do interviews for a living. And they were relentless. Relentless."[34]

GUTSY, FRIENDLY, HONEST:
WHEN SUBJECTS LIKE JOURNALISTS

For subjects who were involved in smaller stories that resulted in only one or a few articles—and therefore, fewer interactions with fewer reporters— many of the most salient aspects of those interactions had to do with how they negotiated the content of the potential news story, which I discuss in the next chapter. When it came to general impressions of journalists, the majority of my study participants liked the reporters who interviewed them and assessed their interview experiences overall in positive terms. Even when reporters were asking more adversarial questions, most subjects said they were friendly, personable, and engaged.

Ruby, for example, immediately liked the *Daily News* reporter who sneaked into the emergency room to interview her after she had been shot. He obviously had guts, or he would not have claimed to be her cousin to get past security—he was white and she was black. But she also liked his demeanor:

RUBY: Gutsy. Friendly. Honest. And he was genuinely into his job, and I liked that. The questions he asked were professional questions. And they weren't demeaning. They were to the point and about the subject—y'know, me getting shot.

Q: So when you say that he wasn't demeaning or anything like that, do you think that reporters usually are?

RUBY: I see it on TV. Some of the questions they ask and the way they talk to the people. And the people don't realize that these questions are geared to make them look like assholes. So they're not intelligent enough to see this and they fall right into it.

Q: But you felt like [this reporter] was respectful.

RUBY: Oh, he was.[35]

As Ruby does here, many interviewees judged the reporters they met against preconceived ideas of what journalists were like. Those ideas were not necessarily based on past experience with reporters (although for

some that was the case) but instead on their impressions as media consumers, or what they embraced as the conventional wisdom about reporters.
Those preconceptions were largely negative—I was told repeatedly that
journalists and the media in general are not to be trusted, do not care about
individuals, and often get things wrong. But many interviewees were remarkably quick to make exceptions for *their* reporter, provided his or her
behavior seemed to contradict those stereotypes.

The subjects who had liked their reporters were also the ones who said
they had felt most relaxed during interviews—that the encounter actually
felt more like a friendly chat. In theory, treating a journalistic interview
like a casual conversation would make subjects more likely to reveal information that might not be in their best interest. That is Malcolm's con artist–victim model, supported in some ways by Goffman: since a journalistic
interview is intended for reframing later, the perception that it is just another friendly encounter is a misreading of the encounter frame, likely to
result in the subject presenting an inappropriate face. And yet those interviewees who perceived the interaction as a friendly one were not necessarily
more likely to feel they had said anything inappropriate than those involved
in more formal or adversarial interviews. In fact, it was often the subjects of
more confrontational interviews who let something slip they later regretted. Many who said the interview felt more like a casual conversation had
no regrets at all.

I think these unexpected findings can be explained in two ways. First, I
found it was possible for many subjects to feel the interaction was pleasant
and friendly without completely losing sight of the true frame of the encounter—that it was intended for reframing later. Patricia, a Tea Party activist
describing her interview with the *New York Times*, illustrates this well:

PATRICIA: I felt a heavy responsibility to the movement. I wanted the
movement as best represented and as honestly represented as I possibly could.

Q: And you were aware of feeling that way during the interview?

PATRICIA: Oh, every moment of it, yes.

Q: So it sounds like it felt to you more like a formal interview than a casual
conversation?

PATRICIA: No, it was a casual conversation, and [reporter] is a good interviewer and does put you at ease, but I've been involved in this
[movement] long enough to know that you don't go into it trusting.[36]

Patricia corrects my preconception here. As she suggests, appreciation for a friendly interlocutor and extreme caution about one's face-work are not necessarily mutually exclusive.

Second, as I discuss at greater length in the next chapter, subjects are capable—not always, but often—of judging whether the trigger in question could lead to potentially harmful coverage. Some triggers are simply less risky than others. When topics are essentially fluffy or consensual—think Fourth of July Parades, or kids planting trees in a local park—subjects may sense it is safe to let their guard down because no matter how their performance is repackaged later, their reputation and goals will not be damaged. In such cases, their intuition may well be supported by the behavior of reporters, who are unlikely to seem adversarial or to include hard-hitting questions that demand that subjects really defend themselves. Not every interview is a sting operation, after all.

PUSHY, PHONY, FAKE:
WHEN SUBJECTS DISLIKE JOURNALISTS

While the majority of my interviewees had good impressions of reporters and described their interactions as positive overall, that was by no means unanimous. Some described their encounters in extremely negative terms. The most-cited criticism of individual journalists was that they were pushy and insensitive, focused only on "getting their story." In other words, subjects felt those journalists were prioritizing the instrumental side of the encounter over the basic norms of human interaction.

Subjects' responses to aggressive tactics varied. Sometimes pushiness seemed to have the desired effect during the interview, just as it did at getting subjects to agree to be interviewed in the first place: subjects found themselves answering questions they would have preferred to avoid. Other subjects felt they were able to fend off intrusive questions, and still others were surprisingly understanding of even egregious attempts to invade their privacy. Take Alegra's assessment of some of the journalists she spoke to about the illness that ended her pregnancy:

ALEGRA: They have to be pushy. I got annoyed with some of 'em, but that's their job, they have to be that way, you know? In order to get the stories that they want. Like CBS, they really wanted a picture of the baby that I lost, and I just refused over and over and they continually asked until the minute they put it on air. But that's their job.

Q: It sounds like you're pretty forgiving of their pushiness.

ALEGRA: I mean, it was annoying and it upset me and my husband, but, like I said, that's their job, y'know? You just have to expect that. They wanna get their story.

As in Alegra's case, complaints that reporters were pushy or insensitive were most often leveled at TV journalists, who many subjects felt were hurried and intrusive. Subjects also criticized TV journalists for seeming phony. In several cases TV reporters made a strong negative impression because they changed their demeanor completely when the little red light went on, leaving subjects feeling unnerved and manipulated. Friendly just moments before, they suddenly seemed adversarial or maudlin, depending on the performance they were hoping to elicit from the subject.

Fatima, for example, agreed to be interviewed for a TV news story about sensitive issues she and other Muslim women faced. A Muslim reporter had traveled all the way from England to tape the interview in her living room. The encounter began well but devolved from there:

FATIMA: So anyway, we sit down and [the journalist] is here, and she's the Muslim correspondent from London. And I immediately see her and we give our greetings to each other and I give her a hug and she's SO nice and we're hitting it off and y'know, she's speaking to me in Arabic and I'm just really clicking with her and she seems like a great person. We sit down on the couches, the camera turns on, and she becomes someone else. So she's just like this total actress. Like she turned on this role, and y'know, she grew up in the Middle East, she's been around Muslim women all her life. I knew that she totally understood my perspective and where I was coming from, but it's like for the sake of the audience she had to act like she was dumb and didn't know anything and just started attacking me. For these people it's like an act. It's like a total act. They have to act this way. It just seems really fake.[37]

A couple of subjects in similar scenarios said they felt so taken aback by the abrupt change in the reporter's behavior it took them a few on-air moments to compose themselves. The reporter's behavior moments before had led them to expect the interview to have a different tone. Instead, they witnessed an abrupt frame shift, from a friendly, intimate encounter to one intended for public consumption.

One could argue that in such cases journalists' behavior was just an exaggerated version of what everyone tries to do when an interview begins: present a face suitable for reframing later. But what to a journalist may feel like a carefully cultivated professional demeanor can seem like a complete charade to amateur news subjects. They may feel ill-used or violated when, at least on the journalist's side, professional conventions appear to trump the most basic norms of civil interpersonal interaction. Even when subjects said they understood the reasons behind reporters' conduct, they did not see the exigencies of news production as valid excuses for disrespectful or seemingly inauthentic behaviors.

Encounters with TV journalists are just the starkest illustrations of what is generally true in journalistic encounters involving ordinary news subjects: as the professional party, accustomed to the routine of abruptly putting on a public face and blocking out all distractions, be they equipment, crowds, or trigger-fueled emotions, journalists do tend to have the upper hand in these encounters. Not only are they better positioned to perform effective facework in the encounter frame, they are in total control of how the interview material is reframed in the published story. Often they will edit out their own part of the interaction altogether, leaving the subject to stand alone like the proverbial cheese.

Janet Malcolm argues in *The Journalist and the Murderer* that the journalist-subject relationship is inherently uneven because of the deception journalists invariably inflict on their subjects.[38] But as the examples in this chapter suggest, the structural disequilibrium of the relationship exists whether the journalist is deceptive or not. It is important to recognize this distinction so we can move beyond blanket condemnations of all journalists and ask more nuanced questions, such as whether a given journalist in a particular situation exploits his or her advantage to an unethical degree.

Given the way the deck appears stacked against news subjects in the interview process, it is even more remarkable that most interviewees assessed it overall in positive terms. Here I think being "ordinary" has its advantages. Many journalistic codes of ethics acknowledge that inexperienced private citizens deserve greater sensitivity than public figures. Moreover, as I have discussed briefly in this chapter and detail further in the next, the stories in which ordinary people appear are not always the kind that warrant hard-hitting, adversarial reporting. Often the reporter is as invested as the subject in a sympathetic portrayal of the latter's most appealing face. As interviewees in this chapter illustrate, friendlier, more honest-seeming reporters generally make for more cooperative, relaxed subjects, and the ensuing interacting does not necessarily lead to a disappointing result for subjects, or to their feeling betrayed by journalists.

But, although many interviewees were not dissatisfied with their interactions with journalists, those who had negative experiences were extremely turned off, and their complaints deserve attention. Being hounded by packs of journalists, feeling intruded on at a vulnerable moment, or watching a seemingly sympathetic figure transmogrify can make a bigger impression on subjects than how well or badly they are represented in the product later. Even interviewees who said they understood that intrusive, insistent, or seemingly phony behaviors were a necessary part of journalistic work were nonetheless rattled, if not outright frightened and disgusted by them. Those were often the parts of their experience they were most eager to discuss.

This chapter explored how subjects made sense of the basic encounter frame in which their interviews with journalists took place. As I have argued, the demeanor of journalists and an array of distractions—on top of the often heady impact of trigger events—can make it difficult for subjects to present a face that would be ideal for reframing in the news product later. To complicate matters further, often subjects hope to use their interviews to convey specific information to the public, in a specific way. In the next chapter, I explore how the journalistic encounter can feel like a pleasant exchange of information or an outright battle over how a story should be told.

4

THE INTERVIEW STAGE PART 2

From Interaction to Story

Annie was working on an innovative mapping project for a state agency based in West City. It was a cutting-edge project, with significant implications for conservation in the state, so she was excited to hear the local newspaper was interested in doing a story on it. A reporter quickly arranged to meet her at her office, and she tried to prepare for the encounter. As she explained, "I was thinking, 'Okay, I wanna try to stress this, I wanna talk about this if he asks me about this.' I tried to run through possible questions he might ask me. Not ever being in the newspaper before I had no idea what an interview was like."[1]

Annie was not sure what to expect of the interview, but, like many interviewees, she still tried to think through what she wanted to say beforehand. She hoped it would help her communicate her preferred message effectively when she spoke to the reporter. And yet, as I detail below, during the interview Annie began to realize that the reporter planned to tell a very different story from the one she had envisioned, and she had to figure out what to do about it on the spot. Give in? Resist? Redirect? How?

In this chapter I explore how interviewees jockeyed with journalists during their interviews over what information should be included in the published news story, and how it should be framed there. Sociologist Herbert Gans calls this process a "tug-of-war" over the news message.[2] He is referring mostly to journalists' struggle with powerful, official sources, not private citizens like those in this study. Nevertheless, I find that the tug-of-war characterization does capture what some interviewees described.

On the other hand, it is too openly adversarial to apply in some other cases and suggests a considerably more equal distribution of power than what still other interviewees said they experienced.

I begin with a short discussion about how journalists seek out subjects to fit into preconceived roles. I then go on to discuss four categories that capture the range of contests over the story frame that interviewees described. In the first two categories, subjects felt they and reporters were on the same page about the story frame. While those encounters were more pleasant than adversarial interviews, they could also be precarious because they raised subjects' expectations that the coverage would be as they envisioned it. In the second two categories, subjects sensed that their own story frame did not align with reporters', so the interview felt like a negotiation, tug-of-war, or outright struggle over what the story frame should be. These last two scenarios sometimes made for uncomfortable or adversarial interviews; however, they also put in the foreground the constructedness and contestability of the story frame. That made it possible for subjects to adjust their behavior during interviews and helped them prepare for coverage that might not quite align with their ideal vision of how their story should be told.

CASTING AND AUDITIONING FOR NEWS STORIES

As I discussed in chapter 2, subjects like Annie often have specific goals when they speak to reporters. They hope to call attention to a cause, witness to an event, or repair their reputations. Depending on their goals and the nature of the trigger, subjects may or may not be highly invested in how the story is reframed for public consumption. For instance, subjects stopped on the street for a quick quote often have little at stake in the story. But many subjects are contacted by reporters because they took part in a major event, have a strong relationship to an issue, or are experts on a topic. In those cases, subjects frequently have a clear idea about what the "true" story is and how it should be told, before interviews even begin.

But journalists, too, often have preconceived ideas about what the story frame will be when they approach potential subjects. In the United States, journalists are not generally supposed to give their own opinions in their stories; instead, they must find other people to voice the various points of view they hope to include. They have to produce stories quickly—more so now than ever before, given the pressures of online production—so it is not uncommon for them to mentally or actually begin composing stories before they have completed the reporting process.[3] That means they often seek out sources to fill in specific gaps—to represent a particular segment of the population, or to supply quotes they more or less already have in mind. One might say they are looking for actors to cast in a play, the script of which they are in the process of writing.

In that spirit, we can think of the interview not just as a performance like any other face-to-face interaction but as an audition of sorts.[4] If the journalist is still in the initial stages of researching a story, the auditioning subjects may have a great deal of influence on how the story is told and how their part is written. Imagine a highly collaborative process in which the playwright tailors the script to the strengths of the actors. But often, ordinary Joes are contacted to provide quotes when a story is near completion, in which case they may sense they are being cast in preestablished roles.

Since journalists ultimately decide how to frame the story and cast it, the interview stage is often subjects' only opportunity to contribute to and influence the story frame—to persuade reporters that a particular way of telling the story to the public is more accurate than, or preferable to, another. However, when reporters approach subjects for interviews they often do not tell them what story frame they have in mind, or how fully formed it is at that point. That leaves subjects with little recourse but to rely on oral and behavioral cues from reporters—the types of questions they are asking, for example, or how interested they seem in certain answers—to judge where reporters stand on the issues under discussion, and how they will probably reframe them later.

Annie illustrates this well. When she greeted the journalist who wanted to write about her mapping project and led him on the winding walk back to her lab, a couple of things surprised her. She was taken aback by how quickly the interview began, and she found herself answering a barrage of personal questions she had not expected:

ANNIE: And he showed up and immediately started interviewing me. Which was really weird. As we're walking he's talking to me, y'know, and I was like, "Oh. He's interviewing me already. [sounding uncertain] Okaaay, this is gonna be fine."

Q: So no real preamble, just like—

ANNIE: No. Just zinged right into interviewing me.

Q: What did you think about that?

ANNIE: Um. [with a little hesitation] I thought it was fine. A little odd. I don't know, just because he was asking me more personal questions, and not about my job. I wasn't expecting that. He would ask me, "Are you married?" That was like the third question. So it was like, what does that have to do with what I'm doing? He definitely caught me off guard.

Annie had no trouble recognizing the boundaries of the interview frame: she correctly interpreted the reporter's cues that the interview had already begun. The abrupt frame-shift took her by surprise, but what really caught her off guard was the type of questions he was asking. She had entered the interview with strong feelings about what the eventual story should look like: it would focus on her map's implications for environmental conservation. She had prepared her comments with that story frame in mind. But as the reporter launched into his questions, Annie began to suspect that he had a different vision, for an article that would focus on her personally, as a kind of heroine explorer.

Based on the cues subjects pick up from reporters during the interview, they can do their best to present a face and a message likely to influence the story frame in their favor. They can make adjustments as necessary if they suspect a journalist wants to take the story in a direction they had not anticipated or do not prefer. Sometimes they may find themselves improvising to try to get the reporter back on track. But, as Annie discovered, that strategy is far from foolproof:

ANNIE: So we went through all these personal questions and I was like, "Oh, great. Here we go." I'm trying to steer it back towards talking about what we're doing at [her state department] for this project, and he just kept asking me very personal—not personal, but I guess I'd call them "human interest" questions. Like, "What do you have for lunch when you're on the road?"

Q: I noticed that made it into the article.

ANNIE: Yes. Y'know, he asked me to describe a typical day while I'm working, what I do. And I think I described it, and then I tried talking about the landscape [starting to laugh] and the project again.

Q: Yeah, trying to get back to the initial bullet points.

ANNIE: The big picture, yeah. What I'm doing and what it's gonna do for the environment. So I remember I kept trying to swing it back that way but he wasn't buyin' that. And he did mention halfway through the interview that this was going to be a human-interest story. And I was like, "Well, that's fine, but we need to talk a little bit, just a *little* bit, about the conservation aspect of the job." . . . And I think while I was being interviewed Robert [her boss] came over, and he started talking about the importance of the project. So we were both really drilling it into him.

She may have had little prior experience interacting with journalists, but Annie was fully aware during the interview that she was locked in a struggle with the reporter over the frame of the story he would later write. She anticipated where the reporter wanted to go with her story based on the questions he was asking, and she took steps to try to haul him back to her vision of what the story frame should be. She even addressed her concerns about his envisioned frame explicitly, by telling him she felt strongly that they needed to talk about conservation at least *a little bit*.

And yet the immediate exigencies of the face-to-face encounter—that she be at least minimally polite, for example—and the fact that the reporter seemed married to a preconceived idea about how to frame the story made it hard for Annie to redirect his focus. She ultimately concluded that, despite her best efforts to control the message, she never really had a chance:

Q: You said that you found yourself trying to steer the conversation back to what you thought were the most important points.

ANNIE: Yeah, and he would go back to the human-interest stuff.

Q: Did you feel like you could control the thing at all?

ANNIE: No. No, you can't. Nope. [Chuckles] No, he definitely, I think, had his mind made up of what he was gonna write about before he came. And he just needed a little more information.

Annie was right: the reporter wrote a human-interest story that told the world she ate tuna for lunch. In her case, the reporter telegraphed exactly where he was going with the story, but often cues are subtle or imperceptible to the subject, who essentially ends up working blind.

To take steps to redirect the journalist toward a particular story frame, subjects must first recognize that such steps are necessary—that the interview is not only an exchange of information for the reporter to use in a news story but also a collaboration, negotiation, or outright battle over how that information will be framed in the published story. Below I describe four categories of story contests, starting with interviews in which subjects did not sense that the story frame was being contested at all, and ending with episodes in which subjects felt they were being completely miscast in roles that did not fit. Dividing the range of frame contests into the categories below is analytically helpful, but in practice these categories blur into one another. Even within a single interview, a subject may fluctuate between them, perhaps feeling at first that the reporter is sympathetic to his frame, then antagonistic, and so forth. As is true of all encounters, the actors were in a fluid, ongoing process of assessing new informational cues from their partners and adjusting their faces accordingly.

"I JUST TOLD HIM WHAT HAPPENED": UNCONTESTED STORY FRAMES

On one end of the spectrum, the journalistic encounter may not feel like a frame contest at all. Some interviewees simply could not imagine a story frame different from their own and saw no signs to the contrary from reporters. That feeling was especially common among people-on-the-street and witnesses of relatively uncomplicated, contained events. They understood they were being singled out to give their perspective on a specific occurrence or issue and saw no reason to expect anyone to contest it.

Take Manuel's description of his interview. A bailiff in a county criminal court, he was featured in the West City paper for tackling and detaining a defendant who attempted to escape. I asked him if he had any reservations about talking to the reporter, to which he replied:

MANUEL: Yeah, I didn't have any problems with it because I knew what had happened. I mean, there was nothing we were trying to cover up. Like I said, I already knew [the reporter], so I felt comfortable with him. I didn't think he was going to word it the wrong way or give us a bad rap or anything. I felt like he was gonna call it the way it happened. . . .

Q: Before you did the interview did you give any thought to what you were going to say?

MANUEL: No. Because you just say what happened. Just like if somebody asked you, "What is your name?" You don't think about it, you just tell them your name. It's the same way. When it's there, it's there. And that's how you answer it.[5]

Although Manuel later said he hoped the story would serve as a deterrent to other potential escapees, he did not have a complex story frame in mind other than "what happened," and he trusted that the reporter's frame would be the same. He knew the reporter and believed the trigger was noncontroversial—"there was nothing [they] were trying to cover up"—which helped. The reporter's behavior also confirmed Manuel's belief that his version of the story was the only one: the reporter did not ask him tricky or adversarial questions or demand that he respond to conflicting reports. As Manuel's example illustrates, absent any pushback from reporters, subjects can emerge from interviews confident that theirs is *the* story frame, and that the reporter's version of events will be the same.

One could easily interpret Manuel's total confidence that the reporter would transmit his story as he saw it as a naïve understanding of the journalistic encounter. All story frames are ultimately under journalists' control, and they always could, in theory, cast the subject in an unflattering role. And yet none of my interviewees who said, like Manuel, that they "just told the reporter what happened" felt they had misjudged the encounter. Although some disliked some aspect of the news coverage later—Manuel felt they chose a particularly unflattering photo—they did not feel their trust in reporters had been misplaced. Perhaps they just got lucky; but perhaps people are better than we might think at discerning when a particular trigger-reporter combination poses little risk. Even the phrase "I had nothing to hide," which popped up in various iterations in my conversations with subjects in this category, suggests they were aware that in some journalistic encounters they *would* need to conceal something—that journalists' job is often inherently adversarial or investigative, their goal to bring light to shameful behavior. When the topic and subjects' involvement in it are uncontroversial, however, it stands to reason that the story frame would not necessarily be a point of great debate.

I also spoke to some subjects who were interviewed for more complex stories that they realized were open to interpretation but who still felt confident reporters would adopt their preferred story frame. They did not feel that the frame was in dispute because reporters gave no indication that they had a competing frame in mind. In some cases reporters seemed completely amenable to adopting whatever frame the subject wanted. For instance, Thomas, an actor who was featured in a long piece in the *New York Times*, entered the interview stage with strong feelings about what he wanted to get across. He had a physical condition that limited his range of movement, and he was eager to speak about the innovative performance art he was creating with a director-choreographer at the time. He hoped it would drum up interest in the work and increase ticket sales.

It turned out the reporter had a child with a similar condition, and he and Thomas got along quite well. The reporter even attended rehearsals, which happened to include exercises that seemed to be increasing Thomas's range of motion. During the interview process Thomas, like Manuel, did not feel any pushback from the reporter against the version of the story he was presenting. This reporter, unlike some Thomas had encountered previously, seemed completely open to having Thomas write his own script:

> THOMAS: He never tried to tell us the story that he wanted—y'know, to get us to tell him the story that he thought he wanted to write. . . . So he just reported, asked us some questions, interviewed some other people in my life, like actors I had worked with and whatnot. So he did a lot more work than what actually appeared in the article itself. 'Cause in addition to his two or three visits in rehearsal we had a good three-hour-long interview, in which I talked about so many more, much larger issues than what appeared in the article.[6]

Thomas's last comment here hints at the potential danger of journalistic encounters in which the story frame feels completely uncontested or uncontestable. They can raise the subject's expectations that the reporter will adopt his version of events whole-cloth. Those expectations might be met, as they were for Manuel, but they might not be. Thomas eventually came to love his article, but when he read it the first time he was pretty disappointed. The reporter had centered the story on those motion-enhancing exercises:

THOMAS: I remember my mood was like, [sounding let-down] "huhh." I was ambivalent about it—or, I didn't feel so good.

Q: Well, do you remember what it was that you were sort of disappointed in? If that's even the word.

THOMAS: Yeah, that would be fine. I think the initial thing was it wasn't really—our concern was that the focus would be on the art and the project and the process, but really [the final article] was this sort of weird quasi-medical story about the physicality of what these two sort-of outsiders are doing.

Thomas describes a classic clash between the story frame he, the subject, had envisioned—focused on the performance art he was creating—and the one chosen by the reporter to tell the story—about the surprising medical benefits of the exercises he did during rehearsals. As his example illustrates, if subjects feel during the encounter that the story frame is not in contention, they may not realize they need to take special measures to try to influence how the reporter will tell the story. An atmosphere of pleasant consensus during the interview can also raise subjects' expectations that the reporter will simply tell the story as they, the subjects, envision it, which may lead to disappointment later.

WHEN FRAMES ALIGN

Sometimes subjects are acutely aware that journalists could choose story frames unfavorable to them, usually because the triggers in question are complex or controversial. But during interviews they start to feel reassured by little indications from journalists that their envisioned story frames align. Unlike the previous set of cases, here the story frame becomes more explicitly a point of discussion, negotiation, and collaboration during the interview. Since the tone usually remains constructive rather than adversarial, subjects in these cases may let their guard down to a degree an outsider might think foolish for someone discussing sensitive issues with reporters. However, subjects are confident that journalists are giving off cues that indicate they can be trusted to frame the story in a favorable way. The subject may even feel like he is collaborating with the journalist on a story that will meet both their needs, so there is little to be gained by being hostile or guarded. As in the previous category, lack of tension over the frame can raise subjects' expectations that the coverage will be as they envision it, which is always a risk.

Flora, for example, was contacted by a *New York Times* reporter because she had written an email to prominent members of her ethnic community urging them to unite and act together in the wake of a natural disaster in their home country. Someone had apparently leaked the email to the reporter. Flora was initially tempted to refuse an interview because she had not written the email with a large audience in mind and worried an article would simply air the community's dirty laundry. But the reporter persisted and convinced her that he wanted to write an in-depth article about an issue she considered very important:

> FLORA: I didn't want [the email] to be the thing. But when I spoke to him, it seemed like it was a broader article. And that's when I was like, "Oh, okay." Because I agreed! I had so much to say to him as far as the community and how it wasn't about the [disaster] but really about how we need to be a more unified force. . . .
>
> Q: Is that what convinced you that you did wanna talk to him? Was it this conversation?
>
> FLORA: Yes. Yeah, because I was just like: this is important.[7]

The reporter presented a fairly loose story frame about the lack of unity in the community, but it was one that corresponded with the message Flora wanted to convey. In their initial phone conversation, and later, in their in-person interview, Flora saw continuous hints from the reporter that he was open to her perspective and planned to write an article in which that perspective would be undistorted because it fit what he was looking for. Since their story frames seemed to dovetail, she felt quite comfortable being open with the reporter:

> Q: Did you give much thought to what you wanted to say to him before the interview?
>
> FLORA: No, not at all. I just figured, like I said, he had a direction he wanted to go. And he just asked me various things. . . . It wasn't an interview, it was more like a dialogue. . . . I told him my personal

thoughts. . . . He had his thoughts, but he wanted to know what the community was thinking and feeling, and he really wanted to put that out there. . . .

Q: So would you say you trusted him?

FLORA: I did. Very much. Very much.

That may sound like a setup for a major letdown, but Flora was not wrong. The story exceeded her expectations:

FLORA: I liked everything [about the article]. And I liked the context in which he put it, which was, again, in a nonmalicious way, it was very much informative and it was really to create this discussion and dialogue about an issue that really exists. I felt like, as a writer, he was trying to accomplish the same thing we were. You know how sometimes someone will quote someone but you can tell they're against what they're saying? But I guess he had an idea and he went out and looked for people to support it. . . . So, since I was one of those people that supported his thoughts, I guess I like the article [chuckles].

The same question arises in Flora's case as it did in Manuel's: did Flora just get lucky? In a way, probably so, because the reporter still could have chosen to frame the story unfavorably. But she trusted her intuition that she was being cast in a role that fit, and cues from the reporter all along seemed to confirm that. Looking back on her interactions with the reporter, she concluded, "I felt like his mission was aligned with mine."

Leyla described an even more collaborative experience. She was speaking out on a topic so controversial she changed her phone number before the article came out. The story was about contentious organizing practices at a particular labor union where she had worked. Long embroiled in the controversy, she was hyperaware of competing story frames that might upend her efforts, and she hesitated to cooperate with any reporter who might use her input to bash the labor movement in general. But she was familiar with this particular reporter's past work, and he made it clear from the beginning that he was on her side of the issue:

LEYLA: I was pretty willing to speak to him initially just because I know who he is, although I did ask him what he expected his perspective to be. And he was pretty honest with me that he has been friends with

[the union president] for a long time, and that he had been very supportive of [the union] but that the reports that he'd heard of this
practice were really appalling and he thinks it has no place in the
labor movement. And that seemed like a pretty good perspective to
have. And so we emailed back and forth and spoke on the phone a
whole bunch. And I felt really very comfortable with his handling of
the issue.[8]

Their subsequent encounters felt like a true collaboration to produce
the story they both had in mind. She described an interaction in which she
shared painful personal experiences with a sympathetic interlocutor. In
return, he kept her informed about how the story was developing, and
their teamwork resulted in the story she had come to expect. Looking
back, she agreed that her level of comfort during the entire process was
largely due to the reporter having conveyed to her that his story frame
aligned with her own:

LEYLA: I felt like he was a vehicle for me to get my story out there in this
    situation, and I feel like that's what came out in the article, too. I really
    felt like the story that was out there was the right story.
Q: Well, I wonder to what extent you were able to feel that confident due
    to his being able to tell you right up front that he basically saw the
    story the way you saw the story.
LEYLA: Yeah. I think that was hugely important for me. Absolutely. I
    think that I probably would have spoken to him differently had that
    not been the case. I think I still would've spoken to him, at the end of
    the day, but I think I may have been more planned, or aware, or even
    concerned with exactly how I said everything in a way that I didn't
    have to be because I felt pretty reassured right from the beginning.

Several subjects of long profile stories described a similarly collaborative experience. Their cases are noteworthy because they spent ex-
tended periods of time with the reporters—in some cases many hours
or even multiple days—and the stakes were high since they were the
main focus of the resulting story. But most of the profile subjects I spoke to
felt comfortable in their interactions with journalists, partly because
there was open discussion about which story frame might work well for
the article.

Fatima, for example, was featured in a long *New York Times* profile about Muslim women. A reporter shadowed her for three days. In contrast to her negative feelings about a TV journalist described in the previous chapter, Fatima quickly grew to consider this reporter a friend:

> FATIMA: She was very open and, to be honest with you, the experience with [the reporter] was absolutely the best experience. . . . She really took the time to talk to me and not make me feel pressured, and she was very much explaining to me what she wanted to do. She told me it's not a political piece, it's just supposed to be a profile to just try to show what our life is like, basically.[9]

Fatima described a long, deeply collaborative process. She found the reporter amenable to all her requests—she asked that the photographer be female, for example—and in return she worked hard to get the reporter the kind of story she was looking for. After all, it was the kind of story Fatima also wanted to tell. It helped that the reporter was an attentive listener, open to her ideas about what might work well in the article:

> FATIMA: It was very easy to talk to [the reporter]. I didn't feel any nervousness. Then we actually just kind of became friends. She had specific questions that she wanted answered and so she would use those questions to start the conversation and then I would kind of add, like "I think this is a cool point," or "you should put this in." Or "this is a good story."

Fatima never felt her trust was misplaced; she loved the published story. It captured her life beautifully and, judging by the readers' comments, portrayed members of her community as relatable human beings. She hoped it would help dispel damaging myths about Islam, which was her primary goal.

So what is going on here? The examples in this category contain all the elements of the classic *Journalist and the Murderer* scenario of seduction and betrayal, and yet their outcomes are the exact opposite.[10] Friendly reporters led these subjects to believe they were writing a particular kind of story. In return the subjects were open and trusting, and *that trust turned out to be well placed*. Here, once more, I think it helps to recall that these are not public figures. It is often not in journalists' best interest to go around egregiously misleading private citizens and writing unflattering profiles of them, unless the subjects are implicated in serious malfeasance. On the other hand, there is much to be gained by developing a collaborative-feeling relationship with subjects, especially when writing profiles or stories about sensitive issues. It clearly leads subjects to be more open and honest and helpful during the interview process.

That said, not all interviewees who had believed that reporters' frames aligned with their own turned out to be right, and the result of their misunderstandings ranged from disappointment to a sense of betrayal. Some subjects conceded that reporters had not *explicitly* said they were on their side, but they had still gotten that impression during friendly seeming interviews. For instance Norma, a Tea Party leader who told me she probably spent upward of twelve hours talking with a *New York Times* reporter, said that he came across as exceptionally friendly, curious, and articulate. Others in her local chapter also came to like him and regard him as a friend. One couple invited him on a fishing trip. Norma conceded that she was never absolutely certain where he stood on the Tea Parties, but she *thought* he leaned slightly in their favor.

Norma personally felt well-represented in the article when it came out. However, other members of her local chapter who were also named in it felt quite betrayed by the reporter. She explained to me, "I think they felt they had opened their hearts to him, and really expressed how they felt, and they felt that that was dishonored."[11] I spoke with two other Tea Party leaders who had interacted with the same reporter in different locations. They found him professional and curious, and in one case somewhat adversarial. They did not get the sense that he was feigning sympathy for their cause at all. But I suspect that for some people it is hard to have a friendly conversation with open-minded-seeming reporter without developing a sense that he is on their side. They may then expect him to frame the story in the way they would prefer, even if he never explicitly confirms that that is his intention.

But, as one would expect, interviewees felt even more betrayed if they believed reporters had *explicitly* confirmed that they would use a specific story frame and then wrote a story that did not fulfill that oral contract. In such cases interviewees were not only upset because their expectations had not been met when they saw the published story; they were also angry because they felt that during interviews they had not been given a fair opportunity to adjust their behavior and message because they had not understood reporters' true intentions. Recall Leyla's comment that, had she sensed the reporter's frame had not aligned with hers, she "would have spoken to him differently."[12]

Daniel felt betrayed in just that way. He and his friend Rodney were interviewed separately for an article about substance abuse counselors who had been laid off owing to budget cuts at public schools in the Bronx. Daniel was interviewed first and had a specific story frame in mind. He wanted to convey to readers that this was one of the most drug-infested neighborhoods in the country; that the high school where he had worked had been successfully confronting the problem through aggressive programming; and that these budget cuts would have detrimental effects on the kids.

He spent over an hour talking to the reporter about all the good works he had done and even sent her pictures of the students. He asked her outright—more than once—if all that information would make it into the story:

> DANIEL: We started from my first year at [his high school], and the transition that I made from middle school to high school. . . . I was telling her all of that.
> Q: And was she just kind of letting you talk? Was she interested?
> DANIEL: She was very interested. She was like, "Wow. This is so nice. Wow." I felt betrayal—I felt mad afterwards. Because she seemed like she was so—for us. For our kids, the community. Me. I was excited. . . . We coulda hit a home run! I said [to the reporter], "Most of the stuff we talked about's gonna be in there, right?" And she said, "Yeah, most of the stuff we talked about's gonna be in there." . . . I said, "Okay, because I really want people to know about this." . . .
> Q: Okay, got it. That was the story that you were—
> DANIEL: Originally. "The Bronx is about to lose two good ones. Why are we lettin' these guys go?" That's what she helped me envision when she first got on the phone with me.[13]

Daniel felt he had been intentionally and explicitly led to believe that the story frame would be what he was hoping for—that the reporter had "helped him envision" a complete portrait of his school and the implications of the recent layoffs there. So he felt betrayed when the reporter wrote a short piece focusing mostly on his friend Rodney and the implications of the layoffs for Rodney's family. As Daniel explained, if he had realized that the journalist's story frame did not align with his, he would have modified his expectations for the coverage. He also would have pitched the reporter a concise sound bite that would have conveyed his main message while conforming to her story frame:

DANIEL: I would've been less disappointed. I wouldn't have been that mad because I would've been expecting it. And I also would've said, "Okay. Just mention that this school is in the highest drug-infested neighborhood in the South Bronx, and the kids are gonna need somebody there."

Rodney, who spoke to the reporter after Daniel, had a much more positive experience. During that interview Rodney sensed that the reporter was adopting his own frame for the story, which differed from Daniel's. He and his wife had *both* been laid off, a critical blow to his family's welfare. Based on his sense that the reporter was intrigued by his story frame, he made a point of adjusting his performance to ensure his message would translate well:

RODNEY: When I brought up the situation that my wife also got laid off, it opened up another set of questions that was like, [imitating a suddenly very interested reporter] "Ooh, really? Oh, this is huge. It's not just you. Because your situation, it affects the whole family." . . . I wasn't sure what [the article] was gonna be because you give so much information. You don't know what they're gonna choose. But I made sure to get some key points in. To get the main sound bite in, which was, "Husband and wife laid off."[14]

To be fair to the reporter, she may well have changed her story frame when she spoke to Rodney. Perhaps she had fully intended to focus on Daniel's school and the effects of the layoffs on the students, until she found Rodney's account of the impact on his family a more compelling way to frame the story. Perhaps her editors made the decision. But Daniel and Rodney illustrate a key point: based on their sense of how well their envisioned story frame corresponds with the reporter's, subjects adjust both their performance during the encounter and their expectations for the subsequent coverage. Both Daniel and Rodney believed during their interviews that their frame aligned with the reporter's because of cues they got from the reporter. Daniel was wrong. When he saw the coverage, he felt betrayed. Rodney was right, and he loved it.

A TUG-OF-WAR OVER STORY FRAMES

Sometimes subjects feel acutely aware throughout the interview process that journalists may well choose a story frame that is far from their own ideal. These encounters do not necessarily feel antagonistic; some still feel collaborative. But subjects tend to let their guard down less because reporters do not give off cues that they are necessarily allies. When reporters appear agnostic or skeptical, it can actually benefit subjects, who can make adjustments. They can tweak their presentation in the encounter to present the most convincing possible argument; take defensive measures against potential counterarguments; and modify their expectations for the coverage.

Nikhil is a good example. A surgeon who spoke to a reporter for the West City paper about a controversial procedure to relieve pain, he knew right off the bat that the reporter was a skeptic. She told him so. So he spoke to her as he would a wary patient, sensing it was the best approach to ensure she would choose a favorable—or, at least, not entirely unfavorable—story frame:

> NIKHIL: When I spoke to the reporter, she mentioned that, "I know this thing doesn't work." So I was like, "Okay. Well, I'm not gonna convince you that this works, but I want to at least give you the other side of the story."
>
> Q: So she actually presented herself as someone who was convinced that it didn't work.
>
> NIKHIL: Yeah, she herself was a migraine sufferer. And so she kind of was sympathetic, but she was not fully convinced. So my goal was not to make her a believer but at least to say, "Well, let's keep it in the middle. Let's get you a balance." So I told her, "You're ultimately gonna write the story. But I want you to at least know both sides of it." And I did tell her that this is not necessarily a controversial procedure, it's a new procedure. We just have to figure out who it works on, and I can tell

you it doesn't work on everybody. So, I think when that kind of information was laid out there, she was ready to kind of back off her thoughts and listen to me.

Q: Well, after the interview, how did you feel it had gone?

NIKHIL: I thought it went okay, I did not—the article came out much better than I thought.[15]

Nikhil was fortunate. The reporter told him outright where she stood on the issue, so he could pitch his performance appropriately. His respectful, clinical presentation was probably the most persuasive approach he could have chosen. Her attitude also helped him lower his expectations, so he was pleasantly surprised at how well his views came across in the published story.

Even if reporters did not introduce themselves explicitly as skeptics, if they behaved in a skeptical manner—asking adversarial questions or continually presenting opposing viewpoints for subjects to address—subjects got the sense they needed to maneuver deftly to convey their messages. In such cases the encounter sometimes felt like a negotiation, if not an outright battle with the journalist over how the story should be framed.

Colleen, for example, went through a series of interviews with a *New York Times* reporter for a story about a new private elementary school where she works. The new school was designed to serve an exclusive population, so she was aware going into the interview that it was a controversial story, and she tried to prepare herself for an adversarial encounter. She described a classic tug-of-war with the reporter, in which she tried to censor herself, felt pushed by the reporter to address aspects of the topic she had hoped to avoid, and ultimately gave up more ground than she would have liked:

COLLEEN: There were certain things that she asked me that I was not gonna tell her. And that was tricky.

Q: What did you say when she asked you those questions?

COLLEEN: I said, "I'm not at liberty to talk about that." Or "I'm not gonna talk about that." . . . A couple of times I was—not manipulated, but I was pushed. And I was pushed to the point of being concerned of how it would be represented if I did not answer.

Q: That you would kind of implicate yourself by not responding?

COLLEEN: Yes, that it would be easier to just get it out there than to say, "That's not the point." Which, of course, from my perspective, you're missing the point, but from her perspective, she's writing the article.

Q: Right, and it's exactly her point.

COLLEEN: Exactly. That whole thing about whether or not we have an I.Q. cutoff on a standardized test in order for children to be admitted. We don't, and I can support it six ways to Sunday, but she kept pushing, "but all of your applicants are in the high 90s, right?" And [I said] "Most of them are." "But how many would you say?!" "Most of them!" She's hammering.[16]

Being on the defensive end of an antagonistic interview can be strenuous and exhausting, as Colleen found out. Since the reporter is ultimately the one who will write the story, subjects may feel hobbled in the struggle over the story frame by their dependence on the reporter's good will. No matter how aggressive the reporter might be, it is not usually in a subject's best interest to seem overtly defensive or adversarial in return, as Colleen described:

COLLEEN: Well, having someone ask you questions for eight hours is exhausting, physically and mentally. Then there's the backstory in your mind of "why are you asking me this again?" But I don't wanna say to her, "Why are you asking me that?" Y'know, you don't wanna be antagonistic to somebody who's writing an article about you! It was excruciating because I did feel like I was in a witness box, and . . . because there was so much at stake. It was not a fluffy little, "Tell us about your recipe for chili bread." Y'know, it was not that kind of thing. And even though it may have come across to people reading it that it was just a nice, fluffy, informative piece, that's not what it felt like in the process.

A tug-of-war over story frames can provoke a lot of anxiety in subjects. It can feel uncomfortably antagonistic—especially, as in Colleen's case, if the subject is highly invested in the issue under discussion. But tug-of-war encounters can be preferable to those described in the previous two categories because they bring to the foreground the fact that the story frame is being negotiated, and that the journalist will ultimately make his or her own decision about what it will be like.

That negotiation between unequal players is almost always at the heart of the interview process. And yet it can be more or less evident, depending on the behavior of both actors, especially the journalist. As illustrated by the examples above, since the subject in tug-of-war encounters is always aware that the frame is in play, he can adjust his behavior to present the most persuasive version of his argument. He is also far less likely to feel betrayed by the coverage, even if it is outright hostile, because he will be prepared.

HELP, I'M BEING MISCAST!

Sometimes subjects get the feeling during interviews that reporters are not just asking tough questions but trying to get them to say something specific—to perform roles that the reporters need to cast, but that subjects may not feel represent them accurately. Some interviewees realized they had been miscast only when they saw the published story, and I discuss their reactions in the next chapter. However, I spoke with a number of subjects who sensed during the interview itself that reporters had an entire script written already and were trying to get them to parrot back the lines. Obviously, a reporter cannot come right out and tell the subject what to say, but she may ask leading questions or use other techniques to try to elicit a specific performance.

Interviewees who felt reporters were trying to get them to follow a pre-written script varied in their responses to that pressure. Bella, a university professor contacted by several publications to comment on a new video game about her area of expertise, described her own effort to resist being miscast by one reporter:

BELLA: [The reporter] said he was writing an article on [the game] and would like to know my opinion of it. And I said, "Well, I would like to play it to be able to answer that." And the first really odd thing about it to me was that he said there wasn't going to be time to do that because the article was due out on Saturday. And I said, "Well, it would be very hard for me to give my impression without ever having played it." And basically, he didn't find that a sufficient reason to not give an impression. So I then asked him to describe it. So then we had quite a pleasant conversation in which he described it and I made some comments. But it was very clear to me that he had a storyline for his article, and that involved asking a professor whose field this was, and that that person would be aghast.

Q: How could you tell?

BELLA: Oh, I mean, it was transparent. It really was: did I not disapprove of this? He had that storyline. And I could tell it to such a degree that I had to keep resisting it very consciously. . . . I think he was going to have different kinds of interlocutors, but the professor was going to say, "This is really the end of civilization as we know it. That you would make a video game." He never said those words. I'm telling you what was my sense of what was expected from me. And I had a very clear sense of not wanting to play ball on those terms. . . . It was inaccurate, and I don't like being scripted. I don't! And it was so clear to me that he was scripting me. He was not rude. I don't feel like I had a terrible experience. I just felt like I was part of a scripted, already written piece where I was supposed to be just the line from the Ivy League professor.[17]

Although Bella felt she was able to resist being miscast, she spent so much time in the interview trying to avoid saying what the reporter clearly wanted her to say, she ultimately felt she did not convey anything of value at all. It was disappointing because opportunities to influence the public conversation about her area of expertise were rare. She concluded that "It was too overdetermined. I realized that. I did what I could to engage him, but it just had too many constraints built into it in terms of my being able to say anything."

Subjects varied in their responses to pressure from reporters to say specific things, and some did not fare as well as Bella. Even when they recognized they were being miscast, they had trouble adjusting their performances to avoid it. A few simply acquiesced during the encounter and found themselves saying what the reporter clearly wanted them to say. Others said they talked so much during the interview that the reporter later cherry-picked quotes to suit a predetermined story frame, in some cases misrepresenting the subject's broader point.

I spoke with three young women in three different states who had talked to a *New York Times* reporter for a story about social life on college campuses. All three felt the reporter was casting an already scripted story, and all three felt the roles did not quite fit, but they responded differently to the situation. Shauna described trying to resist:

> SHAUNA: I felt like he really just had an agenda already. He knew what he wanted the story to be like and he just wanted to find quotes or bits of information and work them in. He asked the same question over and over again, hoping that I would eventually give him the response that he wanted.
>
> Q: Well after you hung up, what were your thoughts about how the interview had gone?
>
> SHAUNA: I called one of my friends and I was like, "Yeah, so I had this interview and I really felt like he wanted me to say a certain thing." Like, that was my immediate feeling. I was thinking, "Oh, I probably won't be used because I wasn't saying what he wanted." I felt like I wasn't giving him any supporting evidence that he would wanna use.[18]

But she *was* used, quoted twice, in ways she felt were taken out of context and misrepresented her view completely. Despite her efforts to redirect the conversation during the interview and avoid following the prewritten script, she had said enough for him to pick and choose a quote that suited his purposes.

While Shauna found herself actively resisting being miscast, Monica, another student in the same story who lives in a different state, chose a kind of middle ground. She tried to tell the reporter what he wanted to hear, without entirely misrepresenting herself:

> MONICA: I got the impression that he had his central thesis and he was definitely looking for anecdotes and information that would back that up. And I think I tended to mold things to fit that thesis. I think I still said what I wanted to say, and I said things that I believed were true, but there were other things I could have said that didn't support his thesis that were true as well. Or that I knew that he wouldn't—that he didn't pick up on when I would say them.
>
> Q: So it sounds like you felt pretty comfortable giving him information that shored up his thesis because it wasn't false in your experience, but neither was it—
>
> MONICA: I definitely didn't say anything I felt was untrue.

Q: I guess that's another way of asking the question: whether or not you felt manipulated into saying anything you weren't comfortable with.

MONICA: No, definitely not. That can be true, to some extent, of any conversation you have with anybody. Just based on their reactions to certain things that you say. And so I suppose in that way that was probably true to some extent, but I don't think that as a reporter he pressured me into saying anything.[19]

Monica's last point here returns us to a familiar question: is telling a reporter what he clearly wants to hear really so different from ordinary face-work?[20] As Monica suggests, a skilled reporter can project a face that depends not only on the subject engaging with him but on that subject supplying certain desired information, in a certain desirable way. The subject may well find herself saying things to suit the journalist's story frame. Even Monica, who recognized what was going on while it was happening, was not *too* thrilled when she saw her quote in the *New York Times*. She said it made her come off as "shallow, and materialistic, and a gold digger." She was resigned to it, but it was not how she would have chosen to be cast on a national stage.

As Deanne discovered, it can be particularly maddening to feel an off-camera reporter is trying to manipulate your performance. Recall that she witnessed a woman attempt suicide. She was still in shock when a TV reporter approached her and tried to get her to emote for the camera:

DEANNE: She said, "Did you see what happened?" I said, "Yes." And then it was immediately lights on, here's the microphone in my face. And she said, "Can you tell us what happened?" But I just felt immediately—I just got a fake vibe from this woman. [Phony voice] "Ohh, that must've been hard." And it was like, "Ick." And okay, now you're gonna try to create this big maudlin story.

Q: So you felt like she was, like, milking—

DEANNE: Totally! That's exactly what it was.

Q: And your sense of that came from her tone?

DEANNE: Totally. Just cheesy. It was fake, it was cheesy. Honestly, it was like *Saturday Night Live*. It was like she's giving me these knowing, sympathetic looks and I was like, "How the hell did I get here? What am I doing?" It was sorta like an out-of-body experience. It was like I heard myself talking, but I didn't wanna be talking, and y'know, this reporter might've been a really nice woman, but at that moment I just had nothing but disdain and was like, "Ick. You're another vulture. . . . You're just trying to get some sensational, manipulative, heart-tugging story, and how did I become a part of it? Like, why am I agreeing to this?"[21]

As Deanne vividly describes here, the shock of the trigger event and the immediate demands of the face-to-face encounter, including the cameras and the behavior of the reporter, can lead a subject to not only agree to be in a news story before she can really think through the pros and cons but to present herself in ways she later regrets. When Deanne saw the coverage, she realized she had succumbed to the reporter's efforts. Voice shaking, clearly distraught, she *hated* how she came across.

DEANNE: I think she was trying to get me to really emote. And I did. When I saw it that night, oh, I just hated it. And I hated it because I felt like, y'know what? I allowed this woman to— [pause].
Q: Well, did she try to get you to say certain things that you weren't gonna say?
DEANNE: She did.

Miscastings raise the question of whether the norms of everyday interpersonal encounters are simply incompatible with successful navigation of the news production process. If journalists are putting out cues that their own face-maintenance is predicated on the subject performing a specific role, it can be difficult for subjects not to comply—even if they feel the role is a bad fit. One might think only inexperienced news subjects would fall into this trap, but my interviews suggest that journalists themselves might be particularly susceptible to it. Shauna and Monica were both seniors working at their university newspapers at the time of their interviews. Both said that made them especially eager to cooperate with any reporter, especially one from a prestigious paper like the *New York Times*. It stands to reason that the more invested subjects are in pleasing reporters, the more prone they will be to distorting themselves to suit reporters' needs.

Indeed, Ira, a magazine journalist with a decade of experience, was himself an especially extreme example of a subject contorting himself to accommodate a reporter. The reporter in question was a former colleague who was writing an article about adult men who play video games. Ira does play video games—as part of his job reviewing them, for limited periods of time in his office, and with his wife's blessing. But little by little he found himself responding to pressures from the reporter, and later a photographer, to present himself as a man-child whose video game habit was threatening his marriage. He even found himself enlisting his wife in the charade. They both gave quotes suggesting video games were a point of contention in their home and posed for pictures to that effect:

> Q: Was there any point when you guys said, "No, I'm not gonna do that?" Or did you just kinda play along?
>
> IRA: We were definitely a little resistant. But the thing is, like, that whole experience was so awkward anyway so we were kinda like, [acquiescing] "ehhh." Obviously the photographer knew we were a little bit anxious about it, but we didn't put our foot down. Actually, the whole thing is this like, weird cumulative effect of obedience. Or just an unwillingness to resist.
>
> Q: Yeah, it sounds almost like you were victims of your own willingness to cooperate.
>
> IRA: Yes! Yes.
>
> Q: Because it was the path of least resistance or something.
>
> IRA: Yeah. And it essentially—I think it all boils down to me just wanting to be friendly with an editor.[22]

The published article was humiliating. Technically accurate insofar as no facts were wrong, it failed to mention that Ira played video games *for his job*. But more disturbing than the content of the article was the feeling that he had been complicit in misrepresenting himself and, worse, his wife. As Ira's experience illustrates, although many subjects do successfully resist efforts by reporters to squeeze them into preconceived roles, subjects' familiarity with news production may actually make them more likely to succumb.

———— ✬ ————

In these past two chapters I have explored journalistic interviews from subjects' side of the encounter. The interview stage is especially important to subjects because only through their interactions with journalists can they exert influence over how their own stories are told in the news. Many interviewees expressed frustration with some aspect of the reporting process or the coverage of their stories, but the only ones who used the word "betrayed" were those who felt they had intentionally been led by a reporter to expect a particular story frame. They had adjusted their own behavior and message accordingly, only to discover later that the reporter had chosen to frame the story differently from how they had expected—in a way that was less helpful to their cause or more damaging to their face.

That is the classic *Journalist and the Murderer* scenario, and it can be deeply unnerving. It can lead subjects to question their trust in reporters and their participation in future news stories. It is also *rare*. My findings suggest that ordinary people feeling personally betrayed by reporters is probably the exception, not the rule. Once again, I think this is partly because interviewees were not public figures. Many stories that draw on private citizens' comments, opinions, and narratives are not sting operations designed to reveal some malfeasance or abuse of power.

That said, there is no question that, while public figures and elite, official sources may indeed wield as much power as journalists in their interactions—some scholars argue more—ordinary news subjects like my interviewees almost always have less.[23] Journalists' clout in their interactions with their subjects, whether those subjects are public figures or private citizens, comes from their control over which stories are told in the news, and how they are framed there. This is the classic gatekeeping function. Public figures and other powerful subjects have experience interacting with the media and, often, formal training that help them handle interactions with professional reporters more effectively. Over time, these professionalized news subjects can learn how to block out distractions, present prepared sound bites, and resist pressures from journalists, all of which help improve the likelihood that what they present in the encounter will survive a journalists' reframing intact. They also have an ace in the hole: ongoing access to exclusive information that they can strategically withdraw or selectively bestow, and that journalists need badly.

My interviewees, for the most part, had none of these advantages. Some were hot commodities to journalists for brief periods of time. That was the case for the survivors and heroes of major incidents that I described in this chapter. But their popularity with journalists was short-lived. In theory, they could have parlayed their temporary access to exclusive information into some kind of clout in their dealings with journalists. Some did give interviews only to specific reporters, for example. And yet I found that they were mostly so intimidated by the packs of journalists that had descended on them, they did not feel like they were able to control their interactions with the media very well at all. It did not help that some were still disoriented from their involvement in life-or-death events. If we combine all these factors it is hard to avoid concluding that ordinary news subjects can certainly engage in a spirited poker game with journalists over how their stories should be told, but in the end their chips are few.

After interviews are over, subjects wait and hope. For many, the wait is uncomfortable; the moment they see the coverage, a kind of reckoning occurs. That is the subject of the next two chapters: how subjects react when they finally see the news coverage in which they are named. In chapter 5 I begin by exploring how they assess accuracy.

5

TRUTH (PERCEPTIONS)
AND CONSEQUENCES

How News Subjects Judge Accuracy and Error

I have told Alegra's story in earlier chapters. She agreed to be featured in a newspaper article because she had contracted a dangerous medical condition when she was pregnant and lost her baby.[1] Hers is exactly the kind of painful, private story that might leave readers wondering why she would agree to speak to a reporter at all. But she knew exactly why: if she or her doctor had been more informed about the danger to pregnant mothers, things might have turned out differently.

There were a number of factual errors in the resulting newspaper story, though she had forgotten the specifics until she looked at the article during our conversation. The length of her coma was off by a month. Her "near-fatal" seizure was not really life threatening. And one of her quotes got the gist of what she had said but changed her wording. As she put it, "I've never said the word 'nonchalance' in my whole entire life."[2] When I asked if the errors bothered her, she said, "No, because they were so minimal. It wasn't like, 'Oh my gosh, they really messed this up.'" She explained that the article had achieved her main goal of getting the word out, and the errors did not bother her because they did not interfere with that objective. Many interviewees felt the same way.

Journalists and journalism scholars take for granted that factual accuracy in reporting is *important*. The reasons seem obvious: citizens need accurate information about the events of the day, and errors can damage a news outlet's credibility, not to mention an individual journalist's reputation. But surveys find that news subjects rarely rate errors in their own articles as severe. They almost never ask for corrections. Even when the coverage in which they are named contains errors, they look forward to being in the news again.[3] If both journalists and audiences care so much about accuracy, why would the individuals being written about—those we would expect to care the most—appear to care so little?

This chapter is the first of two chapters dedicated to how subjects react when they finally see the news stories in which they are named. Here I focus on how they assessed accuracy in those stories. Scholars in the past have surveyed news subjects to study journalistic errors—it is one of the few ways they have been systematically studied before—so I begin by discussing what they have found. Those quantitative studies raise questions that my interviewees then help answer in the remainder of the chapter. I explore the contextual factors that influenced how subjects interpreted errors in their stories, then go on to discuss the different kinds of errors they identified, and why they felt some were more severe than others.

Taken altogether, my findings show that, from the perspective of people named in news stories, accuracy assessment goes way beyond simply measuring the facts presented in those articles against external data. News subjects have a complex relationship to accuracy and often assess errors using very different criteria from journalists' own.

QUANTIFYING ERRORS: WHAT SURVEYS TELL US ABOUT HOW NEWS SUBJECTS THINK ABOUT ACCURACY

In 1936 newspaperman-turned-journalism professor Mitchell Charnley developed a method for testing newspaper accuracy. He identified people named in three Minnesota newspapers and mailed them copies of the articles in which they had appeared. He also enclosed a simple questionnaire asking them to count and categorize the errors in those articles.[4] With their direct knowledge of events described in the story, who better to identify inaccuracies than news subjects themselves?

Since then, scholars have tweaked and repurposed the Charnley method to explore errors in many media, formats, and genres.[5] Their methods vary, but when it comes to sheer numbers of errors, findings have been surprisingly steady over the past eighty years. Subjects of newspaper stories consistently report that between 46 and 61 percent of stories contain at least one error. The highest percentage, 61 percent, was found in the most recent and most wide-ranging study—a survey of 4,800 news sources named in fourteen newspapers across the country.[6]

While their findings are sobering, an interesting tension haunts these survey-based studies. Even as researchers try to classify errors with increasing precision—for example, by categorizing them as "subjective" errors, such as over-emphasis and omissions, and "objective" errors of fact, like names and titles—they end up acknowledging that errors are *always* subjective.[7] They continually have to qualify their results with the caveat that they measure error *as perceived by the subject*, and that subjects have unique perspectives. Their findings often illustrate this clearly. For example, when reporters are asked to respond to subjects' allegations of inaccuracy, they frequently disagree about whether an offending item is an error at all.[8] As one researcher dolefully concluded, it seems that, despite concerted efforts to quantify it, "error is largely a state of mind."[9]

And as it turns out, subjects' state of mind is "remarkably tolerant of error."[10] In a 2005 survey, for example, subjects rated subjective errors as more severe than objective errors, but they perceived severity of *all* errors as remarkably low. The most egregious subjective errors were actually those in the "other" category, suggesting that researchers had not anticipated at all the most distressing inaccuracies in the eyes of the subjects.[11] To explain these surprising findings, scholars have concluded that it is likely in the dynamics surrounding a story's publication, such as the subject's level of investment, expectations, and repercussions of the story—all of which lay outside the bounds of their surveys—that we might find the key to understanding how subjects actually assess accuracy.[12]

Those issues are best explored through qualitative methods. For example, a rare interview-based study conducted by journalism scholar David Pritchard in the late 1990s found that consultation with their reference groups was enough to calm unhappy news subjects who had identified errors in their stories.[13] If friends and family could reassure them that their reputations and relationships had not been damaged by the errors, they felt no need to complain to the newspaper. Pritchard's findings seem to corroborate the idea that, unlike journalism professionals who prioritize getting the facts straight in the product, perhaps it is not errors per se but their *effects* that are news subjects' primary concern.[14]

Pritchard also found that, despite his efforts to get news subjects to focus on accuracy, they often wanted to speak about their experiences "making the news" more broadly, or other specific aspects of it, such as their
encounters with journalists.[15] Those findings highlight one of the problems with isolating an article's content from its circumstances and asking
subjects only to assess errors: that is simply not how subjects experience
errors in the real world. As the accuracy literature consistently concludes,
it appears that subjects assess content in *light* of their circumstances,
as part of a larger phenomenon of being in the news that fits into their
lives in various complex ways.

My interviewees were in a good position to shed light on how subjects
actually think about accuracy, and how important it is to them, since they
were discussing it in the context of their broader experiences as subjects of
news stories. For some of them, the trigger overshadowed the attendant
news coverage so completely they did not even want to *see* the coverage, so
they were unable to assess its accuracy at all. Such was the case for a witness
of a fatal plane crash, for example. But, for many subjects, seeing the articles
or broadcasts in which they had appeared was an important moment, one
they anticipated with dread or excitement depending on what the trigger
was, their relationship to it, and how they thought the news coverage might
affect their lives. Below I explore subjects' views on errors, starting with the
contextual factors that most influenced how they interpreted them.

CONTEXT MATTERS: HOW TRIGGERS, GOALS, EXPECTATIONS, AND FEEDBACK AFFECT ERROR PERCEPTION

I did not provide interviewees with a definition of accuracy or predefined
categories of errors. So they were initially free to bring them up, define them,
and emphasize them as they saw fit. If they did not bring up accuracy at all,
I later asked if they were satisfied with the coverage, then if they felt it was
accurate, and to describe any errors they recalled. Finally, we looked at
the articles together, so they could point out any errors they might have
forgotten.

My study does not lend itself well to quantification because many
subjects spoke about multiple articles and newscasts. That said, I would

conservatively estimate that subjects identified at least one error, broadly defined, in 60–70 percent of their news stories. That range is on the high end of what surveys have found, which makes sense given the freedom my interviewees had to define errors broadly. That said, many of the errors they identified did fit perfectly into surveys' "objective" and "subjective" categories.

However, also consistent with survey-based studies, I found that subjects were often quick to disregard those errors. They were most dismissive of small technical errors, but they were often surprisingly tolerant of more subjective errors as well, such as omission, misquotation, and over- or underemphasis. More striking still, many could not remember whether there were errors in their stories at all. Others had a vague memory of mistakes but could not recall what they were until they looked at the article again. It was not unusual for subjects to describe their whole experience without even mentioning errors, until asked directly about them.

In other words, my findings support the idea suggested by the survey literature that, although journalism professionals regard accuracy as a core value, concerns about accuracy are not always equally important to subjects. Other aspects of their experience "making the news" often matter to them more. Furthermore, as accuracy researchers have long speculated, the context—the circumstances and dynamics leading up to and following an article's publication—shapes how subjects interpret errors.

Many factors are at work in error perception and it would be impossible to identify them all, but patterns did emerge in my interviews that help explain why some errors are so easily dismissed while others chafe badly. In what follows I explore three of the important contextual features that affected how interviewees perceived errors: their goals for the story, their expectations for the story, and reactions from their reference groups after the story appeared. Once more, while it is useful to separate these for analytical purposes, they actually interrelate a great deal.

IT DOESN'T MATTER IF IT DOESN'T HURT: HOW TRIGGERS AND GOALS AFFECT ERROR PERCEPTION

As discussed in chapter 2, depending on what the story was about, many interviewees saw appearing in the news as a rare opportunity to fulfill specific goals. Some wanted to witness to an accident or a loved one's character; others wanted to raise awareness about an issue or cause; while still others hoped to publicize their business or an event they were organizing. Many interviewees were invested in the news coverage because they were counting on it to achieve those goals, so it makes sense that they assessed the content of news stories, and accuracy in particular, in light of those objectives. Simply put, subjects were usually willing to overlook errors that did not interfere with their goals.

For example, Jon and Jane were featured in a big story in the metro section of a New York paper because their family business was being evicted for reasons they felt were unjust. They loved the article, which they said completely captured their story and raised awareness about their plight. That was their immediate goal. No, their quotes were not verbatim, and some of the details about how their business operated were off. But, as Jane explained, those errors did not matter. When it came to the bigger picture, the reporter "got it":

> JANE: But not even just the technical stuff, the social stuff. The heart of the matter. The nut of the problem. He totally got the unfairness of what was happening to us and why it was unfair. He didn't quite nail what our business is perfectly right. Which is okay, it doesn't matter. The reason that he was here was not to explain how our business worked. The reason he was here is we were basically being unfairly persecuted, and that he got right. That was the important stuff.[16]

Conversely, when errors undermined subjects' goals altogether, they were especially hard to forgive. As I detailed in the previous chapter, Daniel was quoted in an article about layoffs of substance abuse counselors in public schools. The staff, students, and families had worked hard to improve their school, so when Daniel was contacted by a reporter he was eager to call attention to their accomplishments and the short-sightedness of the layoffs. He spent an hour with the reporter explaining activities he had organized, providing her with pictures of himself with the students, and explaining why these layoffs were disastrous for the kids.

The final story was a cruel disappointment. The photo was not of his students but of another counselor, and the article focused on the financial hardships faced by laid-off school workers in general: nothing about the specific school, nothing about Daniel's work or the potential negative effects on the student body. The most objective error in the story, the state-ment that he had been fired from a previous job (he had not), was just the last straw in a long string of subjective inaccuracies of omission and em-phasis that Daniel felt were much more serious. He perceived all of them as errors and felt they completely undermined his goal to draw attention to the injustice of the budget cuts:

> DANIEL: I'm just disgusted. [The reporter] stayed on the phone with me for an hour. We went over step by step everything that I did with the kids. . . . We talked about everything that I'd done at the Department of Education. The only reason I agreed to do that story was to bring light to the whole situation. To show people that they're letting people go that's good for these kids. I don't know what that was in the paper. She talked about nothing that I did. Nothing![17]

Highly invested subjects, like Daniel, were counting on their stories be-ing told in a particular way in order to achieve their objectives. They tended to interpret coverage that diverged from the story they had envisioned as a bitter letdown, and errors within that coverage as particularly egregious.

STEELING ONESELF FOR ERRORS: HOW EXPECTATIONS AFFECT ERROR PERCEPTION

While many subjects had objectives for their stories, they varied in the extent to which they really expected the news coverage to help them meet those objectives. Interviewees seemed to form and modify expectations at various stages. Some had expectations based on past experience, or stories they had heard from other people about interacting with the media. Many subjects' expectations were affected by their interactions with reporters, either in the interview stage or in any fact-checking stages that occurred postinterview. As discussed in chapters 3 and 4, in those interactions subjects often picked up clues about what kinds of stories reporters were working on and how they planned to frame them. Subjects then adjusted their expectations accordingly.

As survey studies predict, expectations had a powerful impact on how surprised subjects were by inaccuracies, and how severe they perceived them to be.[18] For example, Daniel, the substance abuse counselor quoted above, was especially disappointed in his article because he felt the reporter had explicitly reassured him that much of what they discussed would make the cut:

> DANIEL: I said, "Most of the stuff we talked about's gonna be in there, right?" And she said, "Yeah, most of the stuff we talked about's gonna be in there." Most of the stuff. Yeah. That's not nothing. I said, "Okay, because I really want people to know about this."

Not surprisingly, this exchange raised Daniel's expectations, so the omission of almost everything he had discussed in the interview was especially disappointing.

Meanwhile, Tim provides a good counterexample of how low expectations can cushion the blow of an inaccurate article. He runs a tutoring business and was happy to speak to a reporter for an article about how negative economic trends were affecting companies like his own. He explained to her that his business was actually doing very well and gave numbers to prove it. However, when the reporter called back to check her facts, Tim began to suspect the story might not turn out as he had hoped:

> TIM: I didn't feel during the interview like there was necessarily some kind of a spin on it. I was tipped off a little bit after, when she called back, and she asked me some question about some numbers that she said I gave her that were way off. It was totally wrong. And I was like, "I don't know where you got that from, but that is not at all what I said." And she was like, "Oh, I'm sorry; I don't know where I got that then." ... And then I was like, alright. This probably isn't gonna be so good.[19]

Tim steeled himself for a sloppy story. Sure enough, his article contained multiple errors and misrepresented his business. Tim was disappointed but hardly crushed. After all, he had expected it.

DOWNPLAYING AND HIGHLIGHTING: HOW FEEDBACK FROM OTHERS AFFECTS ERROR PERCEPTION

Feedback subjects received from their reference groups also had important implications for error perception. Dudley described a scenario that illustrates this vividly. On the day the *New York Post* ran a story about an accident near his technical school, a professor invited him into a classroom to see the article in which he appeared. Surrounded by impressed students, Dudley read the article, only to discover he was misquoted:

> DUDLEY: I came in and [the teacher] was like, "Show him the paper." And everyone in the class was like, "Whoa, that's the guy, that's the guy?!" I read the one little line. I was like, "That's not what I said." Everybody started laughing. Then I left. I felt really cool. I told one of my friends, "Hey, I was in the paper." And then I told my mom. And I sent a text message to a friend of mine, that I made it into the *Post*. And then on my way home my dad asked me to get a copy for them and for his father. So I bought copies.[20]

Most striking about this scenario is just how little it matters to Dudley that his one quote was actually an error. He alerted his reference groups and bought multiple copies of an article that misquoted him. He got immediate positive feedback from others and anticipated more. That pattern was common among interviewees. I found that many discovered that being in the news enhanced their status, almost regardless of the content. As long as the coverage did not reflect *very* poorly on them, "making the paper" was generally seen as special. In some cases the positive feedback from others so dominated their experiences that inaccuracies in their stories simply faded into the background.

But just as positive feedback led some interviewees to downplay errors, some who initially felt errors were negligible or nonexistent changed their minds when they got feedback indicating otherwise. Norma, a Tea Party leader featured in a lengthy *New York Times* article about the movement, was initially delighted with it. She quickly bought five copies. Then the emails started rolling in from family, friends, and strangers who read the article as an indictment against the movement because it lumped the Tea Party in with white supremacist and militia groups. They felt that was a misrepresentation of the movement. In light of their comments, Norma began to see the whole article differently:

> NORMA: When I read it the first time I did not read it as negatively as I did the second time. . . . I saw those other groups mentioned as totally separate from our organization. I just didn't make that connection.

I don't think I felt negatively until I realized that people were literally linking—because we were in the same article—they were linking one part to another.

Q: So how did you come to realize that?

NORMA: Partially because my daughter had gotten some emails, and that was talked about. And so she really brought it to my attention. And then after I started seeing other things that were appearing on the net. . . . And right from the start our members were really upset.[21]

While Norma continued to feel that she *personally* was portrayed accurately in the *Times*, she began to think an article that presented her organization alongside racist groups was misleading to the point of being inaccurate. She probably would not have come to that conclusion had she not seen other people interpreting it that way. As I discuss in chapter 7, where I focus on audience feedback, some articles ended up having stigmatizing effects, and subjects found themselves pilloried by the audience for a simple quote. If the subject felt the source of the stigma was actually an error, it was especially hard to forgive.

TYPES OF ERRORS: OBJECTIVE, SUBJECTIVE, AND MORE

Recall that Deanne was in a series of articles because she witnessed an attempted suicide. Many of the stories contained easily verifiable factual errors. The location was almost always listed incorrectly. So was the time of day. The physical description of the scene wasn't quite right. But none of those factual errors bothered Deanne nearly as much as the sensational tone of the coverage and the exclusion of parts of her quotes. She felt those reportorial choices made her come across poorly and were more potentially damaging to the other subjects in the story than technical errors. As she explained:

DEANNE: I mean, obviously saying something about 82nd Street, that's an error. Because [the incident occurred] at 72nd, not 82nd. But just selecting parts of my quotes? That's manipulating. That's manipulating the story, and that's what makes me feel icky. I don't feel icky if someone got it wrong. To me, a factual error, it's not a big—you're not screwing with people's lives with a factual error.[22]

Deanne's comment that factual errors do not "screw with people's lives" nicely captures a fundamental difference between the way interviewees tended to view inaccuracy and the way the news industry generally perceives it. To the subjects in my study, errors of tone, omission, and over- or underemphasis often mattered far more than errors of basic fact. The former were perceived as more manipulative of the story's meaning— "icky" in Deanne's words—and more damaging to subjects' goals and reputations. These "subjective" errors, as they are labeled in the survey literature, are also the kinds of errors that are most disputable. They are frequently rooted in differences of opinion between subjects and journalists about how to frame stories, especially which details to include.

Indeed, many of the details and characteristics of news stories that interviewees identified as inaccurate or misrepresentative would probably not be considered errors by news organizations at all, and some would fall outside the categories provided on accuracy surveys. For example, one interviewee took issue with being described as "living in fear," noting that she had used the expression "I am afraid" during the interview, but in her mind that was a far cry from letting fear dominate her life.[23] Another interviewee pointed out that her quote was set up with the descriptor "she joked." She had not been joking. Moreover, she had emailed that quote, so she wondered how the reporter had come to that conclusion.[24] Or take Ruby, who had been shot accidentally by teenage gang members. The story failed to mention that the injury had interrupted her criminal justice degree. She was studying to become a juvenile probation officer to try to help exactly the kind of kids who had shot her. Ruby felt this ironic nugget was journalistic gold, and its omission an error of reportorial judgment.[25]

As these examples suggest, if interviewees were often quick to downplay or dismiss errors, they were also, when given the opportunity to speak at length about them, more likely to identify a greater variety of errors than people not named in the story probably would have. That is because they were measuring the published account against (1) their experience of the trigger; (2) their in-depth knowledge of what information was exchanged during their interview with the reporter, but limited familiarity with any other research the reporter may have done; and (3) their envisioned story frame—all while sensitive to possible repercussions of the coverage.

Interviewees identified so many inaccuracies of such a wide variety it would be difficult to enumerate them all. Below I focus on the kinds of errors that stood out because they were the most common, or the most aggravating to subjects.

"OBJECTIVE" ERRORS

As noted above, many interviewees were quick to dismiss technical errors like numbers or basic facts because those errors usually had only negligible, if any, effects. They even dismissed some errors that might seem severe to an outsider. For example, Shannon's business was profiled in the West City paper, and her entire goal was to get publicity. Shannon's last name was misspelled in the article, but she was *still* delighted with it, putting the lie to the old saw that "all publicity is good publicity as long as they spell your name right." Shannon pointed out that the reporter did manage to spell her name right at least once, and he included not just a picture but an online video of her on the job. She felt the visuals further increased the prestige of being featured in the paper so, publicity-wise, the misspelling was a minor blip.

Misquotes stood out because they were *extremely* common. Interviewees described misquotes that ranged from words being taken out of context to slightly altered or fabricated completely. Survey-based accuracy studies usually categorize misquotes as "subjective" rather than "objective" errors. I prefer the latter designation. Although there was usually no way to prove incontestably that a quote was distorted, and in some cases even my interviewees were not completely sure, in many cases, when subjects claimed they were misquoted they were so adamant that I was completely convinced. Many—like Alegra, who identified the word "nonchalance" as a word she had never used in her life—were able to pinpoint the exact word or phrase the reporter had gotten wrong.

Predictably, the misquotes subjects deemed most severe were those that, like other severe errors, distorted their statements so much they worried about possible effects on their goals or reputations. For example, Ray was caught up in a feud with a new restaurant over the location of his food cart, a local institution. Ray was eager to rally public support by making his case through the media, and the controversy was covered by several outlets in West City. He felt his argument hinged on the fact that he could not easily just move down the street, as the restaurant owner had claimed. Not only were permits involved, his whole brand was built on a specific street corner:

> RAY: [Reading the article] Like this is a misquote: "I feel like my brand is South Street." I didn't say that. There's no way that that's what I said. That's a whole different meaning. I know that I stated, emphatically— I'm very clear on this—"Our brand is South and San Fernando." That was a bullet point. We've got it on the t-shirts.[26]

The distinction may have seemed minor to the reporter, but to Ray the specific intersection, not the entire lengthy street, was the identifying brand of his business. It was literally printed on the company t-shirts. Saying it any other way weakened his argument since the whole feud was about *that* street corner.

Misquotes are also noteworthy because, even when subjects did not feel they were damaging, many found them oddly disorienting and memorable. Observations like Lynn's were common:

> LYNN: Even though everything is in quotes, somehow it's not exactly my words. I just remember that when I was reading it I was like, "Well, that doesn't sound like something I would say." The gist of it was always right but it bothered me that things were in quotes that I hadn't actually said.[27]

That even "direct" quotes often are not verbatim perhaps should not surprise us since many reporters only take handwritten notes and must do so quickly. But still, most interviewees had previously interpreted quotation marks in the paper—as most readers probably do—as a sign that the quote *was* verbatim. They were surprised to learn firsthand that that was not always the case.

The sheer variety of objective errors interviewees described made it hard to create a clear spectrum of severity. Subjects generally felt that errors that attributed incorrect action, motivation, or views to them were more egregious than technical errors like incorrect names or numbers. That makes sense since the former tended to have greater impact on subjects' goals and reputations. From their point of view, a more accurate version of the old saw about publicity might be "all publicity is good publicity, even if they spell your name wrong, as long as they don't make you look incompetent or like a total jerk."

Tanya, for example, was outraged when her local newspaper erroneously said she had taken actions during the Miracle-on-Hudson plane crash that would have endangered everyone onboard.[28] The paper later apologized, but she refused to deal with them after that. Karen was similarly irate to see a news program describe her as an enthusiastic fan of a new age guru whose unsafe practices had led to a deadly accident.[29] She had always been suspicious of him (in the wake of the accident even more so), and she felt she had made that clear in the interview. Under the circumstances, only a fool would continue to be a devoted fan. Karen, like Tanya, felt the inaccurate description might negatively affect how people thought of her, so she made a point of voicing her complaint to the reporter. As I discuss later in this chapter, subjects only rarely took that step.

"SUBJECTIVE" ERRORS

As defined by the survey literature, subjective errors, such as omission and over- or underemphasis, are the result of reportorial judgment. That distinguishes them from objective errors, which are verifiably wrong. However, interviewees did not make clear distinctions between objective and subjective errors. They often registered errors of omission and emphasis as every bit as straightforward and inaccurate as more easily verifiable errors of fact. In fact, since subjective errors often affected the whole tone or direction of the story, subjects often deemed them more severe than objective errors. Subjective errors are also harder to prove, harder to categorize, and harder to get corrected.

Errors of omission deserve special attention because they were probably the most common type of inaccuracy cited by interviewees. Subjects usually judged what was included in the published story based on expectations they had developed during the interview stage. Unless reporters had told them about the other research they were doing for the story and how they envisioned framing it—which was not the norm—subjects were left to envision coverage based on the limited clues they picked up in their encounters with journalists.

Especially when interviews had been long and involved, subjects often expected to play a larger role in the story than turned out to be the case.

Kim, for example, had spent a lot of time with a newspaper reporter. She told him in detail about the circumstances that had led to her unemployment, her expectations for the future, and the difficulties she faced. He was a terrific listener. Her reaction to the resulting article, which was about a public program to help the unemployed, was common:

> KIM: I thought there would've been more about my personal experience. Like my lifestyle change, background, everything. I really didn't know that [the reporter] had interviewed other people, 'cause he spent a lot of time with me. So I kinda thought it was just gonna be me.[30]

Some interviewees, like Kim, conceded that omissions were not exactly errors but rather choices journalists had made—poor choices, in their view, but choices nonetheless—about what to exclude from the story. Other subjects acknowledged that the omissions were not *technically* errors but argued that they contributed to an incomplete or distorted representation of what they had shared in the interview. Many felt their best points were excluded, while others, like Tea Party leader Patricia, felt their most vapid or nonrepresentative comments were included:

> PATRICIA: No, it wasn't technically inaccurate. I mean, after four and a half hours of interviews I thought there would be a little more meat to what he picked that I would say. I thought, "Of all the quotes you could've picked, why that one? That sounds pretty stupid." Yeah, I probably did say it, but gee, that wasn't the point of it, y'know? I gave him so dang much substance. I mean, I spilled my heart and soul about what this movement is all about, and did he capture that? No.[31]

Unlike Patricia, some subjects felt omissions were indisputably errors. They had a well-defined sense of which key issues and facts absolutely had to be included in order to tell their story without distortion. That assessment was most common in coverage about feuds or controversies, in which subjects felt their side's argument was given short shrift by the exclusion of key information. Those were also often high-stakes stories, in which subjects were depending on the coverage to make their case or to defend their image to the public.

Michelle, for example, identified many factual and subjective errors in the coverage of her lawsuit against a religious group. She was suing them for building a temple in her residential neighborhood. The error that most bothered her was the omission of the fact that she had warned the group in writing of her lawsuit *before* the temple's construction, a warning they had ignored. She felt the omission completely distorted the story:

> MICHELLE: I sent [the reporter a copy of] the letter: "Don't build it! You do it at your own peril. Please don't. You're going to waste your money." And [the reporter] never even mentioned it! And I think that's really pivotal in determining the justness of whether they have to tear it down or not.[32]

Understandably, Michelle felt that the distortion—caused by the omission of this key information—could potentially have negative effects on her reputation and professional life. In combination with other errors in the story, she felt she came across as an unfeeling bigot, and feedback she received seemed to confirm that.

Even when subjects felt the coverage was in all other ways accurate, sometimes they took issue with a story's tone. Several interviewees said they had been familiar with the New York tabloids' often gossipy, sensational tones, but they still found it disconcerting to be written about in such a way. Some felt it misrepresented the seriousness of the trigger as they experienced it. Gina, for example, felt the *Daily News* story in which she appeared made it sound as though she and other jurors on a high-profile murder case had not taken their job as seriously as they had. As she put it, "We were an intelligent group and really debated the points thoughtfully and this makes it sound like we *weren't* deliberate. Like it was a *game*. Come on! We treated it with so much more gravity!"[33]

Some subjects did not pinpoint specifics within the stories as inaccurate but instead felt the larger choices reporters had made about how to frame the story were essentially errors because they completely missed the point or miscast them. For example, Michelle felt the religious beat reporter's assignment to the story about her lawsuit was itself a major error. In her eyes, the story was a question of real estate, not religion. Publishing it in the religion section was already a misframing of the issue because it erroneously implied that her motives had to do with religion at all. As she put it, the reporter, "really picked it up by the wrong handle of the pot."

Subjects invariably felt that misframings and miscastings could have at least minor negative effects on their goals or reputations, so they found those errors particularly maddening. In some cases, interviewees had seen few signs during the interview that they might be miscast and were unpleasantly surprised at the moment they saw the story.

Maggie, for example, was featured in a New York–area newspaper in a story about senior citizens trying to reenter the workforce.[34] She was eager to speak to the reporter largely because she hoped the article might improve her chances of getting a job. She was careful to present herself as an energetic, enthusiastic team player. So she was disappointed to find herself depicted as a "grandma from Hoboken," in an article that seemed to emphasize over and over her—to the young reporter, apparently extreme—old age, at seventy-one. The choice of quotes, the choice of picture—*everything* seemed designed to drive home how very old she was. She felt the emphasis misrepresented her—she is a *youthful* seventy-one. But she also worried it would damage, rather than help, her chances of finding a job:

> MAGGIE: It's making me seem like this little old grandmother. And I'm out there looking to work—not to be described as a little old grandmother, but as a vital, energetic, valuable worker. . . . I don't wanna present an image of a little old grandma. I don't think that way. I don't think my attitude is that way. I don't mean to put down little old grandmothers, but it's just not me.

STARING INTO THE BLACK BOX: HOW SUBJECTS EXPLAIN ERRORS

While some interviewees were dumbfounded at how inaccuracies had crept into their stories, I found many quite understanding of how errors can occur. Some even blamed themselves for errors, either because they supplied the reporter with misinformation or because they felt they had not expressed their views clearly. Many subjects were quick to dismiss small technical errors, not only because they often had negligible effects, as discussed above, but also because they were the most easily explained. Many were obviously simple mistakes. It is hard to attribute malice or bias to a reporter who simply got, for example, a street name wrong. Subjects explained that reporters write so quickly, or deal with huge amounts of information, or don't record, or have limited space, so mistakes simply happen. At least when it came to small errors, many subjects did not appear to be holding reporters to a higher standard than they would anyone else.

More subjective errors of omission and emphasis, which often could *not* be explained as simple mistakes, were more bewildering to subjects. Interviewees speculated about how those errors might have happened. Some blamed reporters for sloppy or careless work. Others concluded more damningly that reporters simply did not understand the issues well enough to write an accurate story, had a bias that influenced the story frame, or intentionally distorted the facts to sensationalize. Subjects were least understanding of the errors they traced to reporters' trying to miscast them in prefabricated roles. They tended to see those as deliberate distortions rather than understandable mistakes. Notably, those were the only cases in which I heard the possibility of a libel suit mentioned.

Some interviewees wondered aloud whether another stage in the news process—editorial or legal review, for example—might have introduced errors into the story. For some that appeared to be an attractive alternative to blaming a likable reporter for disappointing coverage. In follow-up discussions with unhappy subjects, reporters themselves were quick to suggest that explanation. Some version of "I wrote a longer story but my editors cut it" was especially common, although not all interviewees found that excuse plausible or satisfying. For example, Patricia, a Tea Party leader, felt a *New York Times* article unfairly "sandwiched" her group between mentions of blatantly racist organizations, even though the reporter had assured her he would be fair. She explained:

> PATRICIA: [The reporter] said, "No, no, I'm gonna keep this all fair and balanced and exactly the way I said I'm gonna do it," and so still in my mind I just wonder, is this something that happens at the editors' desk where they do the sandwiching, where they attach things to it like the militia and the racism? Was it [the reporter] who did that?

For many subjects, like Patricia, the postinterview news production process was like a black box where anything might have happened. The impenetrability of that part of the process made it hard to level blame at reporters, but also hard to know where else to direct it.

A couple of subjects used metaphors of translation or filtering to explain news production back to themselves. They may not have had a deep familiarity with journalistic processes, but they knew the telephone game when they saw it. Susan, for example, had been interviewed for a story on parks conservation by a reporter who phoned her from the newsroom. A different reporter ultimately wrote the story. Given the process, to her mind it would have been more surprising if the story had *not* contained errors:

> SUSAN: So [the reporter] then ended up cowriting it with a reporter from the *New York Times* who has never even been to this park. So the story has been translated from him to the other reporter, to an editor, to, somehow, this piece of information that is in the *Times*, that gives completely wrong information of what's been going on. What I guessed before, but now I have proof of, is how difficult it is to translate a story from one person to the next. And there were so many people involved and everybody putting in their little things.[35]

(NOT) REQUESTING CORRECTIONS

Although interviewees identified scores of mistakes, very few reported them to journalists or requested corrections from news outlets. Many had not even considered it. When pressed, their most common explanation was that the errors were simply too minor to bother.[36] Others said they doubted that a correction would actually be printed or felt the damage was already done and a correction would do little to help. Sometimes other obligations and real-life demands, trigger related or not, simply took precedence over contacting the newspaper for a correction. As Paul explained, the article about his being attacked by a homeless person—an article that was taken directly from a police report—contained some errors, but he was too busy recovering from the grisly incident to bother contacting the paper:

> PAUL: I mean, at that particular point I was dealing with so much stuff, like having to stay the extra day in the emergency room. I had missed a day of work, and I had to go see my doctor as soon as I got back. You know, there's just kind of a lot going on, and in all honesty, it wasn't a huge deal.[37]

For most interviewees, errors had to be a fairly "huge deal" to warrant reporting them to the paper. As should be predictable at this point, errors deemed that important were the ones interviewees felt reflected poorly on them or that might have negative ramifications for causes they cared about.

Chuck explained that distinction well. He was quoted in a number of outlets as a witness to a residential fire that turned out to be arson. An online version of the story, paraphrasing Chuck, made it sound like the suspect was an important member of the Democratic Party in the neighborhood. An ardent Democrat, Chuck contacted the paper to explain that the suspect was not very involved in the party, and that the story should be corrected to that effect:

> CHUCK: I didn't want that to be used to say "See! A Democrat burned down a house." I didn't want that to happen. It was an error that could have ramifications. I mean, it's a quantitative issue: to what degree does this error make a difference? And, if [the reporter] had said, "The pickup was ten feet farther north," it would have been irrelevant. But the fact that it was reported incorrectly with the Democratic Party made a difference.[38]

As these examples taken together suggest, we can attribute the underreporting of inaccuracies in large part to fundamental differences in the ways news subjects and journalism professionals perceive errors. Those errors news outlets are most likely to acknowledge and correct—verifiable errors of fact—were the ones interviewees tended to care the least about and were therefore the least likely to report. Meanwhile, the kinds of errors and misrepresentations that bothered interviewees the most, like being completely miscast or having a major piece of their argument omitted from the story, were not the kinds of inaccuracies news outlets were likely to correct, so interviewees were not inclined to report those either. Reporters and editors would probably dispute that they were errors at all, and subjects knew they could not be corrected in the kind of brief addenda one normally sees in the corrections section. "The reporter completely missed the boat on the above story," which would have been the only satisfying correction to some interviewees, is not the kind of correction printed more than once or twice a decade by major news outlets, and less if the story is about an ordinary Joe.[39] Interviewees seemed to understand they had little recourse in such cases.

The various ways subjects explain errors back to themselves also seem to contribute to the underreporting of errors. Most interviewees were not particularly invested in improving their local paper for its own sake, or in improving journalism in general by going out of their way to report errors that had minimal impact on their lives and were easily explained. At the same time, larger distortions and misrepresentations were also likely to go unreported, in part because they were *not* easily explained. Subjects often did not know whom to blame for errors of omission and emphasis and believed contacting the outlet would do little good. Moreover, when they did contact reporters, they were often encouraged to blame an editorial process that seemed inscrutable—often only the reporter had a name and a face—and intimidating—there was apparently a whole team of people supporting her. Participants in this study were unlikely to go to bat against that team unless the errors were both easy to prove and likely to do considerable damage if left uncorrected, a confluence that occurred only rarely. These findings suggest that the number of errors actually reported to news outlets is way out of whack with the number perceived by subjects, and the number of corrections actually published even more dramatically so.

In the final analysis, evidence suggests that subjects often do not care about errors and judge them according to criteria that are not always compatible with journalism's own accuracy measures. Media critics and professionals usually judge accuracy by comparing published information to externally verifiable data, and they rate severity of errors based on how far the published material varies from that data. That system defines error very narrowly, as that which can be so verified. But interviewees usually judged errors and their severity on an effects-based scale. They had a much broader understanding of what counts as an inaccuracy because they were comparing the published material to their experience of the trigger, their interaction with the reporter, and their expectations—all while hyperaware of the coverage's potential repercussions. In general, subjects felt that errors that interfered with their goals or posed a threat to their reputations were grave, while errors that did little damage were minor and not worth correcting.

That said, there is convincing evidence that errors damage a paper's credibility in the eyes of readers.[40] Sometimes the same errors interviewees dismissed as not worth correcting seemed to damage credibility in their eyes as well. For example, some said that, since they themselves had been misquoted, they realized they should be skeptical of all newspaper quotes. Or take this telling conclusion from Annie, whose article contained what she felt was a nonharmful fabrication. The reporter said she had traipsed over mountains in her mapmaking work, which was simply not true:

> ANNIE: I now know that they make a few things up. I always kind of speculated that they did that, but I didn't know. But they do that, they really do! And it's not like it's something that's that important. But.
>
> Q: Did it occur to you to contact the reporter and set that record straight?
>
> ANNIE: No. It wasn't that important. To me, it wasn't what the story was about anyway.[41]

Of course Annie did not ask for a correction: other aspects of the story and her experience "making the news" simply mattered more to her. As her reaction illustrates, error assessment was one part of subjects' reactions when they saw their news coverage, but it was not the only one. As I explore in the next chapter, for many subjects, seeing themselves in the news evoked strong feelings, from pride and titillation to embarrassment and even existential angst. Those feelings at times exacerbated subjects' concerns about accuracy and at times eclipsed them altogether.

6

THAT'S ME! . . . BUT IT'S NOT ME

Aesthetic, Emotional, and Existential

Effects of Confronting Our News Selves

Q: You said the first time you saw [the article] it was pretty cringe-worthy.
BILLY: Yeah. I don't see myself very often. The mirror can only give you so
   much. And then when you realize, "Oh, that's what they see when I'm—I
   didn't realize." Yeah, so it's weird. It's funny, it's almost like being detached from yourself. . . . It was almost as if somebody had painted a picture of me and it just didn't look right. But it was a huge picture and it
   was, like, at my memorial. And I'm like, "Aach!" But y'know, it's like,
   that's me. So it was weird to have to come to terms with the fact that that's
   what you look like. On a mass communication.[1]

illy sat for several long, collaborative interviews with a reporter for
the West City paper. A comedian making a comeback of sorts,
Billy cooperated eagerly. He knew a profile in the paper could help
put him back on the map. By the time the article finally came out, he had
invested a lot of time and energy in the process, and the stakes felt high.
The piece, which spanned several pages and included pictures of Billy on-
and offstage, was mostly favorable, and overall he was pleased. But when
he looked at it—even when I showed it to him during our interview—he
positively squirmed. He explained that he felt so . . . weird. The person in
the profile seemed so familiar, and yet so strange and alien and public.
And yet *it was him*.

As I discussed in the previous chapter, scholars have long taken an interest in news subjects as arbiters of journalistic accuracy, and subjects do provide interesting insights about errors. However, my interviewees' reactions to seeing themselves in the news were emotional and multilayered. In many cases, they went far beyond a simple appraisal of whether the coverage was accurate. I had to prompt some of them to discuss accuracy at all.

On the other hand, nearly everyone spoke at length, and without prompting, about how it *felt* to see their own names, quotes, and images in the news. Billy's response, though magnified by the size of the article and the circumstances, exemplifies a fairly typical reaction. Many interviewees described the experience as just plain weird, whether the medium was print or broadcast, online or off. Others described feelings that ranged from excitement to anxiety.

In this chapter I try to get to the bottom of what it is, exactly, that can make seeing oneself in the news feel so strange, exciting, and even scary. I begin by analyzing the news as a form of representation in which the people I have been describing thus far as "news subjects" are converted into objects, viewable from the outside by the individuals themselves, and interpreted and appropriated by others. I then probe in greater depth just how a news appearance differs from other forms of representation, and how those differences can help explain interviewees' emotional, aesthetic, and, in some cases, existential responses to seeing themselves in the news.

In the final analysis, when subjects see themselves in news products, they are seeing a version of themselves that is simultaneously familiar and unfamiliar to them. It may even be completely unrecognizable. And yet that representation will be highly credible, circulate publicly, and potentially bring rewards or ridicule to subjects themselves.

BECOMING A NEWS OBJECT

KIM: It's kinda weird to see yourself on TV. You see yourself differently when you're on TV and it's kinda like, "Whoa! That's me?"[2]

In earlier chapters I used Erving Goffman's term "face-work" to describe how individuals present themselves in an interpersonal interaction like an interview.[3] As I explained, journalists then take the subject's face and re-frame it, by putting it through a decision-making and repackaging process to create a news story.

The resulting portrayal of the subject, whether in text, sound, or image, is a representation in the most straightforward sense: it is an object generated through a process of human and technological intervention that renders present the individual it depicts.[4] No one would claim that the figure in the news product literally *is* the living, breathing subject, but it bears his name and image and thus calls him to mind in the eyes of the audience.

Thus far I have referred to news "subjects" using the definition of the word most commonly applied in journalism and the arts, as that which is depicted, named, or referred to in the product—the person the news story is about, the figure in the painting. But "subject" can also refer to an entity that consciously moves through the world—the *opposite* of the static figure in a story or a painting. A subject in this sense is defined by its agency—its ability to make choices. Thus what I have been describing as the process of "becoming a news subject" could just as accurately be called the process of "becoming a news object," insofar as it is a procedure that strips a living, thinking human of agency and pops him or her out the other end in object form, with no agency at all.

This process is very common. Photographing people is the most obvious example, but describing a person in words, or representing them in any other medium, objectifies them in the simple sense that it reproduces them in object-form. The representational process also makes it possible for the subject to stand before that representational object and see herself *as* an object. That, too, should be familiar: early in life we learn to accommodate an understanding of ourselves as both subjects—actors who see and act—and objects—people who are seen and acted-upon.[5]

And yet seeing ourselves represented as objects *can* still feel deeply unsettling. Although little has been written about the phenomenon of facing-off with our own representations in the news product, theorists reflecting on the weirdness of seeing ourselves in photographs provide relevant insights here. In two classic works on photography, cultural critics Roland Barthes and Susan Sontag write about the inevitable sense of distance—and difference—between the viewing-self and the object-self when we see ourselves in a photo.[6] Both identify a disconcerting "that's me—but not me" sensation. Barthes traces it to questions about ownership: that is me in the photo—but is the photo actually mine, the photographer's, or the public's? A photo, he argues, is the embodiment of the self as a public entity. It follows that when we see a photo of ourselves we may feel that something once private—which perhaps should have remained private— has been made public.

Sontag goes a step further, emphasizing the forcible objectification and appropriation of the subject photography entails, arguing that "to photograph people is to violate them, by seeing them as they never see themselves, by having knowledge of them they can never have; it turns people into objects that can be symbolically possessed."[7] Like Barthes, Sontag argues that seeing ourselves in photographs that can be seen, circulated, and used by others somehow disrupts our sense of the self as a unified entity. We feel the loss of a part of the self but also a loss of the illusion of coherence and control.

But it gets weirder. Barthes adds that when we see photographs of ourselves we may be haunted by the sense that we are confronting our own double, and both Sontag and Barthes associate photography with death. Sontag sees the act of taking a photo as a kind of murder. For Barthes, the relationship between Death—he capitalizes it—and photography is an ongoing theme with multiple variations. He argues that seeing a photo of ourselves reminds us of our own death since the photo recalls the presence of something now absent: when we see ourselves in a photo, we are encountering both a specter of ourselves from a previous moment to which we can never return and a specter of our own death in the future. I see a version of myself I will never be again; time is passing; soon I, too, will be gone.

Seeing oneself in the news is not analogous in every way to seeing oneself in a photograph. However, the comparison is fruitful for a couple of reasons. First, the experiences overlap. Often newspapers include photos of subjects, and obviously TV is image based. Second, and more important, the feeling described by Barthes and Sontag rings true to interviewees' self-described experiences. As I detail below, whether they were talking about seeing photos of themselves in the paper, or confronting their representations in printed words, moving images, or sound, the strange sense of something private having been made public; the weird sensation of seeing themselves as objects; the feeling of lost control; even an eerie sense of being simultaneously annihilated and preserved were all consistent themes in interviews. The similarity is especially remarkable since Sontag and Barthes were writing in the 1970s, at a time when seeing photos of ourselves was far less routine than it is now. One would think the strange sensations they described would be greatly diminished in recent years. Perhaps they are when we see yet another cellphone photo of ourselves. As I discuss further below, when it came to seeing themselves in the news, for my interviewees, the feeling of strangeness was alive and well.

THAT'S THE "REAL" ME AND I HATE IT: SELF-OBJECTIFICATION AND SELF-CRITICISM

Billy struggled to explain exactly why he felt like cringing every time he looked at the profile of himself in the West City paper. He spent a lot of time in our interview trying to unravel his mixed feelings about it. As he said in the quote at the beginning of this chapter, at first just seeing himself from the outside—"what they see"—was weird. It made him feel strangely "detached" from himself. Billy knew that was him, but he was not used to seeing himself from the outside, other than in a mirror, so the figure he saw felt strangely unfamiliar at the same time. The same could probably be said of our reaction to many representations of ourselves. As Sontag says of photographs, the representational object captures us as we could never see ourselves.[8]

As he went on, however, Billy's description did seem to diverge in some key ways from what we normally feel when we see ourselves in object-form. A few things stand out. First, Billy felt that, even though the representation did not look quite right, he had to accept that it was accurate—that that's what he really looked like. Why should that be? Probably several factors contribute. The medium is undoubtedly one: photos were featured prominently in Billy's article. As I discussed in the previous chapter, subjects had no problem contesting quotes attributed to them in text. But they attributed much more authority to photos, videos, and audio recordings of themselves. Even if those representations felt wrong, it was hard for them to deny that *that was them*.

Another likely contributing factor was that the article representing him was made by someone else—as Billy points out, it was like someone had painted a picture of him. As they did with images, interviewees found it hard to contest descriptions of themselves. They did not seem to trust themselves to judge them. Reporter's stories about subjects promised them an outsider's view of how they really were. Seeing their own representations in the news was fascinating to many interviewees partly because they were just plain curious. They seemed to think journalists' portrayals of them, as Sontag said of photography, might reveal something about themselves that they could not have known otherwise. In Billy's words, "the mirror can only give you so much," and they wanted more.

Second, Billy alludes a couple of times to the uncomfortably public nature of this representation. People sometimes wonder what it would feel like to attend their own funeral—to hear people talking about them in a public gathering, making meaning of their lives in a collective ritual. According to Billy, seeing oneself profiled in the news feels a lot like that. Yes, he was seeing how others saw him, but this most intimate of revelations was happening in a public forum—as he put it, in "a mass communication." Seeing an unflattering photo or overhearing commentary about ourselves can feel uncomfortable, even when the experience is private and contained. So it makes sense that such moments would feel even more disconcerting when we know many strangers are watching or listening in.

And not just observing. Judging. Feminist scholars call the process of imagining how others see and judge us "self-objectification."[9] It is generally considered a negative tendency because it can lead to acute self-criticism, which is exactly what many interviewees said they experienced. Once more, Billy offered a particularly vivid description:

> BILLY: I was like, "I need a haircut." Or like, "I shouldn't have worn that." Critical. Hyper [critical]. I don't mind being photographed, but when it's on that level, it's weird. Because people judge you. . . . I know people are looking at it and they're like, "Who's this guy?"

Especially when photos or videos were involved, interviewees almost always responded with some version of "I hated how I looked/sounded." They winced to see their verbal ticks, bald spots, and tummy rolls so brutally laid bare. And yet, because the representation was presumably objective, they felt they had to accept that this was what they really looked or sounded like. For some, an unflattering photo felt like a further confirmation of its truth, a corrective to their more flattering delusions about who they really were. In the words of Ray, a food truck owner who spoke to journalists about his feud with a nearby restaurant, "You're like, 'Ugh. Who's that thinning-haired, middle-aged guy?' Yeah, it's awful. It's brutal.

'Cause it's just like, you're face-to-face with it, you know. You still have this myth about who you are."[10]

As I discuss later in this chapter, the fact that these particular representations appeared in the news, a genre that makes authoritative truth claims, meant that for some subjects they seemed even more disconcertingly like proof of reality.

THE PARTIAL, CIRCULATING SELF

By the time interviewees saw themselves in the news, they had mostly come to accept that they had given up control over how they would be represented there. As I have discussed in earlier chapters, subjects usually came to that realization at the various stages of agreeing and submitting to interviews. And yet once their story was out in the world, they were confronted with a whole new part of the process they could not control: how the representation of them circulated and was received. They could not control where it would go, who would see it, or how it would be interpreted. In other words, like Sontag said of photography, the news production process "turns people into objects that can be symbolically possessed."[11]

I noted already that many subjects said they imagined an audience judging them. We can now add that they also imagined that audience constructing an image for them based on the bits and pieces used to describe them in the paper. For some interviewees, that reconstructed person felt familiar, but for others it did not. Even when the bits and pieces used to describe them did not exactly feel inaccurate, they almost always felt partial, and therefore distortive of the whole. Tim, for example, found it strange to see himself depicted as a "math whiz" in the paper.[12] Yes, he and his wife ran a tutoring business, and sometimes he helped out with the teaching, but he was hardly a math *genius*, and he had other qualities that were more central to his identity. No, the description did not reflect poorly on him, but it wasn't *him*, and it felt strange to imagine people out there thinking that it was.

As I discussed in earlier chapters, we all present different faces or versions of ourselves in different social settings.[13] But representations of us can circulate beyond the original context, which sometimes means a face appropriate for one setting winds up being seen by a different audience. Some subjects emphasized this as particularly strange-feeling. The partial representations of themselves they saw in the news were not inaccurate, exactly, but they emphasized one of their many faces—one they normally preferred to show only to a select audience. In fact, part of Billy's discomfort stemmed from being featured in the newspaper for his work as a comedian, an intimate part of his persona that felt incompatible with the one he adopted at his day job in the stockroom of a department store:

> BILLY: After the interview came out the people at [department store] put it up on the bulletin board at work in the break room, and I didn't go to the break room for like, a week or two after that, because I don't like to have the conversations about it. It's like an intimate peek into my world, and so I didn't want the people at work thinking they could just ask me about stuff, because you know . . . having an article in the paper is kind of an important thing. Y'know, in a person's life. But I don't know how to tell the 65-year-old woman who works customer service, who's on break at the same time I am, what it all means, and how I'm doing comedy and trying to justify why I dropped outta college to try to do this. So I just avoided the break room altogether.

Social media scholars describe a similar phenomenon called "context collapse."[14] They argue that the boundaries between different social spaces disintegrate online, complicating our efforts to present different versions of ourselves to different audiences. Billy's description illustrates how the news production process combines context collapse with usurpation of one's presentation-of-self. If it is difficult to adjust your face for a broad, unknown audience when self-broadcasting on Twitter, it is basically impossible when someone else is broadcasting you. First, you do not get to generate and control the details of your own representation—the journalist does that. Next, that always-partial representational object—which bears your name—will be presented to a broad public, not necessarily the narrow one for whom it might feel more appropriate or preferred. Once more, something private becomes a bit too public, and subjects' faces slip further out of their control.

THE UNCANNY

Seeing a presumably objective representation of yourself and finding it simultaneously familiar and unfamiliar; knowing it has been broadcast in a public forum; imagining the audience envisioning you based on just a few quotes and descriptions; hearing a rising chorus of judgments in your head. These are all factors that can help explain why it feels so odd and even uncomfortable to see ourselves in the news. However, truly capturing a *feeling*, especially one that interviewees themselves described as almost ineffably weird, is singularly difficult, even impossible. Ultimately, the best I can do is say it was "uncanny" in all the maddening, hard-to-pin-down senses of the term that psychoanalyst Sigmund Freud identified in his famous essay by that name.[15]

In what is either a great literary feat or simply an inadvertent illustration of a key feature of the concept, Freud cannot quite capture the ghostly feeling he is trying to define. He begins with a series of definitions of the term, and a survey of its counterparts in other languages. That step yields the insight that an *unheimlich* or uncanny feeling can be produced by that which, like the German term *heimlich* ("homey," more or less), is somehow simultaneously itself and its opposite, both familiar and unfamiliar at once. Freud notes that "something which ought to have remained hidden, but has come to light," might be another partial definition of the uncanny.[16]

Unsatisfied with those definitions, however, he goes on to describe examples, each yielding another layer to the concept: objects that make us question whether they are alive or dead, such as automated dolls or ghosts; events or objects that confound our distinction between imagination and reality; our own doubles or any indication of them. Indeed, the "That's me!—but it's not me" response described by photography critics and my interviewees captures very well the sensation Freud describes. We are faced with something that is simultaneously familiar and unfamiliar, alive and dead, private but come to light. Recall that even the term "subject," like the *heimlich* itself, can mean both itself and its opposite.

Freud notes that some people are more sensitive to the uncanny aesthetic than others, and it is true that not all interviewees found the experience of seeing themselves in the news so strange or disquieting. Experience seemed to diminish the uncanny effect: subjects who had seen themselves in the news before did not seem to feel as disconcerted as novices. Today, many people are so accustomed to seeing selfies and other photos of themselves, they probably do not feel even a twinge of the uncanny when they do. Perhaps with exposure we can simply get used to the particular equilibrium between the familiar and unfamiliar we feel when we see ourselves represented in any medium, format, or context. But unsettle that delicate balance by altering the experience in any way and the uncanny may peek out from under the bed again. If the object-self seems either more or less familiar than we have come to expect, it could reawaken an uncanny sensation. For example, a photo that captures us at an unusual angle, or in a time and place we do not recall, can still feel strange. For some people who rarely hear recordings of their own voices, it can feel so weird it almost hurts.

For many news subjects, that this particular representation is being displayed as part of the news product is probably itself novel. Even if the description or photo seem perfectly familiar, their placement in the product alone may have enough of a distancing effect to make seeing one's representation in the news feel quite odd. The multilayered process necessary to create the story, the sense that it appears in a space normally reserved for other people, especially public figures, and the knowledge that it is being widely seen and circulated can all make the object seem still more removed from us than we are accustomed to—uncanny. And variations in the process can make one's news representation seem even more unfamiliar. A number of interviewees said it felt especially bizarre to see themselves in news outlets if they had not spoken to reporters representing those outlets. Their stories had been picked up by other publications and circulated far beyond the original context, in other states and countries. Asked what it felt like to see herself quoted in publications she had not spoken to, Deanne said:

DEANNE: Weird. Weird. Yeah. Seeing myself in the publications I had talked to did seem strange, but it was like, okay, I talked to them. Again, I knew what I was doing. To see myself quoted in a little newspaper online in Alaska?! I'm like—with someone in Alaska reading my name, and reading the story. Who are you? Like, why?[17]

Several interviewees had not agreed to speak to any reporters at all and had the truly uncanny experience of later seeing themselves in the news anyway, as though their object-self had escaped them completely and was putting on a public show of its own:

BARBARA: They were showing me on *Fox News*, which I don't know where they got the footage, but they got the footage of me at an event speaking. . . . I never talked to them or anything like that. And to see—I catch myself speaking, and it's just on there for a second or two, and you see your face and you hear your voice and it's just—it's just—weird. Wow![18]

The more unfamiliar the object-version seems, the more uncanny it is likely to feel. But we also find evidence of the opposite argument in Barbara and Deanne's comments. The uncanny aesthetic can also be exaggerated when the object-version seems all too familiar, not because we recognize ourselves, which goes without saying, but because the object behaves a bit too much like it has its own agency—like a subject. The most uncanny scenarios of all are those that blur the line between the animate and the inanimate: the doll moves of its own accord; I look in the mirror and my reflection winks back. If my object-self is out there, the last thing I want is for it to have a life of its own.

WHAT'S SO SPECIAL ABOUT BEING IN THE NEWS? FAME, STATUS, GENERATIVITY, AND EVIDENTIARY FORCE

So far, I have argued that the news production process generates an object that represents the subject. The subject can then confront himself in that representational object—see himself from the outside—which can produce a sensation best described as uncanny. The feeling of uncanniness is heightened by subjects' seeing the representation in a format and context that is simultaneously familiar and unfamiliar—familiar because they are accustomed to seeing news products as consumers but unfamiliar because it is rare to see themselves there, in a product that will be seen and judged by a large audience. It is to these last characteristics, the large audience and the specific genre of the news, that I now return. They contributed to the weirdness my interviewees described, but they also elicited other strong feelings.

In this section, I explore the epiphenomena of fame, status, and a kind of existential confirmation interviewees said they felt upon seeing themselves in the news. These epiphenomena, and the feelings interviewees associated with them, are made possible by several underlying factors that differentiate a news appearance from other forms of representation. I discussed these in slightly different terms in chapter 1, but they bear revisiting because they are especially relevant at this stage, when subjects finally saw themselves in the news coverage.

First, when you appear in the news you are one of a chosen few. Because there is limited space in the news product, being chosen to be depicted there, especially for a private citizen, is to be singled out from the crowd for a special distinction. Interviewees explicitly contrasted being chosen to appear in the news with being represented in social media, where anyone can opt in and space seems infinite.

Second, interviewees noted that the size of the audience distinguishes a mainstream news appearance from being represented in other contexts. The news audience, even for the smaller papers in which some interviewees were named, was much larger than they thought they could access by other means, and quite likely larger than they would ever access again.

Third, appearing in the news is exceptional because professional journalists control how you are represented there. Other forms of representation available to ordinary citizens may involve some form of human intervention to generate the product—the person who takes the photo, for example, or myself when I create a Facebook profile. But it is very unusual for many of us to have a third party size us up and use their professional acumen to generate a more involved interpretation of us. Recall Billy's comment that seeing his profile in the paper was like seeing a huge, public painting of himself. Insofar as an authoritative professional creates the representation, being turned into a news object really *is* more like having your portrait painted than like having a friend take a snapshot.

Subjects also associated the news product with credibility, which is the fourth distinguishing feature that seemed to have a strong effect on how subjects felt when they saw themselves in the news product. I did not ask interviewees outright if they believed that mainstream news in general or particular news sources were credible or trustworthy. Rather, I am referring here to a consistent underlying assumption that emerged in my interviews about the news as a genre, and the audience's relationship to it. Simply put, interviewees were fairly sure the audience would believe what was said about them in the news, and they subsequently saw indications that that was true. As I discuss further below, they assumed readers and viewers would take the news as a kind of evidence or proof of something that really happened. Taken together, these factors—the news's high barriers to inclusion, the size of its audience, its fleet of anointed representation professionals, and its evidential power—set the stage for some of the most striking sensations subjects said they felt when they saw themselves in the news. I explore these below.

THE THRILL OF FAME AND THE PRIDE OF STATUS

Wendy appeared in a story about a proposal to build a controversial art installation celebrating cancer survivorship in West City. She felt strongly about the issue because her own mother had died of cancer the year before. And yet even though the topic was a serious one, she still got a kick out of seeing herself in the paper:

> WENDY: It's neat. There's a little rush. [laughing] If you sound good! So that was fun. Y'know, it was just fun.
> Q: It's interesting that there can be that fun feeling when there's kind of a lot of gravitas about the issue, but there can still be—
> WENDY: Yes, there is. Like [squeals a bit] Ooh! Ooh! When I saw it [my reaction] was more—juvenile is the word that comes to my mind. Like [excited, childlike voice] "Look! There's me!"[19]

Like Wendy, many interviewees felt an immediate thrill when they saw their own quotes or images in the news, even in serious or somber stories. It is always hard to say *why* something is fun exactly, but some of them explicitly connected it to the feeling of being, however briefly or undeservedly, a little bit famous, the object of more attention than they usually received. Marcel, for example, was briefly quoted in a TV news story about proposed transit fare hikes. As news appearances went, it was pretty minor. And yet he, too felt a thrill:

> MARCEL: It's like the fact that people see you. That's fun. The word that's coming to mind is celebrity, but it has nothing to do with real celebrity. But I feel like there's something about that. This idea that if you show up on this thing, and then you show it to your friends, it's like, this way of getting noticed. In a different way than you're noticed usually.[20]

As I discussed earlier in this chapter, the idea of "getting noticed" by a lot of people made some interviewees feel anxious because they imagined those people judging them harshly. But others, like Marcel, emphasized the upside of being seen by many: they felt visible at a time when getting noticed is increasingly difficult. It felt like a little taste of fame, even if, as Marcel points out, it had "nothing to do with real celebrity." A number of subjects explicitly referred to their news appearance as their "fifteen minutes of fame," and it was clear they enjoyed it. Given that fame today is often considered socially desirable in and of itself, regardless of how it is achieved, it makes sense that subjects would find it gratifying.[21]

The thrill seemed to be magnified for some interviewees by the sense that this particular kind of fame, inclusion in the news product, was hard to achieve. You had to be *chosen*, and if you were, it meant you were important. Jessica, who was featured in the *New York Post* for participating in a demonstration, and Isabel, who appeared in the *New York Times* for her work as a schoolteacher, illustrate this well:

> JESSICA: I didn't know if it was gonna be interesting enough for them to put it in the paper or on TV or what have you. But it was exciting. . . . It says that it's an act that was interesting enough for somebody to write about it and for it to get in the paper. Because not everybody has an article in the paper about them. So it was great.[22]

> ISABEL: It's the fact that the *New York Times* thought we were a worthy story. Y'know? They thought that our dedication to this school was important enough for an entire city to read. Y'know? I think that's what it was. It was that they thought we were important enough to be an article.[23]

Isabel later went a step further, explicitly comparing a news appearance to receiving an award. Several other interviewees made the same comparison, including, remarkably, Alegra, who had appeared in several news outlets for a story about a medical condition that had ended her pregnancy. Given the trauma of the underlying story, it was all the more striking that when I asked her if she could think of another experience similar to being featured in the news, she responded, "Hmm. Probably like an award ceremony, or something where you have to go up onstage to get an award or something. Because you're in front of people and in the spotlight."[24]

That people appearing in such different news outlets, and for such different stories, all identified a similar sensation is remarkable. What they described illustrates "status conferral," one of the key social functions sociologists Paul Lazarsfeld and Robert Merton attributed to the mass media in an influential essay written in 1948. They argued that "the mass media bestow prestige and enhance the authority of individuals and groups by *legitimizing their status*. Recognition by the press or radio or magazines or newsreels testifies that one has arrived, that one is important enough to be singled out from the large anonymous masses, that one's behavior and opinions are significant enough to require public notice."[25]

That the mass media confers status is practically taken for granted today, and I discuss the phenomenon further in the next two chapters on the effects a news appearance can have on subjects' lives and reputations. Feedback subjects receive from others, the focus of chapter 7, is the best evidence that a news appearance boosts subjects' status in the eyes of the world. But even before they started getting that feedback, some interviewees could feel a change. Many felt proud, some felt self-conscious, and a few felt the reward was ill-deserved. But even ambivalent subjects sensed what communication scholar Peter Simonson calls the "metaphorical aura" of status emanating from them.[26] Thomas's description of the feeling probably captures it best. A performer who was profiled in the *New York Times*, he said he woke up at five in the morning to buy the paper at the deli. He disliked how the story was framed, but he felt like "dancing in the streets" after he read it:

THOMAS: You throw somebody up on television and suddenly they're different. You put somebody in the newspaper, and suddenly for a brief period of time they have this energy around them that crackles. There is a sense of fame . . . fifteen seconds. Whatever. But it does exist. And I felt it personally, too. Something lifted in me. I was abuzz. And it felt great.[27]

For many subjects, like Thomas, the aura of status and fame that comes from a news appearance *does* feel great. Being depicted in the mass media anoints you as one deserving of public attention, an official person of interest. But as that phrase, with its criminal connotations, reminds us, status conferral has a negative converse in stigma, which I also explore in greater depth in the chapters to come. For now it is important to recognize that subjects' status will increase even if the content of a news story is not particularly flattering. However, if the underlying trigger or the coverage is *un*flattering or controversial, being held up for public scrutiny can elicit very different feelings. Emma, who was featured in a controversial story in West City for having euthanized her critically ill husband, described that feeling:

> EMMA: When I first saw it I kind of got almost an adrenaline rush, because it was front page above the fold. So it was like, "Oh my God! What have I done?" I got nervous. I got nervous about, "Are people going to recognize me?" I still worry about it. I still worry about, "Are people judging me?" And if people disapprove of what I did, how will that affect how they relate to me?
>
> Q: Is that something that had crossed your mind before the article came out?
>
> EMMA: Well, I thought about it. I think you can think about things like that and you can't really imagine how it's going to be until it actually happens. I felt very exposed.[28]

In other words, the same combination of factors that can make seeing ourselves in the news a source of pride and thrills can also elicit horror, anxiety, and a sense of acute vulnerability if the circumstances and details of the representation are less favorable. As Emma points out, little can prepare subjects for the sense that a huge judgmental audience is bearing down on them. It can feel invasive, if not downright frightening. As I detail in chapter 8, news subjects like Emma often go on to see their fears materialize in the form of judgmental reader comments and direct feedback from audiences, who can easily contact them directly.

I EXIST AND I WILL LIVE ON: EXISTENTIAL AFFIRMATION AND GENERATIVITY

I noted earlier that subjects were curious to see how they would be represented in the news because they thought they might learn something new about themselves. Some interviewees went a step further, describing a kind of existential affirmation they felt upon seeing themselves immortalized in the news product. Shauna illustrates this well. One of several women quoted in a *New York Times* article about gender on college campuses, she strongly disliked the article and felt she was miscast in it, but seeing her name in print in the paper made a big impression. As she explained:

> SHAUNA: It gives you validation, in a way, of your existence, on a larger scale than just your friends, your family. It's not necessarily other people seeing it, it's just the fact that print, in a way, can be forever almost. And so having your name there shows that yes, I was here at some point. It makes your existence, which is such an intangible thing . . . a tangible thing. There's my name. Like, "Here I am." Even for my own benefit I can look at it and it's like, "No, no, I *am* real." . . . I guess for me, what I probably enjoyed most about seeing my name was just realizing that, okay, I did live, I was around, and here's documentation of my existence.[29]

Again, Barthes's observations about photography are relevant here. He argued that the essence, or *noeme*, of a photograph is "that has been."[30] While one may quibble over the accuracy of photographs, especially now that their digital manipulation is so easy, they can still function as proof of the existence of their referent in a particular time and place. It follows that upon seeing a photograph of oneself, "I was here/there" will be a basic response: Here's me in Singapore! There I am in Taiwan! Although she was looking at her name and quotes in print and not at a photograph, Shauna seemed to describe a similar sensation, if clearly more profound. If we take the analysis a step further, psychologist Orville Brim breaks down our desire for individuality into the twin sensations of uniqueness and presence: "I am me"—different from all other people but similar enough to be socially accepted by them—and "I am here," which aligns closely with Barthes's photographic *noeme*.[31] As interviewees like Shauna described it, being named in a news product can feel like a confirmation of both uniqueness and presence: I am obviously unique and special because I have been chosen from the crowd for a highly valued position in the limited space of the paper. I also clearly exist: not only do I see myself in the product, others are seeing me there, thinking about me, and reacting to me. As Shauna puts it, "It makes your existence, which is such an intangible thing . . . a tangible thing."

And there is one more layer here. Scholars studying fame have theorized that celebrity may be attractive to people partly because they associate it with "generativity"— living on after death.[32] As Shauna says, print seems to endure forever. Like Shauna, a number of interviewees said being in the news felt not only like an affirmation of their presence in the here and now but also like documentation of their life that would live on as part of the historical record.

NEWS AS PROOF: EVIDENTIAL FORCE

Shauna also says that seeing herself in the news made her think, "No, no, I *am* real." Similarly, some interviewees noted that seeing events they had experienced documented in the news somehow made those events "more real," especially when they were out-of-the-ordinary or hard to digest. Beth felt that way about seeing criminal charges against her reported in the paper. The charges themselves felt surreal, but she said seeing them in the paper "made it seem more real. It's like having a thought in your head, It's like having a thought in your head that you would never want anyone to hear . . . printed in the newspaper!"[33]

Others said they had been eager to see their own stories in the news partly because they were hoping to find out more about what had "really happened." That idea came up often among victims or witnesses of breaking news stories, whose knowledge of events was limited to what they themselves had seen. They were eager to learn, for example, who the shooter was, or what had caused an accident. Like Beth, they, too, seemed to be looking for confirmation that surreal events had really taken place. Eve, a survivor of the "Miracle on the Hudson" plane crash, described that feeling:

> EVE: I wanted to go back [to the news coverage] and see what happened. I wanted to see what the facts were, what they were saying about it, because I still didn't know a lot of the facts. There are still times when I think, "Oh my goodness, this happened in my life, and my life went on, but it still happened, and it was so big that the impact still occurs to me every day." So going back and reading it over and over, or looking at it again just says to me, yes, this really happened to you. And yes, it was a miracle.[34]

As all these examples suggest, my interviewees spoke of and treated the news as a representational product that was intended to document reality, and they believed audiences would do the same. While the written word may not have the immediate power to verify existence that a photograph has, in the minds of my interviewees the genre of journalism appeared to share with photography at least some of what Barthes calls "evidential force."[35] Trust in the mainstream news media was already at an all-time low at the time I conducted these interviews, which made it all the more striking that interviewees clearly relied on the news for proof of events and assumed the audience would as well.[36]

While my interviewees seemed to associate evidential force with the genre of news in general, within the genre, differences in media did matter to them. Interviewees generally saw images as having what I would describe as a more indisputable evidential power than text. Once more, that makes visual representations of oneself both fascinating and high-stakes: a photo promises to show you as you really are—or really were in that moment—but it is also extremely difficult to negate should it not match your self-image or your sense of what really happened: I can deny that I said a quote that appears in print, but if I see a video or hear a recording of myself saying it, well, there's the proof.

Ironically, news subjects are in an excellent position to discover that the news's evidential force is at least partly built on sand. They learn firsthand that news coverage is always partial, often deficient, frequently arbitrary, and sometimes technically inaccurate. But that just makes it feel even weirder to know the audience is likely to believe it. In extreme cases, interviewees felt like their representation in the news actually had more credibility than *they* did, which was uncanny indeed. Feeling like the "real you" has been displaced by a media-generated imposter can destabilize your sense of self even when the representation is flattering. One interviewee, a hero cop, described just that. A personable, well-adjusted man, Keith played a key role in averting a major terrorist attack in New York City. The New York Police Department paraded him around town, and the story got a lot of local, national, and even international press coverage. Like other interviewees, initially, he said, "It was fun. It's nice getting recognition."[37]

But after a few days of constant media attention, dinner with the mayor, a call from the president, and seeing himself elevated to hero status by the news media, Keith found himself depressed. No doubt many factors contributed to his sudden breakdown, not least of which were sheer exhaustion from all the attention, and the slow realization that he could easily have died in the events that had gotten him so much recognition. But he believed that the source of his depression, confusion, and distress was seeing himself depicted as a hero over and over in the media and feeling that the hero character was not really him:

> KEITH: I'm being paraded all over the city. Y'know? Then you get quiet time and the id and the ego start playin' ball in your head. I don't feel like superman, but everyone's telling me I am. "I'm a normal guy." "No, you're not." "I'm Keith." "No, you're not!" It's like I'm on 'shrooms. I find myself every night at three in the morning staring at my refrigerator. "What's going on? What the fuck is going on in my life? This is really fuckin' weird." I think the media caused this. Depression set in. For no fucking reason. I'm like, depressed?! What am I depressed for? Why am I here at three in the morning, staring at the refrigerator and crying? This is really fucking weird. And it was the battle in my head between being superman and "No! I'm not superman." But everybody tells you you are. You're torn between what the media says you are—and meanwhile I'm still the guy that yells at his dog and you know, fights with his wife and y'know, road rages on the way home and probably drinks too many beers. But I'm still Keith. And it was really weird. Everything was going cool with it, until one day I'm driving in, listening to the radio. I'm almost at work, and I'm like [mimes tears suddenly coming down his cheeks] I'm like, "What the fuck?! What is this?" I pull over and I just start "whoosh" [mimes torrential crying].

Keith felt like he knew who he was, and he knew that the guy he was seeing in the media was not him—*but everyone else seemed to believe it was.* Confronting representations of ourselves may always have the potential to disquiet or destabilize us. But, as Keith's experience illustrates, seeing an unrecognizable self in the news can take that feeling to a new level because subjects are accustomed to looking to the news for documentary evidence of reality and are surrounded by people who are doing just that. If the "real" version of themselves that the news reflects back to them seems unfamiliar, it can understandably provoke existential angst.

Opening the paper or turning on the news to find an unrecognizable representation of yourself is particularly distressing if the story depicts you as having behaved badly or committed a crime. That experience combines the surreal sensation of being wrongly accused of criminal behavior with the reality-making process of having it depicted in the news. Rich, a building superintendent arrested for kidnapping someone he had never met, described that experience:

Q: When you saw the articles, what was your reaction to them?

RICH: I was shocked! It had me listed as an ex-con. I've been workin' since I was thirteen years old! Whaddaya mean "ex-con?" I'm like, "What the hell?!" . . .

Q: Well, did you have the thought, "That's not me?"

RICH: Yeah, of course I had the thought! I knew! But it was! They were sayin' it was me. But it's not! No! I didn't do it! I didn't do it. I was fixin' the fuckin' boiler! I felt violated! It was wrong. It was wrong. It was wrong.[38]

Here, the uncanny morphed into the Kafkaesque. As I describe in the next chapter, some of the most disturbing stories I heard were from subjects, like Rich, who were shocked to find that their friends and family seemed more inclined to believe negative things said about them in the news than their own explanations and denials.

THE CREDIBILITY PARADOX

This brings me to the central paradox of news subjecthood. Because it provides a platform for private individuals to be chosen for public display by an authoritative third party, the news has the power to bestow fame, status, and credibility on individuals—three qualities of tremendous social value. If one is eager to publicize a venture, speak out about an issue, or simply call attention to oneself, that combination is gold. You cannot attain it via advertising, because self-promotion lacks the credibility of production by a seemingly impartial, legitimizing third party. You can only rarely attain it via social media for the same reason, and because the social media audience for a given message is usually a fraction of even a small news outlet's.

But—and here's the rub—this triple whammy of fame, status, and credibility can be attained only by giving up control of your own message to a news outlet, then sitting back and hoping it produces a representation that meets your hopes, needs, and expectations. That process can be terrifying because, whether or not the representation falls short, it *will be credible and widely seen*. You must agree to be made into an object that, once published, may take on a life of its own, as it is circulated, commented on, and interpreted by strangers. A news appearance may still benefit a subject, even if the representation is somewhat disappointing or inaccurate, because the publicity and status are so valuable. However, a representation that emphasizes all the wrong things, disseminates misinformation, or depicts a subject in a negative light can be damaging in ways that are difficult to rectify. In extreme cases, like Rich's, it can feel like an evil double is wreaking havoc on your life, leaving you to pick up the pieces.

As I have argued in this chapter, confronting one's representation in the news goes far beyond cold assessments of whether the representation is accurate. It can be deeply unsettling or profoundly gratifying, but it is almost always weird. Many sensations described in this chapter arose from subjects' awareness that other people would see the representation they themselves were seeing, and that it would lead to social rewards or punishments. The next two chapters explore those repercussions of appearing in a news story.

7

CELEBRATION, CONDEMNATION, REPUTATION

Audience Feedback as an Indicator of Status and Stigma

When Michelle and her husband decided to sue a religious organization for building a temple in their neighborhood, they did not imagine that the lawsuit would be covered in local and national newspapers, much less that the coverage would spawn cyber harassment. But that is exactly what happened. They had brought the lawsuit because their neighborhood was zoned for only residential buildings, and they were concerned that the temple would lower the value of their home. That was all. In their minds it had nothing to do with religion, just real estate. But reporters framed it as a story about religion and intolerance— at least that is how many people in the audience interpreted it. Michelle got insulting calls and messages and knew of at least one video online that seemed to incite violence against her. She was being branded as a bigot, and she worried her reputation would suffer permanent damage.

When I asked Michelle what role the news coverage would play in her memory of the episode five years down the line, she said, "The hate messages and the *consequences* of the media stuff—that will play a big part. But just the media itself? Not so big."[1] For many interviewees, like Michelle, it was not the content of a news story per se that mattered most but the repercussions it subsequently had on their goals and reputations.

In this and the next chapter I explore how news coverage reverberated in subjects' lives after it was published and circulated. I focus here on audience feedback, specifically how subjects used it to judge whether news coverage had affected their reputations. In chapter 8 I explore how digital publication and circulation introduce a whole new set of potential repercussions for news subjects, often magnifying the effects discussed here.

I begin below by analyzing the role news articles can play in subjects' reputations in general. I then focus on how news stories can confer either status or stigma. I find that the news media can bestow both status and stigma with alarming efficiency, but the two operate somewhat differently. Being named in the news, regardless of editorial content, is itself a status-conferring event. On the other hand, the media's role in stigmatizing an individual is usually to amplify a preexisting or potential stigma, especially behavioral deviance. Ultimately, however, both status and stigma conferral by the news media can have profound effects on an individual's reputation and, since reputation is a key determinant of social inclusion, on his or her whole life. I conclude the chapter by discussing the ethical challenges journalists face regarding possible stigmatization of their subjects and suggest how it might be avoided.

TRANSMISSION AND RITUAL: HOW NEWS ARTICLES SHAPE OUR REPUTATION

As I discussed in the previous chapter, when they first saw themselves in the news, many interviewees said they felt anxious about how people in the audience would judge them, particularly how they looked. For some, the concern stopped there: they felt they looked old or chubby and did not like the idea of other people seeing them that way. But for others, the concerns went beyond the surface. If they looked old in the photo or their quotes made them sound dim, would their job prospects suffer? What if they did not just look or sound bad but were described as having done something awful? Would anyone hire them? Date them? Trust them? In other words, many subjects' most pressing concerns about the fallout from their news appearances were about their reputations.

Reputation is social currency. By definition, reputation is a community's perception of a person's moral worth and trustworthiness, based on the bits and pieces of information available about them.[2] As such, an intact reputation is absolutely essential for even basic social and economic inclusion, and the better one's reputation, the better one's prospects in both arenas. We call the plumber with the best reviews, not the one who got panned; we accept a date with the person reputed to treat others well, not the one known to use and abuse them.

Reputation is also important because it influences how we think of ourselves. Sociologist Charles Horton Cooley famously dubbed this tendency the "looking-glass self": we imagine others judging us, then look to those judgments as a kind of mirror.[3] In other words, our reputations, or what we understand our reputations to be, help us understand who we are and can have profound effects on our self-esteem. For that reason, reputation also operates as a highly effective system of social control. Defying social norms can ravage one's reputation—think of yesterday's "fallen woman" or today's "slut" who dares to defy sexual norms. Since reputational damage can be so personally and socially catastrophic, people usually find it in their best interest to just obey those norms, and the status quo lives on.

So how might a news appearance affect one's reputation? As I discussed in chapter 2, interviewees wanted to appear in the news for transmission purposes—to convey information to the public—but also to enjoy the benefits of ritual display before the masses.[4] Both can have reputational effects.

The most obvious way news articles affect reputation is that they transmit information about subjects, and that information is interpreted by the audience as indicating something positive or negative about the kind of people they are. A citizen depicted as having saved a life will reap the benefits of an improved reputation in part because the article conveys the information that she is selfless and brave. And the opposite is also true: a person depicted as having recklessly endangered the lives of others will suffer negative reputational effects because the news conveys that she is cowardly and imprudent, and not to be trusted.

But the process of singling people out for public attention in the news also has a ritual dimension. Many scholars have made the case that reinforcing social norms and standards is one of the core social functions of mass media in general, and of news in particular.[5] The individuals mentioned in the news are key players in this norm-enforcing ritual. In her seminal study of news production, sociologist Gaye Tuchman argues that even ordinary people briefly interviewed as people-on-the-street or quoted as participants in social movements play an important symbolic role. Sure, they may transmit information, but they also represent a group and show the world how people in that group are or ought to be.[6]

Ordinary people *featured* in the news often play a slightly different symbolic role. Unlike public figures, who may warrant scrutiny because their actions have public implications, ordinary Joes are usually featured in the news only if they have done something out-of-the-ordinary. As Herbert Gans puts it in *his* seminal study of news making, "The Unknowns who appear in the news are, by most criteria, an unrepresentative lot."[7] These are a community's victims, criminals, heroes, activists, innovators, and freaks. Like people-on-the-street, they may well be vehicles for delivering new information to the public. But they are also being held up for display in a public demonstration of which behaviors and characteristics are worthy of communal celebration or condemnation. In this sense, mass media can be understood as closely related to public rites going back (at least) to Greek and Roman antiquity, in which people were paraded before the masses in honor or shame.[8] Held up for public display in the news, subjects thus become symbols of good and bad behavior: This is what bravery looks like, and we celebrate bravery. This is selfish recklessness, and we condemn it. In this sense, ordinary news subjects play an important role in reminding citizens to uphold social norms or risk public punishment. For individuals who must navigate the social world, the reputational impact of having been made one of these symbols in the news can be profound.

The feedback news subjects receive from the public is thus a response to their roles as transmitters of information but also as players in this norm-enforcing ritual. As I discuss below, that means that the amount of status or stigma they experience as a result of a news appearance often feels out of proportion to the information actually being conveyed about them in the news story. That is because the community is not just responding to the information transmitted. It is also expressing a communal understanding of what it means, and how important it is, to be held up for this particular kind of public display and judgment.

STATUS CONFERRAL: NEWS AND THE AURA OF IMPORTANCE

Recall from the previous chapter that sociologists Paul Lazarsfeld and Robert Merton influentially identified "status conferral" as one of the mass media's key social roles: "The mass media bestow prestige and en-hance the authority of individuals and groups by *legitimizing their status*. Recognition by the press or radio or magazines or newsreels testifies that one has arrived, that one is important enough to be singled out from the large anonymous masses, that one's behavior and opinions are significant enough to require public notice."[9]

Sociologists usually use the term "status" to refer to the relative po-sitions of groups or individuals in an established social order. One's socioeconomic status, for example, can be high or low relative to other groups. However, since Lazarsfeld and Merton's influential essay, commu-nication scholars have tended to adopt something closer to the popular definition of the term, as an individual's importance and value in the eyes of the community. An appearance in the mass media may or may not in-dicate exactly to which status group one belongs, but it certainly tells every-one in the audience that you are important—worthy of confidence, credi-bility, and attention.[10] Lazarsfeld and Merton are specifically focused on how inclusion in the mass media can affect one's reputation for the better; in fact, they use "status conferral" and "status enhancement" synony-mously, and I do the same here.

The idea of status, whether one is using a more or less hierarchical defi-nition, almost always implies what economist Thorstein Veblen famously called "invidious comparisons" with other people.[11] Others assess our status—and we assess our own—by comparing ourselves favorably or unfavorably to others, with all the emotional baggage that implies. As such, much like having a positive reputation in general, having high status relative to others brings social benefits but also affects our sense of self. Author Alain de Botton has put this well, noting of status that, "If our position on the ladder is a matter of such concern, it is because our self-conception is so dependent upon what others make of us. Rare individuals aside (Socrates, Jesus), we rely on signs of respect from the world to feel tolerable to ourselves."[12]

Status must be communicated and perceived by the community—otherwise how do we know where we each stand?—and for that status symbols are key.[13] An appearance in the mass media is itself a status sym-bol, and evidence of one's *past* news appearances—copies of articles, video clips, links to archived news stories—operate as status symbols as well. When a news article names us and we post it, whether in the window of our local business or on our Facebook page, we are trafficking in these symbols. They inform or remind the community that we have been anointed by the mass media as people worthy of special attention.

One of Lazarsfeld and Merton's key points about status conferral is that it operates independently from editorial endorsement. Although they acknowledge that being depicted favorably by a prestigious institution might enhance status, it is not necessary. It is the fact of having been chosen for attention by the mass media at all that confers status, not the details of the content.[14] As I discuss below, I found that to be true in many cases, but in others the content most certainly did matter, either because it augmented the status conferred or because it nullified it altogether.

RITUAL STATUS CONFERRAL: WHEN CONTENT DOESN'T MATTER

Many interviewees received congratulatory calls, emails, and comments from loved ones, associates, and strangers following their news appearance. The amount of feedback varied depending on many factors, including the extent of the news coverage and how much it circulated via social networks. But it was common for subjects to say their parents bought multiple copies; friends got in touch from around the world; and coworkers, including superiors, suddenly knew their names and seemed to go out of their way to mention the news coverage. Positive attention helped reassure subjects that their appearance in the news had accomplished goals, such as raising awareness or publicizing a venture, and helped convince them that any flaws or errors that had bothered them at the outset were, in fact, quite minor. And nearly everyone, including subjects who had described themselves as spotlight-shy, said they found it just plain gratifying to be the focus of so much positive attention.

But some noticed something strange about all the congratulatory feedback: it seemed to have little to do with the content of the article at all and, in some cases, seemed outright inappropriate given the topic of the story. Tim, for example, hated the *Daily News* article that used his company—erroneously, he felt—as an example of a struggling business. No, the article did not exactly reflect poorly on the services he was providing. However, the article was rife with errors, and he felt that "owner of struggling business" was not exactly a flattering way to be cast. Yet he, too, got a lot of congratulatory feedback. I asked him to describe how his friends and family had reacted to the article, and he replied:

> TIM: I don't know if they read it carefully. 'Cause they're like, "Hey! I saw you in the paper. I saw you in the *Daily News*." But it wasn't like, "Man, that was a rough article." It was 'cause they saw us. I guess they saw our picture. So I don't even know if they read the article. It was a congratulatory kind of a thing.[15]

Tim's reference groups did not seem to know or particularly care what the article was about. As he said, it seemed like some people had not read it at all. Other interviewees said they were congratulated for appearing in stories about being unemployed, potentially evicted, and victims of violent crimes. The positive feedback struck them as incongruous with the content of the news story, which they felt was either unworthy of congratulations, grim, or outright embarrassing.

All these congratulatory responses perfectly illustrate the type of status conferral Lazarsfeld and Merton predicted: subjects' reference groups were celebrating them for having made the news at all, regardless of the stories' content. And responses in many cases went beyond a quick "congratulations." As communication scholar Peter Simonson suggests, status has an aura, and others are drawn to its glow.[16] Friends and family shared the articles via social media, playing up their own connections to the subject as though status conferral were, in fact, contagious: Look! My cousin/ sister/friend/colleague made the news! Schools and employers circulated articles and highlighted subjects' moment in the media spotlight in newsletters, packets of press clippings, and school newspapers, as though they reflected well on the whole institution.

University professor Bella, for example, felt her quote in the *New York Times* was too brief and insubstantial to be at all noteworthy, especially alongside her other professional accomplishments. And yet it was included in the press clippings the university circulated internally—which had never happened to her before, despite her many academic accolades:

> BELLA: It was interesting because nobody referred so much to what I had said, which in fact I hadn't said much of anything, but what was clear to me was that just having your name in the *Times* meant something.
> Q: What kinds of feedback were you getting?

BELLA: Oh, it was positive. "Oh! I saw you in the *Times*." It was like people wanted to say, "Oh, I saw you in the *Times*." . . . I made it onto the
Monday cite list or something.

Q: This is the press clippings for the week?

BELLA: Yes! And I made it to there. It was because of being in the *Times*.
And nothing I'd ever done before ever got me there, but that one little
nothing statement—which I think we can both agree was a nothing
statement—got me there.[17]

In these cases, the ritual dimension of news subjecthood is especially
clear. Reference groups responded positively to subjects having been
chosen for display at all, even when stories were trivial or bleak, and
subjects' roles in them minor.[18] This is the classic "Congrats! You made
the paper!" formulation. It did not matter *why*. Making the news at all
was treated as worthy of celebration, and the community celebrated.

TRANSMISSION AND RITUAL COMBINE: WHEN CONTENT DOES MATTER

In some cases, however, the editorial content of the story clearly did influence status conferral, by either negating it altogether or enhancing it further. As I discussed earlier in this chapter, part of the news's function is
to transmit new information about individuals, including their opinions,
expertise, and things they do that are so out-of-the-ordinary they warrant
public attention. Those kinds of information, especially remarkable acts
and achievements, can be status- or stigma-conferring in their own right.
Interviewees who were portrayed as holding morally questionable views
or as having behaved in a morally reprehensible way, such as criminals,
found themselves stigmatized by the content of their news articles. As I discuss in the second half of this chapter, in their cases it was clearly the information conveyed about them in the articles that hurt their reputations. Yes,
they were held up as important enough for public attention, but the audience responded so negatively to the information transmitted about them
that their status took a nosedive.

A second way editorial content can influence status is by boosting it
even more. Isabel, for example, was quoted prominently in a *New York
Times* story about the school where she teaches. The reporter had spent an

entire day in her classroom researching an article about how public schools were preparing students for standardized tests, a perennially controversial issue. During the reporting stage, Isabel had seen no indication that the reporter would frame the story positively, so she felt relieved when the published article praised her and her fellow teachers. After accolades started rolling in from people who had known her at all stages of her life, including the school principal, she concluded that being named in such a story functioned like a publicly bestowed reward for all her hard work:

> ISABEL: It sort of felt like a reward. . . . From then on we started getting more recognition from [the principal], which was good . . .
>
> Q: Is there anything else that could've happened that would have gotten you that amount of positive attention?
>
> ISABEL: I don't think so. Because let's say I got some sort of promotion to this great position. . . . Who would know? It's that everyone knew. . . . And it's funny because even now, almost a year later, I still get people being like, "Weren't you in the *Times*?" . . .
>
> Q: So that was one category of feedback: was straight up, "Saw you in the *Times*?"
>
> ISABEL: "Saw you in the *Times*. Good job." . . . Then there were a couple that were like, "So proud of you." "Proud of my family." And close friends were like, "We're so glad that your hard work is paying off. You're being recognized. Your school sounds like a great place to work."[19]

Here Isabel describes two layers of status conferral. The first, expressed in accolades for her having appeared in the news at all, was not tied to editorial content. The second, expressed as congratulations for having been praised in the *Times* for her good work, clearly was. As Isabel rightly points out, her work may have been praiseworthy before, but without a news article about it, no one would have known. For those interviewees depicted as exceptionally skilled workers, dedicated altruists, underdogs made good, and performers of heroic deeds, the news appearance itself was status conferring, but the articles also announced other information, which was *also* status conferring in its own right. To borrow Carey's model once more, having one's work framed positively in a major news outlet confers status in a ritual sense—this person is worthy of notice and attention—but also in a transmission-of-information sense—this person is especially good at her job.[20]

STATUS CONFERRAL AND THE LEGITIMIZATION OF PROBLEMS

Other subjects described feedback that seemed to suggest not exactly that their status had increased but that the news coverage had somehow legitimized their condition or situation. I interviewed a number of people who were unemployed and featured in stories about economic trends, or whose businesses were threatened in some way. Their cases stood out because I had expected them to have qualities of stigma, since unemployment and financial duress can have stigmatizing effects.[21] And yet, instead, most of them described an outpouring of sympathy and offers of help.

Rodney, for example, was featured in a *Daily News* story for having been laid off due to school budget cuts. His mother was so proud she bought seven copies of the article. The reactions from his reference groups were overwhelmingly positive—even the drug dealer on the block offered to help him out—but not in a way that necessarily suggested Rodney's credibility or authority had been enhanced. Instead, they seemed to interpret the article as having presented him as a person with legitimate problems, worthy of public attention and support:

> RODNEY: What happened was that I got a lot of calls from individuals saying, "Here's some opportunities coming up. You should check this out now," versus, if you had just got laid off, and you gotta reach out to your friends. The reverse happened and my friends were reaching out. . . . There was really no "congratulations" because it's not really a "congratulations" type of article. It was an "Oh wow, how can I help?" type of thing.[22]

As in the previous section, ritual and transmission combine here. People learned the facts about Rodney's situation because they read them in the paper, but the story appearing in the paper at all gave it importance. Although he was not overtly congratulated, the status aura was probably part of what drew people to him, with their messages of help, hope, and support.

In cases like Rodney's, in which audiences could easily have interpreted the news coverage in a more negative light, the way the story was framed in the news appeared to matter a great deal. He and several other unemployed people I interviewed were presented as victims of broad economic trends beyond their control. The articles did transmit information about their individual cases, but they also depicted subjects as representatives of large swaths of the public facing similar challenges, and not as individuals who were responsible for those conditions. As I discuss further below, perceived accountability matters a great deal in stigmatization processes: people who are perceived as responsible for their conditions are usually stigmatized more.[23] As Rodney's example suggests, depicting subjects as caught up in complex circumstances, rather than as blameworthy for their situations, can reduce the likelihood that news coverage will have stigmatizing effects. It may also increase the likelihood that subjects will experience at least some status effects instead.

STATUS CONFERRAL CONTRIBUTING FACTORS, DOWNSIDES, AND BENEFITS

My study was not designed to explore how specific outlets, technologies, and other factors might be more or less status conferring.[24] Future research could shed light on those different factors. But I do want to emphasize that the status conferral interviewees experienced was not inherent in a given outlet or technology but rather was a matter of perception on the part of their communities. Interviewees, like Rodney, whose primary reference groups read the *Daily News* got as much praise for having appeared in that paper as did those who appeared in the *New York Times* whose primary reference groups read and admired that outlet. For others, an appearance in the *New York Post* carried a great deal of weight with friends and family. As I discuss further in chapter 8, when subjects shared an article or news clip on social media, congratulations rolled in from all corners, with little regard for which outlet had published the original story.

That said, in nearly all cases status conferral increased in proportion to the amount of space devoted to the subject and leapt to a whole new level when the subject was pictured (the larger the picture the better) or featured in a supplementary online video. Several interviewees said they were surprised to receive feedback from people who treated them as though they were the protagonists of the news story, when they themselves had considered their own roles fairly minor. They concluded it was probably because their picture loomed large in the product. As Leyla noted, "I feel like the photo of me made people talk to me as though it was about me, and *my* story. If I could have changed that I think I would have, because it put the focus in the wrong place."[25]

As Leyla's quote suggests, status conferral has some downsides. She points out that it can distract one's reference groups from other aspects of the story that subjects feel are more important. Other interviewees, especially those who were heavily featured in celebratory stories, found the amount of attention they received—although it was almost uniformly positive—overwhelming and stressful. As I will discuss in the next chapter, becoming a celebrated (or not-so-celebrated) public figure in the news today also means becoming the subject of online commentary, which can quickly take a negative turn. And status conferral can even cue backlash from one's reference groups. Interviewees described responses ranging from good-natured teasing, apparently intended to keep the positive attention from going to their head, to jealousy radiating off colleagues who might have reaped the same rewards had the chips fallen differently.

But the upsides of status conferral can be tremendous. Some interviewees described new professional and personal opportunities opening up to them as an immediate result of their news appearance. They received job offers or invitations to speak at events. Those quoted as experts were approached by other media outlets seeking their now-legitimized expertise. But the benefit interviewees mentioned most was that their reference groups simply treated them as worthy of greater attention and deference than before.

A longitudinal study, which this was not, could shed light on whether and how long such benefits might last. The benefits could be social and economic, such as increased name recognition and professional advancement, but they could also be psychological. When I asked Mike if he had any concluding thoughts about having been featured in a *New York Times* article about seniors using social media, he responded, "No—other than having all of your grown kids totally proud of you."[26] There may be little more gratifying than that.

While the long-term effects of status conferral *may* extend far into the future, experimental evidence suggests that, sad to say, status-enhancing events are far more quickly forgotten than stigmatizing ones.[27] For some interviewees who found themselves at the center of a whirlwind of attention from reference groups and media professionals, one of the most notable and disconcerting aspects of the phenomenon was how quickly it died down. And yet even as the cameras and calls faded away, token reminders that they had once been anointed as worthy of public attention lingered. Husband and wife Jon and Jane described both phenomena in the aftermath of a *New York Times* article about their small business:

JON: It's just like, wow, it's like a tornado comes running through and then it's quiet.

JANE: I don't know, I think I have a slightly different take on it than you in that regard. I don't feel like it's gone away. Because every single person that we meet or talk to is like, "Oh, you're that guy," or "Oh, I read that." I don't think people have forgotten it yet.

JON: They might not have forgotten it, but the mad press rush thing was a bit of a tornado.

JANE: Yeah. It was a total tornado.[28]

STIGMA CONFERRAL: NEWS AND SPOILED IDENTITY

Although many social scientists since Erving Goffman have explored stigma, his 1963 book on the topic is essentially an exhaustive definition of the term and remains a core text. As he explains, the Greek word "stigma" originally referred to marks literally inscribed on individuals, "to expose something unusual and bad about the moral status of the signifier. The signs were cut or burnt into the body and advertised that the bearer was a slave, a criminal, or a traitor—a blemished person, ritually polluted." He goes on to explain that the term "stigma" has evolved to refer to a feature, attribute, or behavior so deeply discrediting it casts doubt on an individual's fitness for social inclusion.[29] On a status ladder, stigmatized people cling precariously to the lowest rung.

Goffman identifies three main categories of stigmatized people: those with physical disabilities, members of marginalized groups, and behavioral deviants whose actions indicate "blemishes of individual character."[30] All bear signs or symbols, sometimes visually apparent but often carefully concealed, that mark them as having failed to comply with community norms and expectations. Noncompliance with those dominant norms may not be an individual's fault, as it clearly is not for minorities or those with disabilities. In such cases, the signs of the stigma cannot logically be interpreted as indications of a moral failing. And yet, through an often unconscious process of attribution, we do associate the stigmatizing feature with a host of moral lapses and imperfections, often to such a degree that the stigma and all it suggests about the person's character come to dominate the way the person is perceived.[31]

Most research on stigma has focused on two of Goffman's three categories of stigmatized persons, marginalized groups or those with physical disabilities. I focus on the third category, behavioral stigma, which differs from the other categories because it is *explicitly* moral in character. When we discover that people have engaged in criminal or deviant activity, we may extrapolate irrationally and unfairly about their other characteristics, but doing so is less of a categorical leap than imputing moral failings to someone who, for example, is sitting in a wheelchair.

Experiments find that people who are seen as blameworthy for their stigmas—as behavioral deviants often are—are subject to more punishing treatments than those who are not because, simply put, we feel they deserve it.[32] Evidence also indicates, however, that we continue to treat even *acquitted* criminals as though they were unclean and deserve to be avoided.[33] In other words, like the irrational associative processes that may lead us to marginalize the person in the wheelchair, when we respond to behavioral deviance we are not simply fitting an appropriate punishment to a perceived crime. Mere proximity to the realm of behavioral deviance, rather than actual guilt, may be enough to stigmatize an individual in some cases. As with status, then, stigma has an aura. It can cast a shadow: friends and family of someone accused of misbehavior may find that their own social circles suddenly seem to shudder and contract.[34]

Just as having high status can be good for one's opportunities and self-esteem, so being stigmatized can limit opportunities and badly damage one's self-concept. As such, stigmatized people benefit from concealing the signs of their stigma to the extent they can. An ex-con, for example, will probably not want to shout it from the rooftops. Here, too, behavioral stigma differs from other kinds: it is the least visible, since it usually pertains to one's past actions rather than being written on the body. Since it is not immediately evident, the indicators of behavioral stigma must be communicated in other ways.

The news is one way. The mere fact of being in the news is not, in itself, stigma conferring—quite the opposite, as we saw in the section above on status conferral. However, when deviant behavior, which is only *potentially* stigmatizing when unknown, is reported and becomes known, that stigmatizing potential can be activated. A news report essentially outs the behavioral deviant to the world, then pins itself to their person, scarlet letter style.[35] The information being transmitted is interpreted by the public as casting such a negative pallor over them that the person's overall status and reputation are blackened. Ritually speaking, the person and the act are still anointed as important enough for public attention, but the ritual becomes one not of celebration but of condemnation. Reference groups may subsequently treat these subjects as morally polluted and socially untouchable. Below I detail the different manifestations of stigma that interviewees experienced as a result of their news appearances.

NOT QUITE STIGMA: SNARKY AND MIXED RESPONSES

Interviewees described a range of negative feedback from their news appearances, and not all of it seemed to suggest that they had been stigmatized. Snarky comments about small details of the news coverage and teasing or envious remarks from friends and family did not attack subjects' underlying morals or suggest they were unfit members of society. Most interviewees shrugged them off. It is hard to take it too personally when a reader criticizes your choice of tuna for lunch, as in Annie's case, or when coworkers tease you relentlessly for a silly sounding quote, as Gina described.[36] But some interviewees said they received feedback that questioned their moral worth or attacked them personally, and those cases did have some features of the stigma process Goffman describes.

For example, Michelle, whose quote opened this chapter, was featured in the West City paper and later a major national outlet. The stories reported that she was suing a local religious organization for having built a place of worship in her residential neighborhood. In response to the articles, she received insulting messages from angry readers accusing her of bigotry. Cyber threats made her fear for her safety. Beyond that, however, she was devastated to see signs that the coverage, which she felt was egregiously inaccurate, might be affecting her reputation:

MICHELLE: I have gotten hate messages on Facebook from people as far away as Canada, and as close as here in [town]. I've been called at my work and harassed by reporters. It hasn't been fun. . . . It was very frightening. And it was heartbreaking to me to be portrayed as a racist. . . . I'm not going to lie: it was disturbing to me, it hurt me, to be called that. Some of the messages that I got on Facebook were just like I was some bigot from [home state]. . . . They were trying to paint this picture of me that I was just intolerant. And it was really difficult, because I don't want that to be my reputation![37]

Without the news coverage, the public would not have known about Michelle's lawsuit. When some people in the audience saw it, their feedback indicated that they interpreted it as a blight on her character, a sign she was a racist.

But Michelle went on to say, "When I read horrible things about me it was painful, but there were also positive things. Like when somebody was on our side. So it was helpful in that regard." When feedback came in response to a controversial event or issue, as it did in Michelle's case, interviewees usually received a mix of positive and negative responses, rather than a uniform wave of angry attacks. While these cases do have some features of the stigmatization processes Goffman describes insofar as subjects' moral worth appeared to be badly damaged in the eyes of some, they highlight that stigma is not always consensual in the community.[38] That makes sense, since many norms and values are not consensual, especially about controversial issues. In such cases, subjects did not feel they were facing a community-wide judgment that they had violated a sacred taboo, but rather attacks from people on the other side of a polemical issue.

The distinction made a big difference for them. The supportive comments from the audience buoyed them, at least somewhat. For Michelle, it was an even greater comfort that her friends and family expressed understanding and support. Their responses illustrate that, even in coverage of controversial issues, status conferral can continue to operate:

MICHELLE: The contact that I got from people who I knew was supportive: "I saw you!" like, "Way to go on the Court of Appeals win!" "Hopefully this will be over for you guys." That kind of thing. From somebody I knew [feedback] was never negative it was like, [sounding excited] "Hey, I saw you! Oh my gosh!" That kind of thing.

As Michelle's experience indicates, being on the receiving end of hateful ad hominem attacks is unpleasant, to put it mildly. It can make people feel vulnerable, scared, and deeply hurt. However, if they receive just as many positive comments from those who agree with their position, that can mitigate the reputational and psychological damage that more uniformly stigmatizing news coverage can have.

STIGMA AND "DEVIANT" OPINIONS

Only a few people in my sample described repercussions from having appeared in the news that I would describe as evidence of severe, consensual stigma. Audiences interpreted the news coverage about them as signaling their violation of widely valued social norms. Subjects in those cases noticed changes in the way they were treated by friends, family, and colleagues to such a degree that their quality of life was dramatically affected.

Even a brief quote can have stigmatizing effects if audiences interpret it as an indication that the subject holds morally questionable opinions. Helen, who was quoted in an article about gender on college campuses, felt her quote was taken out of context and misrepresented what she had actually said. She was horrified to see many readers interpret it as an endorsement of infidelity. She faced a barrage of disapproving digital feedback as well as a scathing rebuke from her own university paper. The criticisms were not of the issue or of her point of view but of *her*:

> HELEN: Facebook messages from random people, mostly, across the country. . . . Really mean things, like, "Oh my god, you are disgusting. I can't believe you go to school with me, you have the lowest standards ever!" . . .
>
> Q: So then you said that Monday was pretty much the worst day of your life.
>
> HELEN: Yeah, it was. . . . I got that line, [with a disapproving, judgmental tone] "Oh, you're Helen K? I saw your quote," that happened for about two months after the article. . . . "I saw your article. Wow, you're a slut!"[39]

While the bulk of the responses were from strangers, many were from people on her own campus accusing her of reflecting poorly on the whole school. Helen identified strongly with her university, so those comments wounded her deeply. She noted that others who were quoted in the article did not seem to suffer the same degree of criticism:

> HELEN: I think my scenario was different from theirs because Kara said what she did and she got a lot of harsh backlash, but at least [the article] doesn't make her personally look bad. This is my personal morals in question in the *New York Times*, which so many people are reading.

Stigma can be strongly influenced by the editorial choices made by journalists. When controversial opinions are being expressed, every word counts. There may be little else in an article about the subject to correct, dilute, or counterbalance the controversial quote. Thus a single quote—accurate or not—can easily come to stand in for the person's whole character in the eyes of an audience who knows nothing else about the person.

STIGMA AND "DEVIANT" BEHAVIOR

When news coverage implicates the subject in a crime, negative repercussions can be especially hard for them to manage. As discussed above, these are clear examples of behavioral deviance, which is itself stigmatizing, being broadcast to the general public. Three of my respondents found themselves in that position. Two were falsely accused and later had the charges dropped against them, and one was guilty and had entered a plea deal. All experienced lasting stigma.

Rich, for example, was arrested for kidnapping a politician's wife.[40] To this day he has no idea how he got caught up in the whole saga: cops knocked on his door in the middle of the night and took him away in handcuffs to be arrested in a different neighborhood, for a crime against a woman he had never met. Eventually the charges were dropped for lack of evidence, but not until after the arrest had been written up in several small local papers. The ramifications were devastating. He lost his job and had not found work since. But the most painful part of the whole experience was seeing how quickly his family and friends changed their opinion of him. A niece who had lived with him in the past believed the article; his brother scolded him for reflecting poorly on the family name and potentially damaging his—the brother's—business. And while one could certainly argue that the articles—which contained errors that made the charges seem even worse than they were—were just reporting the arrest, which was itself the true stigmatizing marker, as Rich points out, if not for the articles, *no one would have known.* Not the arrest itself but others' reactions to it were what had derailed his life and alienated him from those around him, and those reactions were a direct result of the news coverage. At the time we spoke he was still trying to figure out how to piece his former life back together.

Beth's case was a bit different. She *was* guilty, of a white-collar crime. But she too felt strongly that it was not the crime itself but the news coverage of it that had stigmatized her. When charges were initially pressed against her, the basics were reported in the local paper of the large city where she lived. She noticed some strange looks from people afterward but little more than that. Even after she agreed to a plea deal and testified against another defendant in the case, she saw little indication that word of her crime had traveled beyond the courtroom. There were no reporters in attendance, and no one outside her immediate family seemed to know what had happened.

Several months later, around the time the other perpetrator was scheduled for sentencing, a scorching article appeared in a national paper. Apparently based on transcripts from the original trial, it depicted her as having betrayed her husband and seduced the accused man into committing the crimes. The change in her social circle was precipitous:

BETH: After the first [article] I was still invited to Christmas. Did they think I was the greatest person in the world? No. But you know, I still came to Christmas. I still was there with the family. They looked at me a little funny. But the second article . . . it is as if a nuclear bomb went off in my life. First of all, I've gained a hundred pounds from the whole thing . . . Secondly, I was always the first person invited to every party. I mean, I've lived here all my life. I know every single person—I mean, this is my world. I know everybody. It was as if every single person I ever knew died.[41]

It struck Beth as strange that the first articles, which documented her indictment but did not include the back story, had so much less effect on people's opinions of her. It was only with the publication of the second round of articles, those that depicted her as having behaved not just illegally but in a morally underhanded way, that everyone seemed to drop off the planet. As she put it, ironically, "The morality stuff is the stuff that stuck more. And if you think about it, that's not even the illegal stuff."

In the wake of the damaging news coverage, she had to move her kids to a new school. Her husband's family disowned her and pushed him to divorce her. She considered suicide. For a long time she just hid from everyone—not that anyone wanted to see her anyway. As she put it:

> BETH: My husband's stupid family. I'm dead to them. And they've written off my kids, they've written off anything that has anything to do with me. To all the people [in the neighborhood] I'm just this pariah. I'm just this total, total pariah. And I don't even know myself.

Little wonder Beth had trouble recognizing herself. If reputation is a social mirror that affects how we think of ourselves, a reputation distorted by stigma is truly like a funhouse mirror. In an effort to start life anew, at the time of our interview Beth was pursuing a new career in a new city, and, as I discuss in the next chapter, she had taken steps to conceal the online trail of the story. But she was haunted by fears of being found out by new friends, new colleagues, and potential employers. In that way, too, she perfectly resembles one of Goffman's stigmatized individuals. She may not have already been discredited in her new social circles, but she would always be discreditable.[42] Ultimately, the experience was so traumatic that Beth concluded:

> BETH: My entire life died. This was a death. I mean, I've had a daughter die. This was a death. This was a death of my life. You have to go through the whole grieving process: shock, denial, all those things. . . . And just like with a death, the only thing that cures—not cures—but the only thing that makes you ultimately recover from losing a loved one is time. And not "recover" but survive it.
> Q: Well, how do you think your experience would have been different if there had been no press coverage?
> BETH: That's what killed me.

While in Beth's case one could argue that she herself was responsible for the source of the stigma she endured, since she had committed a crime—which she acknowledged in our interview—she was not wrong. Had others not known about that crime, which they only did because of the news coverage, she and her family would have suffered far less.

As Beth's story illustrates, the news has the potential, only unleashed in full force on private citizens when they have behaved in ways deemed socially reprehensible, to operate much like traditional shame punishments. Like the physical branding of criminals intended to mark them as unfit members of society, not temporarily, but for life, a stigmatizing news article can wound a person deeply and for a long time. As scholars across disciplines have pointed out, the problem with shame punishments is that there is no guarantee that they will be proportionate to the crime—and often they are not.[43]

STIGMA AND ETHICAL CHALLENGES FOR JOURNALISTS

That news reports of deviant behavior, especially criminal acts, can stigmatize alleged and actual perpetrators and their families is an ongoing ethical concern for journalists. The strategies they use to minimize potential stigma, and the degree to which they prioritize avoiding it vary by culture. On one end of the spectrum, in Sweden and the Netherlands private citizens who commit crimes are rarely named, unless they have committed very public acts of violence, such as major terrorist attacks. Their names are withheld out of concern for their privacy and possible stigmatizing effects on them and their families.[44] On the opposite pole, in the British tabloid press (and, to a lesser degree, the British elite press), "naming and shaming," or deliberately naming people with the intent to inflict shame on them for perceived immorality, is a long-standing convention. The practice has come under fire recently as part of a broader trend of recklessness toward news subjects in Great Britain.[45]

In the United States, the practice of explicit naming and shaming is not as entrenched, and American codes of ethics often exhort journalists to balance the public good against potential harm to private citizens. Conventions usually prohibit the naming of minors and sex crime victims out of concerns about privacy and potential stigma. For the same reasons controversies periodically erupt over when to name "people of interest" in crimes who have yet to be indicted. But in general, in the United States, as in Great Britain, informing the public is considered more important than protecting private individuals. Adults accused of crimes and misbehaviors are usually considered fair game, and convicted criminals are named without debate.[46]

If reporters do name private citizens who are implicated in a crime or other misbehavior, it is hard to avoid stigmatizing them. The behavior itself is potentially stigmatizing, so even the most straightforward reporting of it functions as a megaphone, announcing it to the world. That activates the negative judgment of the public, which can lead to stigmatization of the individual. But clues to lessening stigma in such cases can be found in some of the stories in this chapter. Subjects of some potentially stigmatizing stories, such as the unemployed people I interviewed, actually faced surprisingly little stigma. They were depicted as caught up in big, complex processes beyond their control, and not as wholly accountable for their situations. Since, as I have discussed, people who are perceived as blameworthy for their stigma are more harshly judged than those who are not seen as accountable for it, this kind of nuanced reporting makes a difference.[47] There is no question, however, that depicting people as caught up in a complex web of circumstance is much more difficult, and much more rare, when those people are implicated in serious crimes. It essentially requires showing that behavioral deviance may not be so deviant after all— that we could all find ourselves behaving in such a way, in such circumstances. That kind of reporting takes time, space, and thinking beyond the conventions that dictate how such stories are normally told in the news.

But it can be done. Emma, for example, was profiled in the West City paper after she faced criminal charges for euthanizing her husband, who had been badly incapacitated by illness. Some of the reader comments she saw online were critical, but she was amazed to see other readers coming to her defense. On the other hand, it made sense because the article framed the event as a tragic love story: husband taken ill, nursed by his loving wife until a barebones healthcare system and bad luck simply took their toll on her psyche, as they would on anyone's. This, the article seemed to imply, could have happened to any of us, and the online comments reflected a compassionate reading: "I hope someday someone will love me as much as she loved him," read one remarkable comment. Another replied, "So do I."

Of course, some crimes lend themselves better to this sympathetic treatment than others. Undeniably, the exigencies and scarce resources involved in daily news production make in-depth reporting on the context underlying criminal or otherwise "deviant" behaviors extremely difficult to pull off every time. But given the potential for articles to inflict stigma disproportionate to a crime, more nuanced reporting in such cases, especially when all the facts remain unknown, should be an ongoing goal. These ethical concerns are even more pressing today since stigmatizing material can adhere to individuals online indefinitely. As I will discuss in the next chapter, the potential stigmatizing effects of news articles are just one of the features of news subjecthood that are magnified in today's media environment.

8

MAKING THE NEWS IN A DIGITAL WORLD

Q: When you guys agreed to do the article, did it occur to you at that point that it was something that was gonna be online?

JANE: You know, it's funny 'cause I sit all day looking at the *Times* online but I didn't really think of that aspect of it, I thought of the print newspaper. Right? I mean, you too?

JON: Right, yeah. The print newspaper. I had no idea.

JANE: Which is crazy. I'm telling you, I spend eight hours, ten hours a day with the *New York Times* website up in my face.

Many interviewees were first contacted by reporters online. They responded to follow-up questions using digital tools of various kinds, researched reporters by Googling them, read their own news coverage online, and shared it on social networks. Their embrace of social media varied, but none was a complete technological neophyte. And yet about half of the people in this study said that when they agreed to be interviewed by a reporter, they did not consider the fact that the resulting news story would appear online, or what that might mean. That was even the case for some, like Jon and Jane, who were habitual readers of the online version of the newspaper in which they were being asked to appear.[1] The other half of my interviewees said they immediately assumed the article *would* appear online, but the number that did not was remarkable—and alarming.

As I discuss in this chapter, online publication and circulation alter what it means to appear in a news story, in some ways significantly so. The basic properties of the internet—"persistence, replicability, scalability, and searchability"—mean that more sortable information is easily accessible, for longer, to a far larger audience than ever before.[2] That obviously includes news articles. The effects discussed in the previous chapter, including the feedback subjects received in response to their news appearances and the ways news coverage enhanced their status or stigmatized them were generally magnified online. Interviewees were struck by how far and fast articles traveled; the ease with which readers around the globe could contact them directly; the way news stories became fodder for extensive online commentary; and the degree to which an appearance in the news could completely alter their online reputations. Below I detail each of these phenomena. I then explore some of interviewees' strategies for managing the reputational effects of appearing in a mainstream news article in a digital world. This is the final stage of news subjecthood, but in many cases it is hard to say exactly when it ends.

ONLINE REPUTATION AND THE ARCHITECTURE OF THE INTERNET

(POTENTIALLY) VAST AUDIENCES

Readers sharing newspapers among themselves, whether in coffeehouses, public reading rooms, or private living rooms, is an old practice. Mailing them to distant friends and family also has a venerable history.[3] But those were slow, clunky, contained processes compared to today's frictionless online sharing. News sharing on social media is more common all the time, with many news outlets encouraging and facilitating it by offering the option to email or post a given article with the click of a button.[4] As a result, when individuals appear in a news story, it can spread like wildfire through their own social networks. Some interviewees got messages from their contacts around world responding to their news appearances before they themselves had even seen the coverage. Many others instigated the process themselves by posting the story to Facebook or Twitter, or emailing their contacts. Some, like Dara, a college student who made the news when she was rescued after fainting onto the subway tracks, said that sharing the story on social media felt almost obligatory. When I asked her about posting the stories on Facebook, she said simply, "I felt like I had to. I was on the news."[5] For her, a news appearance was the kind of event one is simply *supposed* to share.

Sharing news is, of course, not limited to readers passing articles around among themselves. Other news outlets and blogs may pick up an article as well, sharing it with their own audiences in whole, part, or re-mixed form. That articles are republished and repurposed by other outlets, like readers sharing newspapers, is not a new phenomenon. But online, the kind and number of forums that repurpose news articles multiply expo-nentially. Articles are thus introduced to audiences who might not be ha-bitual consumers of news on the original site. News aggregators of various kinds—which are completely new digital tools with no obvious pre-internet corollary—direct readers to specific articles as well. And once those articles are old news, they are no longer relegated to musty file systems, difficult to access or navigate. They now resurface effortlessly thanks to search engines. Audiences for a particular news article can thus expand ever outward but also grow quietly into the future.

All these developments—sharing, remixing, aggregation, and search—can increase visibility for any given news article far beyond what it would have been in a pre-internet media environment. Helen, whom I discussed in the previous chapter, provides a striking illustration of the potential implications of these new developments for news subjects because her article essentially went viral.[6] She was quoted in a controversial story on gender in the *New York Times*. Like many provocative trend stories, it reached the top of the paper's own "most emailed" list and was picked up by many other media outlets, discussed at length on blogs and in reader comments, and shared extensively on social networks. Her quote, which she argued was taken out of context and misrepresented her meaning com-pletely, became a focal point for critics. Helen had not anticipated the origi-nal article being so controversial, so she was disconcerted to find herself, a twenty-one-year-old college student, in the national spotlight as a result of a single remark. The feedback was overwhelming partly because it was so negative but also because there was just so much of it. And for each person who had contacted her, she knew that many, many others had seen the ar-ticle. Who knew what *they* were thinking? She described the day the article came out as the worst day of her life, as digital criticism buffeted her from all sides, and she worried her reputation would never recover.

Obviously, not every news article goes viral. Most do not. Audience size depends on many factors, including what the article was about, whether it resonated with the public, and which outlet published it in the first place. But the fundamental point is that the *potential* audience for any given news story today is dramatically larger than in a pre-internet era. For subjects hoping to raise awareness or generate publicity, or those who especially enjoy attention, often the more the better. For many interviewees, after all, a big part of the attraction of appearing in the news was public display or public address, as I detailed in chapter 2. A larger audience increased the thrills of fame and the pride of status discussed in chapter 7, and a wider reach helped them fulfill their goals of, for example, addressing misperceptions or educating the public about issues they valued.

That said, even for self-described exhibitionists, a massive audience can feel overwhelming. Harry, a professional magician who appeared in an article that was picked up all over the world, was fascinated to see his story in different languages and to know people across cultures were seeing it. He is a guy who likes attention—he had previously appeared on a reality TV show—but he also acknowledged that, in this case, the sheer size and range of the audience made him feel "a little scared."[7] For people who do not like attention, a larger audience can exacerbate an already uncomfortable situation.

As I discussed in earlier chapters, for many interviewees, imagining an audience out there judging them was one of the strangest parts of their whole experience. How audiences would receive and interpret their stories was one more aspect of the news production process that they could not control. Online, they could be—or could imagine themselves being—judged by even more people, and for longer. The potentially vast audience introduced by online publication thus adds yet another layer of uncertainty to what "making the news" might mean. The massive audience, imagined or real, potential or actual, fuels all the phenomena I discuss in the remainder of this chapter.

DIRECT FEEDBACK FROM FRIENDS—AND STRANGERS

After their news coverage was published, many interviewees said they received phone calls but also direct messages of various kinds, including by email, text, or social networks. As I discussed at length in the previous chapter, much of that feedback came from friends, family, and acquaintances and often consisted of just a brief, congratulatory acknowledgement of the news appearance. Because articles circulate far and wide today, and digital tools make it so easy to hit the "like" button, comment, or send a quick message, news subjects undoubtedly receive more friendly feedback from their personal contacts than in the past. But a more striking, qualitative difference between being a news subject today and before the internet lies in the amount of direct feedback subjects receive from *strangers*, in some cases from all over the world. Interviewees were surprised to be contacted by distant readers who had found their contact information easily online. In fact, that is how I contacted most of them myself.

People who contact complete strangers after seeing them in articles usually do so because they had strong reactions to the coverage, whether positive or negative. Interviewees said direct messages felt quite intimate, which made them all the more satisfying when they expressed solidarity, support, or agreement with their views. In some of the most dramatic cases, interviewees saw a whole new community emerge through the positive feedback. Thomas, a performer with a medical condition who was featured in the *New York Times*, was touched and humbled by the positive response he received from others with the same condition. They were eager to share their own stories and clearly thrilled to find a role model:

> THOMAS: The response was so overwhelming. Over email and Facebook. My god, it was just so many people responding in such a positive way. And from this country, from Europe, from Asia. From all over. I think people hadn't ever quite seen a story like this before. I knew personally, for myself, I've been hunting for a role model for quite some time. I didn't really have anyone that was quite like me to look up to and shape my path after. And suddenly I was getting all these emails about "my six-year-old son," "my nine-year-old daughter." "Thank you. Thank you for sharing, thank you for telling." It was just this sort of overwhelming positive wave. Which was great.[8]

Thomas found the feedback deeply gratifying. Another interviewee, Ivan, was featured in news outlets all over the world for rescuing a child from an accident near his home in the Bronx. A neighbor caught the dramatic rescue in a video that turned out to be perfect for television, and many stations eagerly picked it up. Hundreds of appreciative voicemails and Facebook messages from as far afield as Nigeria, Malaysia, and Europe rained in. Ivan said keeping up with all the digital feedback was time-consuming and sometimes overwhelming but ultimately worth the effort. As he explained, "I responded to all of [the messages] individually. It took me a while. But anybody that gets up from their TV to go search for me on their computer and send me a message deserves my answer back."[9]

But not all interviewees received such supportive messages. Some heard from strangers who disagreed with—or simply disliked—their quotes, points of view, or life choices. Even Ivan said he got some messages from people criticizing how he had held the body of the child he rescued, which understandably irritated him. Becoming a target for angry feedback was most common for subjects who had appeared in stories that had struck a nerve with the public, as Helen learned on the day her article about gender issues was published. She recalled:

HELEN: Sunday I was at home and I got this Facebook message from this random girl at [her college]. Who, I have no idea. And she was like, "I cannot believe you said that." She was like, "I don't know you, but you should be ashamed of yourself. You are disgusting, you give us such a bad name."

Public figures may be accustomed to unrestrained personal attacks from strangers, but my interviewees were all private citizens who were not. Some had a bit more experience addressing the public—neighborhood and political activists, for example. They seemed less surprised to get direct feedback and quicker to dismiss the negative; perhaps with practice one grows a thicker skin. But for the majority of the people I interviewed, who were appearing in the news for the first or second time, direct feedback from complete strangers was not something they had anticipated when they had agreed to speak to reporters. Their experiences with direct feedback, positive and negative, highlight one of the oddities of being in the public spotlight in a digital world: the audience may remain largely invisible, but any individual in that audience could reach out and touch you directly. Given that the audience always *could* be enormous, that possibility can add to the thrill of public display—or the anxiety of public exposure.

BECOMING FODDER FOR ONLINE COMMENTARY

The many online commenting options available to news audiences today mean that anyone named in a news article might also become fodder for a visible kind of public discussion. News stories have long been the stuff of conversation, but today many of these conversations are asynchronous, between strangers who will never meet, made visible to the public, and archived for future audiences. Just as not every news article becomes a viral sensation, the amount of commentary a given article receives varies a great deal. It depends on what the article is about, the outlet, and many other factors. Many articles simply gain little traction with the online public, and news outlets themselves do not always turn on the comments feature for stories. In those cases, online commentary may be minimal, or there may be none at all.

When there was commentary on their news stories, interviewees' reactions to it varied. Some interviewees were unaware of online discussions about their articles, and others made a point of avoiding them. However, most respondents said the temptation to read them was simply too great; it is really hard to walk away when we know people are talking about us. Just as seeing oneself in the original coverage can feel uncanny, as I discussed in chapter 6, seeing oneself represented in audience commentary can feel just plain strange. Many subjects had not anticipated it, and the people commenting and discussing them were usually complete strangers, which seemed to add to the uncanny effect. Subjects had not even spoken to these commenters, and yet they watched as commenters in some cases had whole conversations about them and criticized them freely.

In some cases, interviewees' interest in reader comments went beyond mere curiosity. Recall from earlier chapters that news subjects are often so deeply implicated in the trigger issue itself, the interview process, and the strange pressures of being represented before the public that they do not trust themselves to assess the coverage on their own. So they turn to their reference groups. We can now add that these reference groups increasingly include not only people they know personally but others who are visible in online spaces—in this case, those who choose to make themselves visible by commenting publicly on news stories. Although they are usually strangers whom the news subject will never meet, they become key points of reference partly for that reason: they seem more objective than friends and family. Their opinions can also carry great weight because, unlike the direct messages discussed above, these comments are public and often appear right underneath the article itself. As such, they have the potential to influence other readers' interpretations of the article, and their impressions of any people named in it.

Interviewees saw advantages and disadvantages to this new phenomenon. Colleen, a career educator featured in an article about the opening of a controversial new New York City school, pointed out that even when the commentary was not uniformly positive, it could be informative and interesting:

> COLLEEN: It's not like the [print-only] city paper, where somebody reads it and puts it down. Now people can respond. And the response is mixed, but in some ways it's kind of exciting because there's a conversation and you're in it. The conversation is about what you're doing. And there are gonna be people in support of it, there are gonna be people who are detractors. But in either case people who are genuinely interested and have not decided will be part of the conversation and they can decide what they think about it.[10]

As Colleen indicates, it can be pretty interesting to be part of a civic conversation, especially about a topic you care about—in her case, her life's work.

Public reaction made visible in reader discussions can also help subjects assess how well an article achieved their goals, such as raising awareness or dispelling myths. The commentary acts as a kind of audience barometer and can be especially useful for activists hoping to gauge an article's impact. As Tea Party leader Patricia explained, she was eager to read comments on her article in the *New York Times* because "I wanted to know: does this article do any harm to our movement? That's really what I was looking for. Did it help us or did it hurt us?"[11] Based on the reader comments, she concluded that the article, which she had not loved initially, had savagely smeared one of her colleagues, which had not occurred to her before:

> Q: Was it the way she herself was represented that bothered you—or?
> PATRICIA: It was the way she was represented and obviously the way it came across, because the comments were all about what a horrible lady she was. . . . And I guess I didn't react as ferociously to her quotes until I saw the comments. From how other people responded to the article.[12]

As Patricia's example illustrates, some interviewees, especially those associated with hotly debated issues, initially felt their articles were fair but changed their mind when they saw readers responding negatively. Tellingly, Patricia blamed the reporter for having quoted her colleague in a way that inspired critical comments, even though she had not initially found the quotes offensive herself. She did not blame the commenters for having interpreted the quotes in a negative light. That reaction was not universal in my sample; some interviewees blamed commenters, not reporters. But either is a possibility, even if the subject's initial response to the reporter's work was a positive one.

On the other hand, being fodder for discussion and commentary about an article can also enhance subjects' status by increasing their visibility and overall digital footprint. As I discussed in the previous chapter, unless they cast the subject in a very negative light, news articles are inherently status conferring because they signal to the audience that the subject is important enough to be singled out for public attention. Status can increase even more for an article if it makes the "most emailed" lists hosted by many news sites, gains steam in aggregator sites that depend on reader ratings, or generates extensive online discussion across social networks and other forums. The more an article is linked to, cited, excerpted, and commented on, the better it will usually perform in a Google search, which further increases its prominence. As long as the article is not stigmatizing, subjects who ride that wave can benefit a great deal, since online visibility and influence are ever more important measures of one's standing in the world.

However, much like expanding audiences in general, online commentary is a viral effect over which the subject has basically no control at all, and being the subject of so much online attention and discussion has some fairly serious downsides. Audience commentary is usually not subject to journalistic conventions limiting overt opinion and speculation. On the contrary, those are encouraged by the format. Although news outlets moderate comments to varying degrees and many prohibit obscenity and abuse, many interviewees felt comments they saw on news sites were inappropriate, ranging from petty and irrelevant to outright mean-spirited and bigoted. Furthermore, many subjects described seeing comments in other online spaces with more lenient comments policies or none at all, and they mostly did not seem to distinguish between the different forums in which they had read them. Understandably, being insulted at all made more of an impression on them than where, exactly, it had happened.

Interviewees varied a great deal in the degree to which they took petty or vicious comments to heart. While some said they were able to dismiss them precisely because they were so stupid and irrelevant— "little kid talk" as Oliver put it—others found them painful, especially when they touched on a preexisting sensitivity or attacked subjects' ethics and morals.[13] It is much easier to dismiss someone who criticizes you for eating tuna than someone who calls you a liar or a slut. A number of subjects who received nothing but supportive feedback from friends and acquaintances were hurt by critical commentary from strangers, in some cases to such a degree that they said it made them regret agreeing to cooperate with the reporter in the first place. Carmen, for example, a young Hispanic woman who was the victim of an unsolved crime that was featured in the *Daily News*, described her experience of reading the comments there:

CARMEN: Then I started reading comments on the *Daily News* that people were writing and they were being assholes about it. They were saying I made it up. That my boyfriend had done it and I was blaming it on somebody else. That since I'm Spanish it looked like I was letting some drug dealer into my house. When I read those comments I started regretting [appearing in the article].[14]

As Carmen's comment suggests, minorities among my interviewees faced especially harsh feedback. Commenters in some forums seized on anything in an article that could be reshaped into a racial or misogynistic slur.

For some subjects who already felt overwhelmed by the attention they were receiving from the news coverage, the comments were the last straw. Unlike critical messages sent directly to news subjects, these messages were public, so they could be embarrassing even if they seemed absurd, and subjects found themselves with few viable options for addressing them. Some described feeling tempted to dive into the fray to post comments in their own defense, and a few actually did: Ivan was not going to stand by and watch people criticize *his technique* when he put himself in danger to rescue a child. Notably, however, none of them said it made them feel much better.

These public discussions about news articles can foment more critical direct messages, and vice versa, and when an article generates a lot of discussion, the distinction between private and public comments starts to blur, as Helen described:

HELEN: I read the *New York Times* comments about the story and it was maxed out. The comment area. That was the worst feeling ever. I remember I started crying when I was reading the comments. Because it was just like, "How does Helen K go to school?!" Like, "She's so dumb, she doesn't have standards." . . . And then people would Twitter me back and be like, "No wonder you're single!" like, "You're that desperate?" It just makes me so mad because my dream was always to go to [this college] and I had to work really hard to get there. So for the [college] community to ridicule me was really hard. And some of the comments on the *New York Times* were from [my fellow] students, like, "Wow, I'm ashamed that you go to this school with me." . . . Once I read the comments it actually made me feel dumb, like, "Wow, I should've actually seen this coming." Y'know? It made me question myself, even.

Helen's quote highlights a few key points about reference groups and audience commentary. In the whirlwind of commentary and messaging, her immediate reference group seemed to balloon to include everyone who had commented on the article, and all the other readers she could imagine who might be judging similarly. Yes, she was still most bothered by the comments from her classmates, but the comments from strangers mattered, too. They all influenced how she imagined she appeared in the eyes of the world and, in turn, how she thought about herself. Her last observation is particularly telling: reading the critical comments and messages even made her question herself. Feedback can do that. It can sow doubt in subjects' minds not just about their own interpretation of news coverage but about themselves.

THE REPUTATIONAL EFFECTS OF SEARCHABLE NEWS STORIES

As I argued in chapter 7, our reputations are among our most valuable and personal assets. They are constructed from judgments our communities make of us, based on social information, including articles, about our past deeds and enduring characteristics. It follows that when methods for gathering that information change, the way our reputations are constructed by our communities will change as well. Although he was writing in the 1960s, Erving Goffman's work on stigma provides a helpful theoretical framework for dissecting how this process plays out in the digital world.[15]

In most of his writing, Goffman focuses on how individuals adopt different roles and faces in different social contexts. But when he confronts the question of how stigma clings to individuals as they move through the world, he has to explain how people are recognized as they transition from one encounter to the next. To explain the process, Goffman develops the idea of the "identity peg." An identity peg is a unique feature, usually a person's name, that is used to identify him across social situations. With the identity peg as a kind of base, "the individual can be differentiated from all others and . . . around this means of differentiation a single continuous record of social facts can be attached, entangled, like candy floss, becoming then the sticky substance to which still other biographical facts can be attached."[16]

For Goffman, social facts are clues to an individual's past and abiding characteristics.[17] Today, in an increasingly seamless version of the process Goffman describes, we plug a person's identity peg—usually her name, but in the future perhaps her face—into an internet search and gather relevant social facts, like candy floss. And then we judge. Crucially, the social facts that make up an individual's biography are not neutral. They may include status and stigma symbols, and they form the basis of judgments—often moral in character—that can be made about the individual. In other words, these social facts form the basis of the person's reputation.

Constructing an individual's reputation used to be a process carried out by a geographically circumscribed community of people who knew a person and pieced together available information about that individual over time. That information was then judged against shared norms. Today an individual's reputation is often assessed by strangers who know only his name and judge him based on information aggregated by an enigmatic algorithm. People with spoiled reputations once had the option of moving to a new area, perhaps haunted by the ever-present possibility of being found out. Today, being found out is a virtual certainty, and moving to a new town will do little to help. The growth of an industry of online reputation consultants who will, for a fee, clean up one's search results by diluting or removing damaging information is a direct result of this new socio-technological phenomenon.

News articles online, which themselves are social facts but also announce other social facts, can play a potentially distortive role in news subjects' reputations. Search engine algorithms, like Google's, change often and are not open to the public. However, we do know that mainstream news sites and the stories they produce tend to perform well in searches because they have relatively large audiences, are linked to from many other sites, and actively engage in search engine optimization. All those factors help in the ranking of search results.

The visibility of a news article in an internet search for a given individual's name will depend on many factors, including how much information is already available online about that person and when the story appeared. However, a high profile news story that names a private citizen and is picked up by multiple news outlets stands a good chance of taking up not just the first several lines but the first several *pages* of her search results. That kind of news story can play a powerful role in shaping her reputation, for a very long time, and across community boundaries.

Seeing one's search results completely reconfigured by a single article can be disconcerting to say the least, as Patricia, who was quoted in a *New York Times* article on the Tea Party Movement, explained:

> PATRICIA: And then I Googled my name a week after that article came out and I don't know how many times my name popped up just because of that one article. I mean, that one article got picked up on twenty other newspapers, and so each one of those newspapers referred to my name, too. . . . I was just shocked at the number of times it was listed in Google. I had expected it, but not quite to that extent.[18]

This may sound ominous, and it certainly introduces new layers of risk to the phenomenon of news subjecthood. However, since appearing in news articles can also confer status (as can increases in one's online visibility and influence), some interviewees found the appearance of a news article when they searched for their names a welcome development. Almost all interviewees said they noticed at least some change in their search profile after their news appearance. For a few, appearing in a news article was the first time *any* social fact appeared when someone searched for their name. Many were pleased; they figured any increase in their visibility online could be helpful, and they rejoiced to have flattering articles shape their public image.

But some had mixed feelings about their new Google-search-selves. Even when an article did not reflect poorly on a subject, having it redefine their online identity—especially when it depicted an anomalous or otherwise unrepresentative event—could still feel strange. As Dara, who made the news for fainting on the subway tracks, explained:

> DARA: For a while [before the news articles] if you Googled me, you'd come up with me in different fashion shows or me and my art, me in an interview about my mom's business, so stuff like that. It was a nice depiction of me. But now you Google me it's like, "Girl faints on subway," y'know? And I'm like . . . okaayy.
>
> Q: Not exactly the web reputation you were most hoping for.
>
> DARA: Yeah.[19]

At least in Dara's case the distortion was not outright damaging. Liana, whose quote in a single news broadcast about her brother's murder was picked up by many other news outlets, found herself the target of a firestorm of negative commentary online. Googling her own name quickly became a painful reminder of traumatic events, and she worried about how it would affect her future:

> LIANA: I wanna go to law school, but then I was just like, "Oh my gosh; I'm gonna be some kind of big attorney one day, you'll Google my name and this story's gonna come up. Like, my family, when we're choosing a doctor we Google the doctor to see if there are any negative comments, y'know what I mean? So I just feel like your name will be there but it'll be there for the wrong reasons.[20]

Liana is probably right to be concerned. When people do a search for us it *might* be out of idle curiosity, but it is often out of instrumental curiosity. They are trying to decide whether to engage with us in some way, be it as an employee, a roommate, a client, or in any of myriad other potential social and economic relations. This is a straightforward, if streamlined, way we have long relied on reputation to determine trustworthiness. Since people performing the searches may know little or nothing about us besides what appears in an online search, what they find there may be their entire basis of assessment.

Mainstream news articles can influence reputations not only because they occupy a lot of space in search results but also because they have credibility relative to other information online of more indeterminate or unfamiliar provenance. Poll results have long signaled declining public trust in the mainstream news media. However, as I discussed in chapters 6 and 7, my interviewees consistently found that their reference groups were quick to believe what they read in articles and saw on the news and were impressed by the status of a mainstream news appearance. These articles carry the imprimatur of their outlets, and of the legacy journalistic establishment more generally. On the internet, where so much unsourced material flows freely and standing out is so difficult, these familiar stamps of credibility and status can take on new weight, even if not everyone in the audience respects or believes them.

And while many factors affect how long an article will loom large in one's search results, they often do not disappear quickly. A few months after her news appearance, Helen was still noticing the effects. She noted, "Even today I messaged someone about housing in DC and they're like, 'Oh! Are you the Helen K from the *New York Times*?' . . . It still comes up and I still get random Facebook friend requests from really creepy people." Helen had contacted a potential roommate. That person Googled Helen before even responding to her, and up popped the *New York Times* article—and all the commentary about it—once more.

MANAGING THE REPUTATIONAL EFFECTS OF SEARCHABLE NEWS STORIES

As horror stories about people trying to delete humiliating or painful information about themselves from the internet remind us, it is very difficult to remove or hide undesirable material once it has been posted online. It is hard if it is a naked picture taken by an ex. It is even harder if the stigmatizing material is a mainstream news story. These are not embarrassing artifacts posted by lone, vengeful individuals, after all, but the work of professional media institutions whose reputations depend on their *not* capitulating to the whims of their subjects and sources. If the story contains an error, one can request corrections that may or may not be granted, but mainstream news organizations do not generally remove stories from their online archives just because subjects are negatively affected by them.

That means news subjects must manage the reputational effects of appearing in a searchable news story as well as they can. Below I explore two approaches to doing so. They occupy opposite ends of the spectrum of reputation management strategies interviewees described: leveraging the benefits of appearing in a status-conferring news story, and managing the effects of appearing in a stigma-conferring story.

SELF-BRANDING: LEVERAGING THE STATUS OF APPEARING IN A NEWS ARTICLE

Before the opportunity to appear in a news story came along, a number of my interviewees had already poured a lot time and resources into promoting themselves, their businesses, or their pet causes. Most found that a news appearance boosted their visibility more than they had been able to manage by themselves using social networking tools and other techniques. Since they already had the idea to self-promote, and some of the structures in place to do so, they were well positioned to take advantage of the news coverage to further their goals.

For example, Colleen, an administrator at a new private school in Manhattan, said she and her colleagues had struggled to publicize their school through direct mail to parents and family organizations, but the article in the *New York Times*—even though it was not entirely favorable—changed everything.[21] They were flooded with inquiries from interested parents, which was Colleen's entire goal for agreeing to the "excruciating" eight-hour interview process in the first place. As she explained, once the article was posted online it became an ongoing, highly credible promotional tool. School administrators could post it to their website, and curious parties could always find it by searching online.

Others took self-promotion a step further by identifying specific audiences and sending the article directly to them, engaging in targeted self-promotion. Billy, a rising standup comedian who was featured in the West City paper, explained that he was using the same techniques he had used before to promote himself, but the article added value to his self-produced materials precisely because he had *not* written it himself.[22] When he emailed nightclubs he hoped would book his act in the future, he sent along a link to the article as a kind of testimonial, the targeted, digital equivalent of framing a review of his business and hanging it in the window.

Mike combined all these techniques to leverage an article to build his brand. He was trying to restart a consulting business he had left years before. He had joined several social networks to try to multiply his contacts and increase visibility for his fledgling enterprise, but he was frustrated to see how quickly his efforts stagnated. He started a blog to bulk up his online presence but was getting little to no traffic until he appeared in an article in the *New York Times* about older adults using social networking tools. The article was not about his business per se, but his name was all over it, along with an enormous picture. Moreover, the portrait the article painted of him perfectly matched the brand he was trying to create: old school yet tech savvy.

He emailed links to all his contacts, posted the article to his blog, and used his social networks to distribute it. He saw traffic to his blog increase "from zero to sixty" right away:

> MIKE: So I would say, having this [article], it says I'm not the sixty-two-year-old guy with the white beard, I'm modern. I'm contemporary. Is this a direct lead to a contract? No. But it is a direct lead to my blog site, on which there's also even a feature that says, "Look, I got in the *New York Times*." Y'know, I'm a player. . . . And what's nice is it's a crossover because on the one hand I'm very old guard, and on the other hand I'm very new guard, all at the same time.[23]

As Mike went on to explain, there are fewer and fewer ways to set yourself apart online. Appearing in a *New York Times* article confers a kind of status that translates well even today:

> MIKE: I mean, in this case it's the newspaper of record. You're being put in an elite class. Even if it's only for a moment. But, the social media was supported by the *Times* rather than vice versa, even though they were inextricably linked. I think the social media cares about the imprint of something like the *New York Times*. . . . I think one's credibility grows by one's association. . . . Those things still matter. And there are less and less of them.

Of course, the perceived status and credibility of any given news site will depend on one's target audience. Mike knew that the *Times* mattered a great deal to his. But Mike's comment highlights the continued and, in some situations, enhanced importance of the mainstream media in a world in which everyone can participate in social networking and other forms of publishing online. While in *theory* our social networks can continually grow—which is what you want if your goal is to increase your professional opportunities—that growth can be hard to achieve once your network includes all the usual suspects. The mainstream media can help differentiate among the masses, intensifying the exposure and status of a select few. Like Mike, news subjects eager to leverage the increased visibility a news article bestows can position themselves to take full advantage of it using digital tools. Mike concluded that the *New York Times* article had been so useful for his self-promotion that he said of the reporter, "She could've been my P.R. department, for god's sake."

THE SCARLET LETTER IN A GLOBAL VILLAGE: MANAGING ONLINE STIGMA

Promoting status-conferring articles online is fairly easy. Containing stigmatizing articles online is not. Online material is archived by default, replicated almost as automatically, and spreads far and wide, potentially before the subject is even aware that it is out there. As I discussed in chapter 5, only in rare cases do subjects contact news outlets to request corrections. Even if a correction, clarification, or—extremely rarely—retraction occurs on the original site, the uncorrected article usually remains alive and well in other online contexts, and many readers will never be aware of the correction at all. And that is in cases when the stigmatizing material is erroneous. Often stigmatizing articles accurately document "deviant" or criminal behavior, leaving subjects with even fewer alternatives.

Since completely removing an article from a mainstream news site is almost never an option, let alone erasing it from the web completely, for many news subjects, the only viable strategy is to try to cover the traces of the article in their search results. The method used by professional reputation management firms requires creating other material on the internet that will show up ahead of an article when someone searches for your name.[24] Essentially you are trying to dilute your results with innocuous or positive material. It is not enough to just create the sites; you must simulate traffic to them so they will perform well in searches. The process takes a number of steps and a fair amount of technical savvy, which is why people pay good money to have someone else do it for them. With one exception, discussed below, interviewees who expressed concern about reputational implications of articles did not know how to implement these techniques to game the search engines by themselves.

Rich, for example, was arrested for the kidnapping and assault of a local politician's wife. The charges were later dropped, but not until after the arrest was written up in several small local newspapers. Of course, the papers were all available online and, as is often the case when low-profile people are acquitted or have charges dropped, there was no follow-up article clearing his name. He had lost his job as a building superintendent as a result of the articles. As his employer had explained, he knew Rich was innocent, but tenants might see the articles, and then what?

By the time Rich told me his story three years later, he had not been able to get another job. He was convinced—and at least one potential employer had told him outright—that his bad luck on the job market was entirely due to this blight on his past. It was evident to anyone who Googled his name. As he explained:

> RICH: I've never had a problem getting a job in my life. All of a sudden, I can't get a job. I'm a nice guy, I'm personable. I've got skills, I've got references. I got everything. I'm getting a second interview, you know, okay. Third interview, all of a sudden they get cold. . . . I know the reason why I wasn't getting' these jobs . . . is people Google people! It was page one [in the search results]! . . . It wrecked my life, yeah. It wrecked my life.[25]

It did not help that, prior to the arrest, Rich had no online presence to speak of. With his steady work as a handyman he had never had the need, so there were no other social facts available about him online to offset the impact of this apparently deviant behavior. At the time of our interview, Rich was considering hiring a professional to help him manage the problem somehow.

Chris, another interviewee, had been accused of raping a minor. In his case, too, the charges were dropped, but the accusations had been covered in local news media. When I asked him how he felt about the articles showing up in a Google search for his name, the question came as a surprise. He was one of my only interviewees who had not thought of the online trail of the news coverage before I mentioned it. He would also probably be dealing with some of the most stigmatizing effects. Chris's and Rich's stories suggest that many people may well be ill-prepared to anticipate or manage the effects of stigmatizing news articles on their online reputations.

Beth offers an illuminating counterexample. A self-described "techie geek," she was in a good position to manage her online reputation herself when she was faced with a major blow to it. Recall from the previous chapter that she was accused of a white-collar crime that also involved an alleged affair. She had testified against another person involved in the crime as part of a plea deal, and that testimony had provided fuel for humiliating and, ultimately, quite stigmatizing articles in some major papers. Beth watched in horror as her husband's family urged him to divorce her and lifelong friends spurned her. Hers was a classic example of how behavior perceived as morally deviant could have stigmatizing effects.

Part of her effort to rebuild her life, which also involved pursuing her education in a different town, moving her children to a new school, and beginning a whole new career, involved trying to muffle the damaging material online. The articles had been picked up by several major outlets and gotten a fair amount of play on finance blogs, where she had been called all manner of degrading names. In all, the news articles and their repercussions took up multiple pages in her Google search results, including the entire first page. So she took steps to hide her connection to the story as much as possible. Using the same techniques favored by reputation defense firms, she bought URLs using several different versions of her name and created a series of blogs and websites. She then created dummy sites that linked back to them, thereby improving their ranking in her search results. It helped that she had a fairly common name: she hoped that by adding enough other material to her online profile, people would assume the damaging information was about someone else.

In the end, her efforts to dilute the stigmatizing material were fairly successful. As she explained:

BETH: It didn't eliminate everything, it's just that it's mingled in, y'know, it's sprinkled in. Like, on the first page there's I think, five Beth [last names]s that I got up there that are perfectly respectable, or say nothing. . . . And then if you go a little deeper there's a LOT more shit about it. A lot about the bad stuff. But I was worried about the first-page impression more than anything else. . . . You can do it if you try. But.[26]

But: it takes a lot of effort and a fair amount of technical know-how. Beth was quick to point out that her efforts limited the harm but did not completely eliminate it. As she rather despairingly summed it up, "It used to be that if something bad would happen time *would* heal everything. Now it's forever!"

Appearing by name in a news article today is different from in the past for all the reasons discussed above. It is hard not to conclude that it is riskier. While the actual audience for any given article may remain small, the potential audience is always unfathomably huge. We still know relatively little about how long an article will remain prominently attached to a given individual's name. And, short of hiring a professional consultant, news subjects have few viable options for managing how, and how much, articles will shape their online identities and reputations. The digital repercussions of appearing in a news article are thus the final uncertainty in a process that begins with a subject's giving up control to a journalist over how his or her story will be told to the public.

I do not want to overemphasize how common the negative scenarios were in my study. Many interviewees still had good experiences overall and were happy to have an article linked to their name online. Some benefited greatly from it. That said, I believe to really know what you are getting into when you agree to an interview with a reporter today means understanding that the most extreme scenario—that the article will figure prominently in your online identity for the rest of your life—is a real possibility. Leyla's example is a good one to follow. When I asked how she felt about the prospect of her controversial article following her online for a very long time, she responded, "I don't think I would've done it if I weren't prepared for it to be part of my history forever."[27]

Since I completed the interviews for this study, cyber-bullying and online harassment have become increasingly common.[28] Along with considerations about how an article might shape one's online reputation, ordinary people considering speaking to reporters should also take into account that a likely consequence will be some form of cyber-harassment. For minorities or people speaking out about controversial issues, it is a virtual certainty. For journalists, that the consequences of speaking to reporters for private individuals can be so serious in the current digital environment raises important ethical questions: Should they warn potential subjects to anticipate cyber-harassment and other digital effects? Always? Only for certain kinds of stories? Only if the person seems particularly vulnerable for some other reason? Nowadays, these should be some of the first ethical questions journalists consider when dealing with private citizens.

As I have explored in this and the previous chapter, the reputational effects and other consequences of news coverage are absolutely central to news subjects' experiences "making the news." As I discuss in the next chapter, however, it is not entirely clear to what degree journalists do or should feel responsible for the outcomes of the stories they write. Just how much the repercussions of news stories matter is one of several fundamental aspects of the news production process about which journalists' and their subjects' perspectives tend to diverge. In the next and final chapter, I summarize the main findings from this study and explore five of these fundamental differences.

9

LESSONS FOR SUBJECTS AND JOURNALISTS

Journalists' jobs require taking material supplied by subjects and repackaging it in the news product. News subjects supply that material, but, especially when they are private citizens like those interviewed for this study, they are often outsiders experiencing the news production process for the first time. Given their differing levels of familiarity with the processes involved, and differing roles in those processes, some discrepancies between how subjects and journalism professionals understand news production are inevitable. One hardly expects a patient and a doctor to see a medical procedure, or the medical profession, in the same way. But still, I was struck by how some interviewees' ideas and expectations about news work and news coverage seemed outright incompatible with how journalists usually work and think about their profession.

In this concluding chapter I summarize my main findings by discussing five ways journalists and journalism subjects tend to view news production differently, and I relate those differences to current debates. These are general patterns, and there will always be exceptions. Some interviewees seemed to understand journalistic processes almost as an insider would. Undoubtedly some reporters likewise have a well-developed sense of how an outsider would view their daily work. Often, however, that is not the case, and differences in the ways journalists and subjects understand news production raise important practical and ethical questions for both.

Journalists and journalism scholars alike tend to refer to inexperienced news subjects as "naïve subjects."[1] While the term gives subjects some agency and could therefore be seen as an improvement on "victims of the press," it still privileges a newsroom perspective. The term implies that people whose paths cross with journalists' once or twice in their lives *should* have a thorough understanding of how journalism works—that anyone who does not is unsophisticated or unworldly. An unintended effect of the label may be that it makes subjects' uncertainties and complaints easier to dismiss because they can be attributed to a lack of common sense or common knowledge.

Notably, we do not have such expectations about many other professions. Patients are not treated as foolish for not understanding all the ins-and-outs of medical procedures. But perhaps because the news is so visible to the public, we figure the public must—or should—know how the sausage gets made. That is an error. The *products* of journalism are hypervisible, but that does not mean that the *processes* of journalism are transparent to the public. Even to private citizens who cooperate with journalists, reporting and editing processes often remain largely opaque.

The point of this chapter, then, is not to point out the foolish lacunae in subjects' knowledge but rather to flag areas where interviewees consistently thought journalism worked, or should work, differently from the ways journalism professionals tend to take for granted that it does. My aim is not to argue that one or the other is necessarily right. However, given that ordinary news subjects are themselves representatives of the public that journalism presumably serves, especially when it comes to normative questions, their views are legitimate and should not be dismissed out of hand. Interviewees were speaking as private citizens who were—temporarily—more deeply implicated in journalistic processes than other members of the public, but they had formed many of their ideas about journalism over time, from the audience side of the equation. As such, their disappointments, happy surprises, and musings on what they found behind the scenes can also shed light on how other nonjournalists might understand journalism, a perspective that is easily lost when one is immersed in newsroom culture.

Understanding the complex ways citizens view journalism—their "folk theories" about how it does and should work—is especially important right now.[2] When I conducted the interviews that form the basis for this book, in 2009–2011, cut-throat competition and diminishing resources were already raising the stakes for understanding how audiences saw and related to the news. News outlets were developing sophisticated analytics to measure audience engagement online and innovative methods to provide consumers with interactive experiences.[3] But the U.S. election in 2016 suggests that, when it comes to engaging audiences, many news organizations may have missed the forest for the trees. Wide swaths of the American public not only do not trust but do not appear to believe mainstream journalism anymore. Understanding why is urgent, and it is going to require qualitative approaches. Interviewees in this study provide helpful insights into how citizens were already thinking about mainstream journalism leading up to its current credibility crisis, and some hints for how news organizations might begin to rebuild their trust.

1. WHOSE STORY IS THIS, ANYWAY?

Journalistic takes on the role of subjects in the news process—most famously Janet Malcolm's influential *The Journalist and the Murderer*—naturally frame the role of the subject from the journalist's point of view.[4] They emphasize the importance of the interview stage and minimize what takes place before and after the journalist comes on the scene. Of course, the subject's involvement in a newsworthy event or issue—what I call the trigger—lurks in the background as the impetus behind the journalist's interaction with the subject, but narratives tend to focus on the interaction itself and its immediate result, the content of the story. This framing of news subjects' role is frequently echoed by journalism scholars, who tend to see news construction as a process of representation (or misrepresentation) that begins when the reporter appears on the scene and ends when the story is published, while downplaying the role played by real-life occurrences in that process.[5]

But I found that news subjects tended to reverse that emphasis: in their stories of "making the news," the events or issues they had experienced before the journalist approached them loomed large, as did the wide range of repercussions they had to manage after publication. For many interviewees, those factors, rather than their interactions with journalists, were the most salient aspects of the experience. In fact, if I had to identify a single variable that the majority of interviewees considered *the* most important in determining what the experience of being in the news was like, it was the event or issue that set the process in motion—"what the story was about"—rather than their interaction with journalists or anything else we normally think of as part of the news production process. Those other factors—interviews, photographers, and so on—mattered to many interviewees as well. But the trigger events were essential in shaping how they behaved throughout the news production process, starting with whether and why they agreed to speak to reporters in the first place, and affecting how they interpreted everything that came after, including the coverage itself.

Subjects' association with triggers almost always precedes journalists'. It is also usually more personal and in-depth. After all, their firsthand knowledge of triggers is the reason journalists approach them in the first place: the subject was on the plane that went down, or witnessed the explosion, or has spent a lifetime studying the relevant issues. From many subjects' point of view, then, even in the best case scenario the journalist will always be a kind of dilettante appropriator, one who shows up late and leaves early and gets a lot of things wrong in the process.

The contrast between a subject's own investment in the trigger and a journalist's is most evident to subjects when journalists do not appear to be making much effort to immerse themselves in the issue or understand subjects' perspectives on it. Interviewees respected reporters who expressed sympathy for what they had been through, or made an effort to understand their area of expertise: Emma appreciated that a reporter took time to try to understand the circumstances that led her to euthanize her critically ill husband. Scientists Jim and Dave were impressed with a reporter's daylong participation in their fieldwork. He still got a few things wrong; at least he had made an effort. But little wonder that ferry captain Jay was disgusted by the *New York Times* reporter who called repeatedly *while* he was rescuing plane crash survivors from freezing waters, or Bella found it off-putting to feel pressured to squeeze complex ideas about her lifelong area of study into one brief, prescripted quote. Journalists in those and similar scenarios were undoubtedly responding to professional pressures to gather news quickly and inform the public. Subjects tended to find those exigencies abstract and relatively unimportant in the wake of life-altering events, or when asked to speak about issues dear to their hearts or minds.

Which leads me to the crux of the matter, the question of ownership over the news story. For journalists, an occurrence or issue may start out as "*the* story" or "*a* story," especially early on: "This is a big story" or "I'm not sure that's the story." But at some point in the reporting and writing process, "*the* story" becomes "*my* story," because I, the journalist, did the research and writing to fashion raw material into a publishable piece of journalism. If, at any point early in the process, the journalist does think of the story as more the subject's than her own, by the end that is often not the case.

And yet for many subjects that is likely to feel deeply wrong. No matter how much work journalists had done to wrestle events into publishable form, interviewees usually felt they were *their* stories because (1) they had a more intimate relationship to the trigger at the story's core, (2) in the final rendition it was their face and words that were used to tell it, and (3) they had to deal with the consequences of the news coverage after the journalist was long gone. My most consistent finding—second only to the determinant nature of the trigger itself—was that subjects almost always had a visceral realization at some point that they had given up control to a journalist of something they would ordinarily keep firm control over themselves—that is, their public presentation-of-self and its related narratives. While journalists were focused on turning "*the* story" into "*my* story," from interviewees' perspective, this was a major intervention, by an outsider, into the way they presented themselves to the world.

The degree to which a subject feels a news story is *his* story of course depends on his role in it and what the story is about. A man-on-the-street interview is less likely to give rise to a strong feeling of ownership than a longer profile that depends entirely on the subject's cooperation. Individual differences among subjects also play a role: compared to novices, interviewees who had more experience interacting with the press seemed more aware and at ease with the idea that the final product would be more the journalist's than their own.

But it is worth noting that those who felt most strongly that these were *their* stories, including all the heroes and several of the catastrophe witnesses and survivors with whom I spoke, were the same people who ultimately felt most exploited by the news production process. Their unique involvement in remarkable events made their stories feel intensely personal and probably made them feel more vulnerable to whatever happened immediately afterward. It also made them temporarily valuable to journalists, who descended in competitive hordes, projecting an almost vampiric need to extract their stories. Interviewees described TV reporters, especially, as "hounds" and "like sharks attacking," who lined the street waiting for them to step outside, showed up at family functions seeking quotes, and made inconvenient if not outright costly demands.[6] Even when the news coverage was uniformly celebratory, subjects' sense of injustice was inflamed by a growing feeling that they were expected not only to donate their time, effort, faces, and stories but also to pay for them, while journalists, who showed little concern for their well-being, reaped the profits.

Reporters descend on private citizens in aggressive throngs only in the biggest of news stories, which are only a fraction of stories involving ordinary news subjects. Nonetheless, journalists would do well to take note: subjects may feel angry or violated, even when reporters' depictions of them are technically unassailable or even celebratory. The source of subjects' anger is not the product. It is a process in which subjects feel their public presentation-of-self and its component narratives have been wrested away and exposed on someone else's terms.

2. WHAT IS JOURNALISTS' REAL RELATIONSHIP TO POWER?

If giving up control of one's presentation-of-self and story is so uncomfortable, why do so many people do it, and often gladly? Many interviewees said they considered possible negative outcomes when they agreed to speak to reporters but ended up agreeing because of all they stood to gain. Several who had had very negative experiences surprised me by saying they would agree to cooperate with journalists again in the future, in hopes of a better outcome. So what were they hoping for?

Subjects' reasons for participating in the news varied a great deal depending on the trigger, individual differences, and many other factors. The main enticement, however, was usually the unique combination of access to a large audience and credibility that they believed a news appearance afforded. From their perspective, even in a web 2.0 world, appearing in the news was an opportunity to communicate with a much larger public than they could otherwise access. Moreover, they felt that a mainstream news publication bestowed status and legitimacy otherwise hard to come by, and all the more valuable in a hypercompetitive digital environment. Feedback from their reference groups appeared to confirm that belief: even if an article was fluff or presented the subject only briefly or clinically, as long as the coverage was not outright stigmatizing, appearing in the news at all enhanced subjects' status in the eyes of the world. On the other hand, if a journalist chose to present a subject in a negative light, or take a quote out of context, or cover a subject's misdeeds, he or she could cause a lot of long-term damage to subjects' professional and personal lives.

It makes sense, then, that interviewees generally saw the people who held the key to those benefits and harms as occupying privileged positions. From their point of view, journalists could show up with little or no prior knowledge about an issue or event but with the ability and resources to tell subjects' own stories to a broad public and *be believed*. Moreover, the outcome could change subjects' lives for better or worse. Scholarship in recent years has emphasized the declining, threatened, or at least transitional nature of mainstream journalism's authority.[7] However, whether because of the time period in which we spoke (prior to the most recent surge of anti–mainstream media sentiment) or because the focus of our discussions was on their own experiences *as* news subjects, decline and dismissal of the mainstream media's authority were not what interviewees experienced. Instead, at every stage, their experiences seemed to indicate that journalists had good old-fashioned authority, and in spades.

That interviewees felt powerless relative to journalists is actually predictable given what the literature tells us about official and elite sources. Only by bringing to bear a host of resources, such as familiarity with news production and ongoing access to exclusive information, are elite sources able to hold their own in the tug-of-war with journalists over the news message.[8] Private citizens usually do not have those advantages. I found that any sense of power interviewees might have had when they found themselves temporarily well-positioned to provide valuable, exclusive information to journalists—as was the case for survivors and heroes in major stories—was mostly offset by journalists' appearing in intimidating packs, with intimidating equipment.

We can contrast subjects' perspective on journalistic power with one of American journalism's most sacred beliefs about itself: that its core mission is to confront and challenge power and tyranny on behalf of the public—that it is the public's representative in the face of power. Given that job, being perceived as cozy with powerful people or institutions is thought to threaten a journalist's autonomy and, therefore, credibility. Ethics codes do sometimes remind journalists that they are in a position to harm their subjects and must use that power responsibly.[9] Most of the time, however, journalists' own narratives about the news media's relationship to power downplay or ignore the idea that they might be perceived as extremely powerful, potentially tyrannical entities in their own right. Meanwhile, I found that news subjects tended to see journalists in exactly that way: from interviewees' perspective, journalists did not mainly check powerful people, they *were* powerful people.[10]

A wealth of polling data finds that the American public does not trust the news media and in fact trusts it less now than ever before.[11] But polls are not, and have never been, very good at uncovering *why* public opinion is so low, nor what it actually *means* to distrust the press.[12] Interviewees' perspectives on journalistic power provide some possible clues. Again, it is important to acknowledge that they were speaking about the news process from a particular perspective, and at a moment when they were especially likely to be aware of the power inequality between themselves and journalists. But we should consider the possibility that many in the general public share their perception of journalists as very powerful people, with the attendant opportunities to abuse that power. If citizens broadly perceive journalists, as interviewees did, as having automatic access to a large audience, with all the status that comes from it, and with the power to build and destroy reputations with a single story to boot—all of which remain beyond the means of most non–media professionals even today—that could certainly contribute to a broad wariness of the profession. It would likely also reduce sympathy for anything perceived as journalistic misbehavior.

And yet I suspect it is not just that this particular profession has special authority and privileges that truly galls. After all, many professions, such as law enforcement and medicine, have special privileges unavailable to the masses. The more unforgiveable sin may be what comes across as a cavalier attitude about, or even denial of, those advantages. In short, perhaps one reason public opinion of journalists is so low is that audiences perceive them, as interviewees tended to, as powerful people and potential bullies trying to pass themselves off as friends, equals, and even underdogs.

It smacks of the simultaneous arrogance and ignorance of anyone in a position of great power trying to buddy up to someone she has firmly pinned under her thumb.

3. WHEN DOES—AND WHEN SHOULD—A JOURNALIST DECIDE WHAT TO WRITE?

Interviewees assessed their news coverage in many different ways. As I discuss further below, their reactions were profoundly shaped by the effects of the coverage, especially feedback from their reference groups. Some were very pleased with the finished product, although most noted something they would have changed if possible, and many identified what they considered errors. They mused a lot about how, exactly, journalists had converted information exchanged in the interview into the published product, especially how distortions or errors had crept in; but it was clear that in most cases all they could do was guess. The writing and editing process was mostly a black box to them. Some interviewees, especially those who had liked the journalist in question personally, speculated that editors were to blame for errors, or that lawyers had prevented an otherwise competent reporter from getting the story right. Other subjects followed up with reporters, who deflected blame to their editors, whom subjects did not know and probably would never meet. Many subjects were left unsure *whom* to blame for errors or wondered aloud if the reporting process was inherently distortive, since their words apparently had to pass through so many steps. But the aspect of the reporting process that subjects theorized about the most, and that seemed most important to them, was at what point in the process reporters had decided what they were going to write.

In theory, journalists are open to changing their stories based on information gleaned from interviews or other data uncovered during the reporting process. However, due to the logistics, routines, and pressures of writing and producing a news story, a reporter's openness to completely reframing a story often shrinks the closer he is to a deadline. If the interview comes late in the process, chances are good that the reporter already has a well-formed idea, or even a largely written story in hand, and is looking for specific perspectives or information to fill in the blanks.

Many interviewees did not appear to know that, and even if they had, they usually did not have a clear sense of when in the journalist's reporting and writing process their own interview had taken place. They relied on cues they picked up during interviews to guess how journalists planned to frame their stories and adjusted their behavior accordingly. When they saw the published product, some realized they had guessed wrong, which led to a lot of speculation about whether journalists had intentionally misled them about what they had intended to write in the first place.

I found that this question of timing and intent was usually the key to whether subjects felt betrayed by journalists. Interviewees who did say they felt betrayed were absolutely certain, in retrospect, that reporters had already made up their mind about how to tell their stories before they even met and had deliberately misled them about their intentions during the interview stage. The resulting story did not meet subjects' expectations, and it felt unfair because they had adjusted their behavior in interviews based on signals from the journalist about what the latter planned to write. This is, although obviously in a less extreme version, the seduce/betray scenario Janet Malcolm presents as the norm in *The Journalist and the Murderer*. Among my interviewees it was rare, but along with those who felt exploited, these subjects deserve special attention because they were the ones who felt most abused by the news production process.

It was more common for interviewees to say that they realized while the interview was happening that the journalist wanted them to say something specific, and that they had felt pressured to do so. In some cases, the role the journalist obviously wanted them to play aligned reasonably well with their position on the issues. Other subjects felt they were being miscast in a role that did not fit, and even if they knew what was going on, many found it difficult to resist complying with journalists' expectations. In the most extreme cases, subjects found themselves misrepresenting their own positions, which was especially frustrating because they felt they had done it to themselves. They did not feel betrayed—how could they, when the reporter's agenda had been so painfully obvious?—but they did feel manipulated. Interviewees generally felt that journalists *should* be open to changing their stories based on what subjects told them—that approaching subjects with a preconceived story in mind and trying to get them to fill in the blanks according to expectations was manipulative and unacceptable.

And yet, as noted above, that is common journalistic practice. Some ethics codes explicitly state that journalists should not "put words in [subjects'] mouths," but it could be argued that the reporters interviewees described technically did not.[13] Obviously, writing stories as one goes and seeking quotes to fit those stories streamline a high-pressure, deadline-driven activity, so there are clear practical reasons why reporters would proceed in that way. Evidence suggests the practice may be even more common today than in the past, as outlets feel pressured to post stories online as soon as possible.[14] But I am not sure to what degree journalists realize that *subjects* realize they are being squeezed into a predetermined role, or that they may well feel manipulated by the process and misrepresented by the result. Quotes and other representations of subjects' views that are produced under these kinds of pressure may not be technically inaccurate, but many interviewees felt they were unequivocally wrong.

4. WHAT'S "FAIR AND BALANCED" IN A CONTROVERSY?

If giving up control over one's own representation is always at least somewhat risky, it is all the more so when the trigger event or issue is inflammatory. Ordinary people who make the news about controversial subjects tend to be invested in them as activists, experts, or concerned members of the public with strong opinions. If it is hard to judge objectively any news story in which one appears, it is even harder when that story is about a divisive issue.

It is hardly surprising that interviewees had strong reactions to their news coverage in such cases. One could argue that subjects of controversial stories will probably believe they were right, be highly invested in being right, and dislike any news coverage that does not present them as *in the right*. Perhaps that is true. Even so, I found that the perspectives of interviewees who had appeared in controversial stories revealed important differences in the ways ordinary people and journalists think about journalistic fairness.

I spoke to a number of people who had appeared in polemical news stories about lawsuits, political movements, disputes with local organizations, and hotly contested municipal policies. All said they had expected the reporter to cover both sides of the issue. The exchange Natasha recalled with a reporter was typical: "[The reporter] said, 'Well, you know, I'm not gonna advocate for one side or the other.' And I said I didn't have a problem with that at all. I said, 'If you just get the information, if you report the information, I won't have a problem with whatever you say.' "[15]

But Natasha *did* have a problem with what the reporter said—or rather, what she *did not* say. In her view, the reporter had failed to report adequately. Specifically, she did not vet the information given to her by both sides. The reporter parroted the claims made by the other side with no effort to fact check them and omitted key information essential to making Natasha's own case. As a result, the published story made the issue seem like a personal feud, with both sides equally valid. Michelle described a similar scenario. She was featured in stories in both the West City paper and a national publication about her lawsuit against a religious group that had built a temple in her residential neighborhood.[16] She was outraged by the reporter's uncritical printing of the other side's quotes, which were easy to disprove: They claimed to live on the property but did not. They claimed not to have known before they constructed the temple that neighbors might sue. Michelle herself had shown reporters a letter in which she had warned the group of her lawsuit before the temple was built. But the articles omitted any mention of the letter. Michelle argued that just a bit more investigation would have revealed the dishonesty of her opposition's claims and the validity of her own.

As Natasha's and Michelle's cases illustrate, interviewees tended to define fairness as the reporter speaking to people on both sides of the issue, researching the veracity of the claims made by both sides, then presenting them in such a way that an average reader would clearly see that one side—their own—had greater merit. What is striking here is not that subjects wanted to be depicted as having the stronger argument, which is predictable, but rather that they expected the journalist to research the evidence and ultimately to come down on one side or the other on the strength of that evidence—to make a judgment, at least implicitly.

Weighing the veracity and validity of both sides of a contested issue and passing judgment on their relative merit may seem like a reasonably fair approach to a dispute under most ordinary circumstances. It is not, however, the way fairness in reporting on controversies has come to be defined by journalists themselves over the past century or so. The objectivity norm clearly dictates that both sides of a controversy must be represented

fairly, but in practice that is often interpreted to mean talking to representatives on both sides and giving equal time or space to their claims, ideally
in the form of direct quotes. Reporters often intentionally minimize their
judgments as to the validity, veracity, or persuasiveness of those respective
claims to avoid any semblance of partiality, and the public is presumably
free to make up its own mind. In other words, neutrality, rather than rea-
soned judgment, is seen as the basis of fairness.

The neutral approach, laudable in theory, has come under fire by media
critics in recent years as "he said, she said reporting," "automatic equiva-
lence," or, most recently, "false balance." Critics argue it is irresponsible
for journalists to present both sides of an argument as equally valid without actively fact checking their claims, especially if (1) qualified experts all
support one side, or (2) the advocates vastly outnumber the detractors, or
(3) for whatever other reason one argument is evidently stronger than the
other. Reporting on climate change is probably the most oft-cited example
of the phenomenon.[17]

Although this discussion among media critics has been percolating for
years, the clash between public perceptions of what would constitute journalistic fairness and the way those steeped in newsroom culture perceive it
was thrown into especially sharp relief in 2012, when the New York Times
public editor, in a naively headlined article entitled "Should the Times Be a
Truth Vigilante?," posed the apparently innocent question of whether reporters should probe the truth of what politicians were saying rather than
just reporting what they had said.[18] The public responded vociferously in
the comments section, mostly expressing indignation that journalists were
not *already* applying their judgment to the truth and accuracy of those
political statements.

The same debate was revived in the 2016 election. Media critics cried
false balance when journalists presented the candidates' respective misdeeds as equally egregious, and yet another New York Times public editor
deafly defended the practice.[19] In the aftermath of the election, polled
Americans were divided on how much they said they wanted the news media
to interpret the facts, but a vast majority—81 percent even among those who
did not want interpretation, and even more (83 percent) among those
who did—said they did believe it was news organizations' responsibility to
engage in fact checking. It is particularly telling that most of the news consumers in that poll did not apparently equate fact checking with inappropriate interpretation of those facts.[20] All this suggests a divide between the

way media critics and the general public perceive fairness in reporting on controversial issues and the way journalists do.

Interviewees' experiences add a new dimension to the discussion of false balance: what it feels like to have one's own story reported according to these still-entrenched, if controversial, norms. Not good, as it turns out. If it is frustrating for audiences to see reporters uncritically printing politicians' statements, it is enraging for subjects when reporters parrot meritless or deceptive claims made by an adversary or neglect to mention key information that validates their own position. Again, perhaps some subjects will find wanting any coverage that does not come down decisively on their side. And yet if journalists' understanding of fairness continues to be so at odds with the popular understanding of what it means, members of the public who get caught up in the news process are likely to continue to feel misused by it.

5. HOW MUCH DO THE EFFECTS OF NEWS COVERAGE MATTER?

Just as news subjects tend to perceive their role in the news production process as beginning before journalists show up on the scene, for them that role continues after journalists have published the story and moved on to their next project. Journalists themselves disagree about how much they should consider the potential effects of their stories on their subjects at all, as I discuss below. However, for subjects themselves there is no question about it: the effects of news coverage on their lives and reputations are of utmost importance. They have to live with them, after all.

This is perhaps the biggest discrepancy in how subjects and journalists experience the news process. From interviewees' point of view, repercussions of the coverage were absolutely central to their assessment of what "making the news" meant. They judged everything about their involvement in the news production process, from the trigger events, through their interactions with journalists, to their judgment of the accuracy and overall quality of the published story, in light of the effects that story had on their immediate goals, reputations, and long-term prospects.

That repercussions of news coverage can influence how subjects come to view all aspects of their experience is perhaps most obvious in how subjects judge the accuracy of the stories in which they appear. In theory, errors—at least, technical errors of fact—are objectively determined. But interviewees tended to assess accuracy and the gravity of errors not, as journalists do, based on how far the facts in the article were from the facts of an objective reality. Instead, they judged errors in light of the positive or negative effects they caused. Interviewees often, in retrospect, perceived choices made by journalists about how to tell their stories—omission of key information, emphasis on certain details, heavily edited quotes, a dismissive tone—as errors if they had damaging ramifications, even if they were not factually inaccurate. On the other hand, they were quick to dismiss even seemingly severe factual errors that had minimal effects relative to the benefits of the news story.

One reason subjects often downplayed errors was that they were being congratulated right and left for having appeared in the news at all or were enjoying other benefits of the exposure. My interviewee Shannon, for example, dismissed *even the misspelling of her name* as unimportant—a typo, essentially—because she was featured in an article that was otherwise great publicity for her business. As her example reminds us, one of the most common effects subjects experienced as a result of appearing in a news story was the enhancement of their status. Being plucked from the crowd for inclusion in an exclusive product was generally seen as a special opportunity. Several interviewees likened it to receiving an award, which nicely captures one of the key features of status conferral by the mass media: it is a response to the ritual display of a person before the public, which itself confers on that person an aura of importance.[21] As such, most news appearances that are not overtly stigmatizing will confer status, regardless of the details of the content. Even subjects whose role was negligible, or who initially felt they came across badly, received congratulatory feedback from others. When the content of the story *also* reflected positively on subjects, status conferral was overdetermined by both the ritual of public display and the transmission of information that was, itself, status conferring.[22]

On the other hand, if the substance of the coverage was stigma inducing, the negative effects could be far-reaching and traumatic. The news coverage announced bad behavior to the world in ways that brought about a whole new set of punishments, as strangers sent hate messages and loved ones shunned them. Some subjects discovered that even their own friends and families interpreted the negative version of events they saw in the news as more credible than their own. Negative consequences of news coverage felt even more unjust to subjects who were not actually guilty of the crime or unethical behavior being reported, as was the case for an accused kidnapper and an accused rapist in my study. But even when subjects were guilty, the stigmatizing effects of news coverage were so great they raised serious questions about their proportionality to the crimes committed.

Both positive and negative effects of news coverage are generally magnified by digital publication. As I argued in chapter 8, in the current technological environment, news articles can profoundly distort private citizens' digital reputations because those articles often perform extremely well in online searches. The fact that negative material online can have such a lasting impact gave rise to the Right to Be Forgotten movement. A European Union Court of Justice ruling in 2014 known by that name requires search engine operators in some cases to remove links to damaging content so they will not show up in searches for a person's name. But such a law is inconceivable in the United States, where freedom of speech outweighs privacy concerns. The Intimate Privacy Protection Act (IPPA), recently introduced in the U.S. House of Representatives, aims to criminalize the nonconsensual distribution of sexual images, also known as "revenge porn." It addresses an extremely narrow aspect of the broader issue of how online material can destroy a reputation but has still raised the hackles of civil rights groups.[23]

But neither IPPA nor the Right to Be Forgotten addresses the *immediate* effects of appearing in a stigmatizing article, which in extreme cases can lead to what amounts to harassment by a cyber-mob, as some interviewees described. Opportunities to comment directly on news sites, and the ease with which readers can locate and directly contact subjects of journalism, create a whole new set of potential effects of appearing in a news story. Audiences can now take punishment of any perceived breach of social norms into their own hands. Since I completed these interviews, there is every indication that cyber-bullying, especially of minorities who speak out online, has gotten worse.[24]

While the effects of news stories can play a huge role in subjects' lives, it is not entirely clear to what degree journalists do or should take potential effects into consideration when they contact and write about ordinary people. According to ethical guidelines such as the Society of Professional Journalists code of ethics, journalists should weigh the potential harm to subjects against the public interest value of a story.[25] Conventions have evolved over time to streamline the public-interest-vs.-private-harm calculation so it need not come under discussion every time. In the United States, stories about individuals who clearly pose a threat to the broader public, such as accused and convicted criminals, are usually published without debate. Periodically, however, controversies surface over whether and when it is acceptable to name "people of interest" who are not yet formally charged with a crime, or people who may have violated a social norm that is not clearly damaging to the public.[26] Such debates attest to the broad gray area in which the private-harm-vs.-public-interest calculation is not so clear-cut.

In fact, in many cases the calculation can be exceedingly difficult because the interests of individual private citizens and the broader public are not easily separable but entangled in multiple ways.[27] Ordinary news subjects like those in this study *are themselves* members of the public that journalists are presumably serving. Moreover, it is often not clear to what degree that public would actually *be* served by knowing damaging information about them, nor what degree of damage would be going too far. If the subject gets fired from his job, would that be too much? What if the story leads to weeks or months of online harassment by vigilante readers; is that now a journalist's responsibility? And how can journalists be expected to predict all possible effects, especially since all the ways people can use digital media to channel and influence those effects are as yet unknown?

Perhaps these ethical knots are the reason some veteran journalists argue that reporters should not concern themselves with the effects of their stories at all. Legendary American journalist Walter Cronkite once said, "I don't think that it is any of our business what the moral, political, social, or economic effect of our reporting is. I say, let's go with the job of reporting—and let the chips fall where they may."[28] That position may seem callous, but one could certainly argue that weighing all possible effects on all news subjects for every story is impractical, if not impossible. Some scholars have argued that journalists should take a lesson from social scientists and prioritize the well-being of their subjects or even seek informed consent from all of them.[29] But there is surely merit in the obvious response that timeliness is of the essence when reporting the news. It also seems convincing that for some professions (soldiers, surgeons), worrying too much in the moment about consequences down the line would interfere paralyzingly with getting the job done.

But the main argument against overconsideration of effects is that it is incompatible with objectivity. Selectively protecting subjects from possible negative effects certainly appears to be the flipside of intentionally publishing material to promote their interests, which is an obvious no-no. Scholars consistently locate a key source, if not *the* key source, of journalism's authority and credibility in its autonomy from outside interests. When journalists deal with powerful public figures that seems clear: journalists themselves often regard *not* worrying about possible damaging effects of a story, such as being banned from press conferences or otherwise denied direct access to a powerful source, as evidence of a reporter's objectivity and professionalism.[30]

In most cases, however, the public's interest in knowing about its representatives or other powerful public figures seems to *clearly* outweigh those subjects' claims to privacy or protection. There is no dilemma there. The scale seems less clearly tipped in cases where the subject is a private figure with, as the Society of Professional Journalists code of ethics points out, greater claims to privacy and compassion. As I discussed in chapter 7, not all cultures find prioritizing the protection of subjects' privacy and dignity incompatible with other journalistic values. In some countries it is common practice to not name criminals, or to use only their initials, to minimize stigmatizing effects.[31] That approach is rooted in a different value system that seems hard to square with American journalism's deep-seated commitment to inform the public above all else. My interviewees provide no easy answers, but, as noted above, they do suggest that the potential for a stigmatizing news article to do persistent, if not permanent, harm to private citizens is greater than it was pre-internet. That development should, in theory, give greater weight than before to the private citizen's side of the scale when placed opposite the public interest.

Looking back at these five fundamental differences between how subjects and journalists see the news production process, we can identify a key underlying discrepancy in their views. Journalists tend to see upright, ethical practice through the lens of factual accuracy, and they focus on *processes*. They prioritize seeking and reporting the facts, and informing the public about both sides of an issue in a factual way. Focusing too much on outcomes of reporting is seen, at best, as a distraction and, at worst, as downright unethical, crossing the line into advocacy. The intention is rarely, if ever, to damage a private citizen; however, informing the public is the top priority, and sometimes the odd subject gets hurt in that process.

Meanwhile, news subjects do care somewhat about reporting processes, insofar as they want to be treated with respect and not pressured, manipulated, or besieged by journalists. But basic factual accuracy is far less important to them than the *outcomes* of news stories, in two respects: first, in terms of the holistic accuracy of the news story, and second, in terms of the story's repercussions.

By "holistic accuracy" I mean that the story feels to subjects like it accurately captures the larger meaning of events as they experienced them. Interviewees did not care much about minor factual details of a news story if the story as a whole felt like it completely missed the point or presented two sides of an issue as equally valid when subjects felt they clearly were not. By repercussions, I am, of course, referring to the effects of the stories on subjects' lives. For subjects to feel that journalism is valid and fair, they must feel that the repercussions of news stories are themselves fair. If, for example, news stories trigger cyber-abuse or lasting reputational damage that is far out of proportion with the acts or opinions they portray; or if reporting fails to vet an opponent's claims, badly hurting a subject's own cause, then those stories will likely feel inaccurate, inadequate, and unjust to them.

When journalism falls short in these two respects—in terms of holistic accuracy or in terms of fair repercussions—it often feels wrong to subjects, even when it is factually accurate and all sides are technically included. From their point of view, these outcomes are the result of journalists' choices, so the argument that journalists should not concern themselves with those outcomes—that doing so dilutes, threatens, or even contravenes journalism's core mission to inform the public—is likely to make little sense. It may even sound outright unethical.

NEWS SUBJECTS' "DEEP STORY" ABOUT JOURNALISM

As political communication professor Stephen Coleman has observed about voting, "The sustainability of any social practice depends to a large measure on how it feels to participate in it."[32] News subjects' feelings about participating in the news have implications for the long-term sustainability of journalism in two ways.

First, in purely practical terms, people are not going to want to cooperate with journalists if they think they will be mistreated in the process, or
if the risks of doing so simply seem too great. That goes for people who
have appeared in news stories in the past who are considering whether to do
so again in the future, and for audiences watching how other people like
themselves are treated in the news. As I have discussed, many interviewees
did not feel abused by news processes, but some did, and their complaints
about being pressured, manipulated, misrepresented, and harassed deserve
close attention.

In a digital media environment, the risks of appearing in a mainstream
news story are greater than in the past. Although the benefits are usually
not diminished (in some ways they are magnified), new developments like
social media now provide alternative paths to communicate one's ideas
and display oneself publicly. Those paths may lead to smaller audiences, but
at least the subject has more control over the message. These factors may diminish the appeal of cooperating with mainstream journalists in the future,
so it is especially important that doing so not feel unfairly onerous, exploitative, or damaging.

Second, and even more important, news subjects' feelings about participating in news processes provide clues about more widespread negative
perceptions of the mainstream news media, which pose a serious threat to
its well-being. No doubt, dislike of the news media is overdetermined by
many factors, including political antimedia rhetoric, increasing tabloidization of journalistic content, and cynical reporting.[33] My interviewees'
perspectives highlight another probable contributing factor: that the
relationship between journalists and the private citizens they cover—and
who make up the public they presumably serve—is fundamentally unequal
in some key ways, and that people feel it.

My interviewees experienced the fullest expression of this inequality,
but it is likely perceived by audiences as well, for it also applies to them.
That journalists have ongoing access to a large audience and the status associated with it already sets them apart from most of their readers and
viewers. When members of the audience are singled out to appear in the
news, they get a piece of that status, but on journalists' terms: Journalists
have the authority to choose who to include in the product and to control
how they are represented there, while the subjects they pick can only hope
for the best. Journalists then move on to the next story, while consequences
for subjects can be extreme—and extremely damaging. Journalists get paid

to do this; subjects receive no compensation. As I have discussed in the preceding chapters, often consequences for subjects are actually positive, but the unequal nature of the relationship is always there, with the attendant opportunities for abuse and exploitation.

I found that whether interviewees had had good or bad experiences navigating these structural inequalities, they explained their experiences back to themselves, and to me, by fitting them into a broader narrative about the news media that they already believed. This is what sociologist Arlie Hochschild calls a "deep story."[34] A deep story is one that *feels* true to people and helps them make sense of their world. It may not be factually verifiable or even rational, but that is not the point. The deep story resonates with people's identities and worldviews and can influence their choices. The deep story for my interviewees was this: The news media is extremely powerful—much, much more powerful than most citizens. Journalists are primarily motivated by profit and status, rather than public service. And yet, outrageously, journalists claim the mantle of public defender. Thus hypocrisy and the potential for abuse define the news media's relationship to the public.

Interviewees' deep story surfaced through focused conversations about their experiences interacting with the press, but those experiences were not the origin of it. The deep story clearly predated their immediate experience. It had cohered through long-term exposure to news products and immersion in a negative climate of opinion about the news media. It also flies in the face of journalism's most sacred self-concept and mission: that journalism serves the public and fights on its behalf. It likely also clashes with many journalists' firsthand experiences of their own work, which is often low-paid, underresourced, and hard. And yet if mainstream journalism institutions want to ensure their sustainability and regain long-waning public trust, my findings suggest that one of their central tasks will be to address public perception that the news media is essentially a big bully.

HOW TO REBUILD PUBLIC TRUST

In 2011, when I completed the fieldwork for this study, social media and many online news sites already existed, though they have flourished and multiplied since then. At that time, interviewees considered journalists powerful gatekeepers and gave a lot of weight to the credibility and authority of the mainstream media in general. But they also expressed suspicion and dislike of the news media. Although many were quick to make exceptions for the individual reporters who had interviewed them, in general they thought of journalists as powerful people who always could and sometimes did exploit people like themselves.

Their reflections on the mainstream press take on new significance in the wake of the presidential election of 2016, an event that throws into question the long taken-for-granted influence of the mainstream media. The explosion of media options has led many people to turn to alternative sources of information, contributing to such extreme audience fragmentation that large segments of the public ended up disagreeing about even the basic facts of the election.[35] Anti–mainstream media rhetoric in the presidential campaign, strongest on the Republican side, appears to have resonated with a large portion of the American public and contributed to a Donald Trump victory. It appears that long-simmering public distrust in the media has finally translated into a significant number of Americans disregarding and outright disbelieving much of the reporting and editorializing done by mainstream news outlets. Today, one has to wonder if my interviewees would make the same assumptions about the credibility of the mainstream press or feel the same level of credulity themselves that they did just a few years ago.

However, read in light of recent developments, this study also contains some potentially helpful insights for anyone concerned about the crisis of public confidence that appears to be facing mainstream journalism today. My interviewees shared a deep suspicion toward the mainstream media, and a sense that journalists were always potential bullies, even if they did not act that way in every particular case. How might news institutions begin to address these entrenched attitudes? Putting resources toward more and better journalism (a laudable goal, without question) and telling audiences in a one-sided fashion how journalism works (also interesting) are probably not going to work very well to address audience perceptions that journalism is fundamentally arrogant and exploitative. My findings suggest some alternative strategies to address the issue, although they will not be easy to implement, especially at a time when most newspapers across the country face badly depleted resources, and all news outlets face tremendous competition.

Interactions with specific journalists, when those reporters showed listening skills, humanity, and compassion, did help interviewees start to see that at least some in the profession were actually cautious, concerned, and, in many cases, very good at their jobs. Those interactions did not completely change subjects' negative preconceptions about the media, but they did seem to soften them a bit. Efforts by news outlets to engage their audiences by giving them limited space to comment online, or by encouraging journalists to post on social media, usually lead to little meaningful interaction between the two groups. More personal encounters, in which citizens see evidence that journalists actually care about them and their views, could start to chip away at deep-seated mistrust. Conscientious outreach to the community by news organizations could facilitate that. The *Texas Tribune*'s recent appointment of a "community reporter," whose job is not to justify the outlet's choices to the public, as is so often the role of public editors, but instead to ensure that community concerns drive coverage, is a step in the right direction.[36]

I also found that journalistic processes were largely opaque to interviewees, even though, as news subjects, they were briefly brought into presumably intimate contact with those processes. Journalism professionals may not realize just how unintelligible and inaccessible their work appears from the outside. Interviewees did not understand how or when journalists made decisions about what to include in stories, how errors had happened, or whom to hold accountable if they were unhappy with the process or product. Outreach efforts should aim not only to increase interaction between journalists and audiences but also to help audiences feel less intimidated and more informed about how journalists research, edit, and produce the news.

The challenge is to explain these processes in a way that is truly audience-focused and does not come across as self-aggrandizing and self-promotional, which can be even more alienating to audiences than saying nothing. More real interaction with audiences could help journalists understand what they do not know and how they see journalism, so they could pitch explanatory efforts appropriately. But the most important first step is to ensure that efforts that do aim to break the fourth wall—such as the *New York Times*'s "Times Insider" content, which gives readers a behind-the-scenes look at how the news there is produced—are available to everyone. "Times Insider" is behind a pay wall; even subscribers have to pay extra for it. I am very sympathetic to the *Times*'s efforts to get money where they can, and the pay wall probably makes sense for short-term revenues. News junkies—people already hooked on what the *Times* is producing—will pay extra money for every drop of insider information.

However, the higher pay wall is not only a practical impediment to broader understanding of the newspaper's work, it also actively cultivates the idea that consumers are entering a kind of exclusive inner sanctum that is not accessible to ordinary people. It is the opposite of outreach. Such strategies are not going to convert nonbelievers or turn people back if they are already headed for the exit. If *any* content on the *Times* website should be available to everyone, it is the content that helps readers understand how they are getting the work done.

Another possible outreach initiative concerns public editors. As I have discussed in this chapter, nonjournalists, unsurprisingly, see journalism differently from journalists. For exactly that reason, the role of the public editor, whose job is to interface between a news institution and its audience, is almost always filled by a veteran journalist. Presumably, only an insider can really understand journalistic work. But there is another side to that coin. If the job really is to explain the profession to outsiders, and to bring audience concerns to the powers that be at news institutions, I frankly doubt whether someone steeped in newsroom culture is the best person for the job. Often their responses seem way out of touch with how audiences think about journalism. Regarding the concerns of news subjects in particular, since journalists themselves are so accustomed to addressing a large public, I question whether they can easily understand the significance of a news appearance in the life of an ordinary person. The experience is meaningful, often enduring, and potentially profound for subjects because, for them, communicating with such a large audience is a rare occurrence in their lives.

If news organizations really want to bridge the gap between themselves and the citizens who make up their audiences and populate their products, they would do well to appoint a community representative—or a whole team of them—to work with their public editors to help facilitate *mutual* understanding. That and other community outreach initiatives will take resources at a time when many news institutions are struggling to make ends meet. But given the very real alternative that audience dislike and suspicion of the news media will further devolve into their not believing much of what journalists have to say, perhaps such initiatives are worth the investment.

Getting the facts straight about the events of the day is hard. Tweaking processes to ensure the facts are ever more accurate is also not easy, especially when resources are scare and getting scarcer. Altering the public's deep story about journalism is going to be much, much harder. It demands a change in orientation, away from solely providing information to the public and toward engaging directly with the public in a more ongoing way. It is going to require tactics that are outside standard operating procedures for journalists and their employers, beginning with their listening to audiences in ways they have not before. But it is important that they do it. Rekindling the belief that journalists care about the little guy—really care, enough to listen to him, and fight for him—may well be more essential to mainstream journalism's long-term sustainability than the quality of the news itself.

NOTE ON METHOD

I began this study in 2009. After considering various ways to study the experience of being named in a news story, I concluded that in-depth, qualitative interviewing was the most appropriate. In-depth interviews are often used for phenomenological and exploratory studies such as this one because they allow researchers to include of a wide variety of perspectives, while still giving respondents the freedom to use their own words to reflect at length on their experiences.

I also decided to focus on newspapers, for a couple of reasons. As has been well documented, the broadcast media get many of their story ideas from newspapers, which means that many people who appear in newspapers subsequently appear on television and radio.[1] I knew that if I contacted people I saw in newspapers, they might be able to talk about and compare their experiences across a range of media. Newspapers were also undergoing rapid and unpredictable changes, so I felt like it was now or never—not only because print newspapers in many markets might soon disappear but also because subjects might have interesting insights about those changes.

Since I lived in New York City at the time, it made sense to focus on news subjects who had appeared in newspapers there, so I could do interviews in person. I contacted people named in the three highest-circulation newspapers in the metropolitan area, the *New York Times*, *New York Post*, and *New York Daily News*, but a few interviewees volunteered to speak about their appearances in other New York–based publications like the

Wall Street Journal. Since the New York media environment is anomalous in the United States in terms of the number of local papers and size of the market, for the sake of comparison I also interviewed twenty subjects (out of the eighty-three in total) who had appeared in the newspaper in a more typical midsized, one-newspaper city in the western United States.

I recruited participants for this study by combing the newspapers daily, searching for subjects' contact information online, and reaching out to them by phone, letter, email, or social media. I also recruited a few additional participants through Craigslist and referrals. Following a grounded theory-based approach, I began by trying to include variety in all categories, including demographics, type of story, and the subject's role in the story.[2] As I determined that the type of story and role in it were absolutely central to news subjects' understanding of their own experiences, I increasingly focused on trying to include as much variety as possible in those areas. In the final sample, most of my eighty-three interviewees had appeared in the paper between September 2009 and October 2010, but several volunteered to speak about experiences going back to 2006.

Interviews were semistructured and recorded, ranging from forty-five minutes to four hours. I met participants at a time and location of their choosing, including in cafes, parks, workplaces, and homes, and did interviews by phone or Skype when necessary for geographic reasons. I began interviews by asking subjects if they had ever been in the news prior to their recent experience. That gave me a sense of how novel their recent news appearance was for them, and whether they had had especially positive or negative dealings with the press in the past. I then transitioned by asking them to "tell me about this experience." Some subjects then launched into lengthy descriptions covering most of the material I would have asked about anyway. Others zeroed in on the most salient or memorable aspects of making the news for them—in many cases, the trigger events or the after-effects of their news appearances. I then asked more detailed questions covering their entire stories, from the events that had led them to be in the news in the first place through any feedback or repercussions that had occurred as a result. I brought copies of the articles so that, after discussing their experiences at length from memory, subjects could look them over and make any additional observations. Although I had contacted them about a specific news appearance, often interviewees were eager to speak about *other* times they had been named in the news, whether for the same trigger but in other outlets or for completely different triggers at some point in the past.

At the end of our conversations, I asked participants to complete a brief questionnaire about their demographic information. No one received material compensation for their participation, although I paid when I met people in cafes or restaurants. Interviewees signed an Institutional Review Board (IRB)–approved consent form in which I promised anonymity. Immediately following each interview, I wrote up field notes identifying main themes that had arisen in our conversation and my general impressions, followed by a short narrative summarizing the subject's experience. I then followed a grounded theory–based approach to analyze my interview data: I transcribed all interviews, identified themes and coded for them, juxtaposed segments according to code, developed theories about how they related to one another, and chose exemplary quotes to illustrate those themes.[3]

At the writing stage, I found that anonymizing without sacrificing the detail of respondents' stories was tricky because, even though I gave everyone a pseudonym, they had almost all appeared in publications that were readily available online. In many cases, a detailed description of their stories could identify them. To avoid that, in many places in the text I have been deliberately vague about details or altered identifying factors. Ellipses indicate where I shortened quotes, and I have removed some verbal ticks for readability.

SAMPLE BIASES AND LACUNAE

Contacting specific individuals, rather than groups of people who can all be approached in the same place, makes recruiting participants both arduous and inefficient—it is less like shooting fish in a barrel than trying to hook a series of specific, one-of-a-kind fish. As such, getting participants for this study was quite challenging, and I was not eager to reject anyone who came forward willing to be interviewed. So while a certain discrepancy between the sample frame (those identified and solicited for participation in the study) and the actual sample (those who agreed to participate and did so) is common in both quantitative and qualitative studies, this one may have especially suffered from it: I did not have a wealth of potential participants whom I was willing to turn away in favor of people who fit less-represented categories. For example, the final sample was heavy on unemployed people who had appeared in stories about the recent economic crisis but short on people associated with crimes. The former had the time to participate in my study, while for obvious reasons it was harder to recruit the latter. Accessing accused and convicted criminals was especially difficult, since those currently in the justice system were mostly unavailable, and IRB restrictions prevented me from contacting actual inmates.

One might wonder if people who had had very negative experiences interacting with the press were disinclined to participate in my study, which would mean unhappy subjects were also underrepresented in my sample. That is a valid question and, while possible, it is hard to know the answer. One could just as easily predict that people who had been burned by the media would want to speak out so others might learn from their experience, and some of my participants said exactly that. I also spoke with a number of people who declined to be interviewed, and of those only two said it was because they had had a bad experience with the media. Other decliners gave completely different reasons for not participating, such as lack of time or disinterest.

An area in the sample that varied more than would have been ideal was how much time had lapsed between when subjects' stories had been published and our discussions about them. I quickly found that contacting people too soon after an article came out was impractical: they almost always declined to be interviewed because they were still dealing with the aftermath of the trigger and/or the news coverage of it. Subjects who had appeared in the news only a day or two before were also unable to speak much about repercussions, so after a few misfires I learned to wait at least two weeks before contacting each person. In many cases, however, a month or more had lapsed before we actually sat down to an interview, and in several cases (these were the few that were recruited via my personal contacts or Craigslist) the primary stories we were discussing had been published multiple years before.

Obviously, this introduces the troubling issue of memory. On the one hand, I was able to gather valuable information about what was important to subjects about this experience based on what they were and were not able to remember after some time had passed. For example, that a number of interviewees did not remember whether there were errors in their articles at all but recalled in detail their interactions with reporters or the reactions of their reference groups was an important finding. On the other hand, the fact that the amount of time varied among my respondents sometimes made comparisons difficult. Often those for whom a lot of time had passed understandably remembered fewer details than those for whom the memory was fresh. In my analysis I tried to compensate for this by not making claims about, for example, salience of some aspects of the experience over others if I thought the mere passage of time was a plausible explanation for it.

SO HOW IS THIS DIFFERENT FROM WHAT JOURNALISTS DO?

By using in-depth interviews for this study I was re-creating some of the dynamics of the journalistic encounter, but there were important differences as well.

First, some of the similarities: for most of my interviewees, being solicited by a graduate student for participation in a study was a novel experience, much like being contacted by a reporter for a news story. I sensed that, as is often the case when subjects agree to a journalistic interview, for many of them the novelty was part of the appeal. And there was also no doubt that, as is also often true for subjects of news stories, the opportunity to tell their stories to an attentive listener was also part of the draw.

As I discussed at length in chapter 3, journalists cultivate, and are often formally trained in, "empathic listening."[4] Social scientists doing in-depth interviews undoubtedly traffic in it as well. I certainly engaged in generating a kind of "pseudo-intimacy" in the encounter that was conducive to getting subjects to talk, sometimes about feelings or experiences they might have hesitated to share with others, so that I could use their input for my own project.[5] They supplied the material, and I made the decisions about how to present it in writing. In that sense, I undoubtedly re-created the uneven power structure discussed in my analysis of the journalistic interview. That structural inequality is probably the most important feature my interviews had in common with journalistic interviews.

But although there were areas of overlap between my approach and journalistic methods, there were important differences as well, some of which turned out to be central to what was meaningful to my subjects about making the news. The design of a systematic study necessitates systematic interviewing: few journalists would ask eighty-three people the same questions in more or less the same order, for example. Nor would they transcribe and code every word. I had far more time to soak up interviewees' stories and analyze them than most journalists normally would.

I also promised anonymity and only a very small guaranteed audience. That meant both the potential benefits and the risks of participating in my project differed from those afforded by a news appearance. I could offer no status or fame at all. The opportunity for public address and public display, with the status and attention they afford, are the main reasons people agree to appear in news stories. Status and publicity affect what it feels like to talk to journalists, to see oneself in the product, and any subsequent repercussions. Taking them off the table thus introduced a crucial difference between what it meant to participate in my project and in a more journalistic one. It altered subjects' motives for participating, reduced the excitement and many of the uncertainties subjects experience during the journalistic process, and essentially eliminated all the reputational and other repercussions news subjects must manage.

Anonymity also reduced the risks for subjects because it meant they would not have to deal with negative repercussions of publicity, or of having something they did not write themselves linked to their names online. While at times I felt ridiculous promising anonymity to people who had already been named in multiple news outlets and, in some cases, seen by many millions, in the end I am very glad I did. If, as I argue, the power balance between subjects and those who write about them is inevitably uneven because only one party will ultimately write their version of events, one way to try to reinstate a bit of equilibrium is to protect subjects from the repercussions of stories written about them, but over which they have little control.

NOTES

1. VICTIMS OF THE PRESS?

1. Todd Gitlin, *The Whole World Is Watching: Mass Media in the Making & Unmaking of the New Left* (Berkeley: University of California Press, 1980), 17.

2. Art Swift, "Americans' Trust in Mass Media Sinks to New Low," *Gallup.com*, September 14, 2016, http://www.gallup.com/poll/195542/americans-trust-mass-media-sinks-new-low.aspx.

3. Gitlin, *The Whole World Is Watching*, 109.

4. In this sense, my findings align with recent newsroom ethnographies that find much continuity in journalistic work, even as they identify emerging routines and values. See C. W. Anderson, *Rebuilding the News: Metropolitan Journalism in the Digital Age* (Philadelphia: Temple University Press, 2013); David M. Ryfe, *Can Journalism Survive?: An Inside Look at American Newsrooms* (Cambridge: Polity, 2012); Nikki Usher, *Making News at the New York Times* (Ann Arbor: University of Michigan Press, 2014).

5. While not focused on ordinary folks as news subjects per se, David Paul Nord's history of American newspapers and their readers documents changing reporting practices and ideas of what counts as news, two areas where ordinary citizens' roles have changed greatly over time. Nord shows that even the earliest American news reports in the seventeenth century included remarkable occurrences about ordinary people, deemed newsworthy for their religious significance. David Paul Nord, *Communities of Journalism: A History of American Newspapers and Their Readers* (Urbana: University of Illinois Press, 2006).

6. Kathy Roberts Forde, "Discovering the Explanatory Report in American Newspapers," *Journalism Practice* 1, no. 2 (June 2007): 227–44, doi:10.1080/17512780701275531; Stephen Hess, "Washington Reporters," *Society* 184 (1981): 55–66; Michael Schudson and Katherine Fink, "The Rise of Contextual Journalism, 1950s–2000s," *Journalism* 15, no. 1 (2014): 3–20, doi: 10.1177/1464884913479015; Daniel C Hallin, "Soundbite News: Television Coverage of Elections, 1968–88," in *We Keep America on Top of the World* (New York: Routledge, 1993), 133–52.

7.   Kevin G. Barnhurst and Diana Mutz, "American Journalism and the Decline in Event-Centered Reporting," *Journal of Communication* 47, no. 4 (December 1997): 27–52, doi:10 .1111/j.1460-2466.1997.tb02724.x.

8.   David Pritchard, "Why Unhappy Subjects of News Coverage Rarely Complain," in *Holding the Media Accountable*, ed. David Pritchard (Bloomington: Indiana University Press, 2000), 39–40.

9.   Irene Costera Meijer, "Practicing Audience-Centred Journalism Research," in *The SAGE Handbook of Digital Journalism*, ed. Tamara Witschge et al. (Los Angeles: Sage Publications, 2016), 546–61.

10. Since the 1970s, newsroom ethnographies, content analyses, and studies of media coverage of significant historical events have consistently found that the vast majority of mainstream news sources—almost always over 70 percent—are these "official" or "elite" sources. For influential examples from the 1970s and 1980s, see, in ethnographies, Herbert J Gans, *Deciding What's News: A Study of CBS Evening News, NBC Nightly News, Newsweek, and Time* (New York: Vintage, 1979); Gaye Tuchman, *Making News: A Study in the Construction of Reality* (New York: Free Press, 1978). For content analyses: Leon V Sigal, *Reporters and Officials: The Organization and Politics of Newsmaking* (Lexington, Mass: D. C. Heath, 1973); Jane Delano Brown et al., "Invisible Power: Newspaper News Sources and the Limits of Diversity," *Journalism Quarterly* 64 (Spring 1987): 45–54, doi:10.1177/107769908706400106. For studies of media coverage of historical events: Gitlin, *The Whole World Is Watching*; Daniel C. Hallin, *The Uncensored War: The Media and Vietnam* (Berkeley: University of California Press, 1989). Since those early studies, many content analyses have explored the lack of diversity among news sources, such as Cory Armstrong, "Story Genre Influences Whether Women Are Sources," *Newspaper Research Journal* 27, no. 3 (Summer 2006): 66–81; Daniel C. Hallin, Robert Karl Manoff, and Judy K. Weddle, "Sourcing Patterns of National Security Reporters," *Journalism Quarterly* 70, no. 4 (Winter 1993): 753–66, doi:10.1177/107769909307000402; Lynn Zoch and Judy Turk, "Women Making News: Gender as a Variable in Source Selection and Use," *Journalism and Mass Communication Quarterly* 75, no. 4 (Winter 1998): 762, doi:10 .1177/107769909807500410.

11. Janet Malcolm, *The Journalist and the Murderer* (New York: Vintage, 1990).

12. Ibid., 3.

13. For a deeper discussion of the influence of the *Journalist and the Murderer* and the debates it has inspired, see Ruth A. Palmer, "The Journalist and the Murderer Revisited: What Interviews with Journalism Subjects Reveal About a Modern Classic," *Journalism*, March 11, 2016, doi:10.1177/1464884916636125.

14. For example, see Isabel Awad, "Journalists and Their Sources," *Journalism Studies* 7, no. 6 (December 1, 2006): 922–39, doi:10.1080/14616700600980702; Sandra L. Borden, "Empathic Listening: The Interviewer's Betrayal," *Journal of Mass Media Ethics* 8, no. 4 (December 1, 1993): 219–26, doi:10.1207/s15327728jmme0804_3; Tom Luljak, "The Routine Nature of Journalistic Deception," in *Holding the Media Accountable*, ed. David Pritchard (Bloomington: Indiana University Press, 2000), 11–26.

15. Scott Maier, "Accuracy Matters: A Cross-Market Assessment of Newspaper Error and Credibility," *Journalism and Mass Communication Quarterly* 82, no. 3 (Autumn 2005): 541,

doi:10.1177/107769900508200304; Philip Meyer, *The Vanishing Newspaper: Saving Journalism in the Information Age* (Columbia: University of Missouri Press, 2009).

16. For example, see Joshua Gamson, *Freaks Talk Back: Tabloid Talk Shows and Sexual Nonconformity* (Chicago: University of Chicago Press, 1998); Laura Grindstaff, *The Money Shot: Trash, Class, and the Making of TV Talk Shows* (Chicago: University of Chicago Press, 2002), Laura Grindstaff, "Self-Serve Celebrity: The Production of Ordinariness and the Ordinariness of Production in Reality Television," in *Production Studies: Cultural Studies of Media Industries*, ed. Vicki Mayer, Miranda Banks, and John Thornton Caldwell (New York: Routledge, 2009), 71–86.

17. Matt Carlson and Seth C. Lewis, eds., *Boundaries of Journalism: Professionalism, Practices and Participation* (London; New York: Routledge, 2015).

18. Matthias Revers, "Journalistic Professionalism as Performance and Boundary Work: Source Relations at the State House," *Journalism* 15, no. 1 (2014): 37–52, doi:10.1177/1464884913480459.

19. German Lopez, "The Daily Beast Tried to Prove Olympians Like Sex, but Instead May Have Outed Gay Athletes," *Vox*, August 12, 2016, http://www.vox.com/2016/8/11/12440186/daily-beast-olympics-gay; Alyssa Rosenberg, "Gawker's Relaunch and the Role of Niceness in Journalism," *Washington Post*, July 27, 2015, https://www.washingtonpost.com/news/act-four/wp/2015/07/27/gawkers-relaunch-and-the-role-of-niceness-in-journalism/; Peter Thiel, "Peter Thiel: The Online Privacy Debate Won't End with Gawker," *New York Times*, August 15, 2016, http://www.nytimes.com/2016/08/16/opinion/peter-thiel-the-online-privacy-debate-wont-end-with-gawker.html.

20. Jay Rosen, "The People Formerly Known as the Audience," *Pressthink*, June 27, 2006, http://archive.pressthink.org/2006/06/27/ppl_frmr.html.

21. "The Audience Turn in Journalism (Studies)," panel at the International Communication Association, San Juan, Puerto Rico, May 22, 2015.

22. Costera Meijer, "Practicing Audience-Centred Journalism Research"; Mirca Madianou, "Audience Reception and News in Everyday Life," in *The Handbook of Journalism Studies*, ed. Karin Wahl-Jorgensen and Thomas Hanitzsch (New York: Routledge, 2008), 325–37.

23. Joseph Turow, "Audience Construction and Culture Production: Marketing Surveillance in the Digital Age," *ANNALS of the American Academy of Political and Social Science* 597, no. 1 (January 1, 2005): 103–21, doi:10.1177/0002716204270469; Anderson, *Rebuilding the News*, 8.

24. Adrian Furnham, *Lay Theories: Everyday Understanding of Problems in the Social Sciences*, ed. Michael Argyle (Oxford: Pergamon Press, 1988); Rasmus Kleis Nielsen, "Folk Theories of Journalism," *Journalism Studies*, April 6, 2016, doi:10.1080/1461670X.2016.1165140.

25. See, for example, Stephen Coleman, Scott Anthony, and David E. Morrison, *Public Trust in the News* (Oxford: Reuters Institute, 2009), https://reutersinstitute.politics.ox.ac.uk/sites/default/files/Public%20Trust%20in%20the%20News%20A%20Constructivist%20Study%20of%20the%20Social%20Life%20of%20the%20News_0.pdf.

26. Furnham, *Lay Theories*. For an example of this method, see Susan Herbst, *Reading Public Opinion: How Political Actors View the Democratic Process* (Chicago: University of Chicago Press, 1998), 73.

27. Interview by author, February 11, 2010.

28. Julian Petley, *Media and Public Shaming: Drawing the Boundaries of Disclosure* (London: I. B. Tauris, 2013), http://reutersinstitute.politics.ox.ac.uk/publication/media-and-public-shaming.

29. Hanne Detel, "Disclosure and Public Shaming in the Age of New Visibility," in *Media and Public Shaming*, ed. Julian Petley (London: I. B. Tauris, 2013), 77–96.

30. Interview by author, December 17, 2010.

31. Kristin Luker, *Salsa Dancing Into the Social Sciences* (Cambridge, Mass.: Harvard University Press, 2010), 125.

32. Barney Glaser and Anselm Strauss, *The Discovery of Grounded Theory: Strategies for Qualitative Research* (Chicago: Aldine Transaction, 1999).

33. James W. Carey, "A Cultural Approach to Communication," in *Communication as Culture* (Boston: Unwin Hyman, 1988), 13–36.

34. Erving Goffman, *Interaction Ritual: Essays on Face-to-Face Behavior* (New York: Pantheon Books, 1967); Erving Goffman, *Frame Analysis: An Essay on the Organization of Experience* (Cambridge, Mass: Harvard University Press, 1974); Erving Goffman, *Stigma: Notes on the Management of Spoiled Identity* (New York: Simon & Schuster, 1986).

35. Roland Barthes, *Camera Lucida: Reflections on Photography* (New York: Hill and Wang, 2010); Sigmund Freud, "The 'Uncanny,'" in *The Standard Edition of the Complete Psychological Works of Sigmund Freud, Volume XVII (1917–1919): An Infantile Neurosis and Other Works* (London: Hogarth Press, 1919), 217–56; Susan Sontag, *On Photography* (New York: Picador, 2001).

36. Ann Swidler, *Talk of Love: How Culture Matters* (Chicago: University of Chicago Press, 2001), 3.

37. The concept of "deep stories" comes from Arlie Russell Hochschild, *Strangers in Their Own Land: Anger and Mourning on the American Right* (New York: New Press, 2016).

38. Mark Fishman, *Manufacturing the News* (Austin: University of Texas Press, 1988); Tuchman, *Making News*; Usher, *Making News at the New York Times*.y

2. WHAT'S IN IT FOR THEM? WEIGHING THE PROS AND CONS OF BECOMING A NEWS SUBJECT

1. For academic examples, see Isabel Awad, "Journalists and Their Sources," *Journalism Studies* 7, no. 6 (December 1, 2006): 932, doi:10.1080/14616700600980702; Sandra L. Borden, "Empathic Listening: The Interviewer's Betrayal," *Journal of Mass Media Ethics* 8, no. 4 (December 1, 1993): 219–26, doi:10.1207/s15327728jmme0804_3. For journalistic examples, see Michael Kinsley, "Speaking Candidly, Journalists Are Truly Snakes," *Bloomberg*, November 4, 2011, http://www.bloomberg.com/news/2011-11-04/speaking-candidly-journalists-are-truly-snakes-michael-kinsley.html; Jack Shafer, "Unsolicited Advice for Future Subjects of Magazine Profiles," *Slate*, June 23, 2010, http://www.slate.com/articles/news_and_politics/press_box/2010/06/unsolicited_advice_for_future_subjects_of_magazine_profiles.html.

2. Interview by author, October 30, 2009. All quotes from Alegra are from this interview.

3. Gitlin, documenting his own decision to speak to the press about the first Gulf War, makes this point. Todd Gitlin, *Media Unlimited: How the Torrent of Images and Sounds Overwhelms Our Lives* (New York: Metropolitan Books, Henry Holt, 2007), 122.

4. Michael Schudson, "Four Approaches to the Sociology of News," in *Mass Media and Society*, ed. James Curran and Michael Gurevitch (London: Hodder Arnold, 2005), 172–73.

5. Ruth A. Palmer, "The Journalist and the Murderer Revisited: What Interviews with Journalism Subjects Reveal About a Modern Classic," *Journalism*, March 11, 2016, 7, doi: 10.1177/1464884916636125.

6. Interview by author, March 3, 2010.

7. Interview by author, November 18, 2010. All quotes from Albert are from this interview.

8. Interview by author, November 29, 2010.

9. Interview by author, March 2, 2010.

10. Interview by author, November 25, 2009.

11. Interview by author, November 14, 2010.

12. Interview by author, March 3, 2010.

13. Interview by author, April 28, 2010.

14. Interview by author, October 14, 2010.

15. Interview by author, August 6, 2010.

16. Interview by author, August 5, 2010. All quotes from Sophie are from this interview.

17. Interview by author, November 16, 2009. All quotes from Jon and Jane are from this interview.

18. Interview by author, October 9, 2009.

19. Interview by author, January 6, 2011.

20. Interview by author, July 26, 2010.

21. Interview by author, November 5, 2010.

22. Interview by author, August 29, 2010.

23. Interview by author, February 11, 2010.

24. Interview by author, January 5, 2011.

25. Interview by author, May 21, 2010.

26. Interview by author, August 4, 2010.

27. Interview by author, May 6, 2010. All quotes from Barbara are from this interview.

28. Interview by author, April 28, 2010.

29. Interview by author, November 12, 2009.

30. Interview by author, November 9, 2009.

31. Interview by author, January 8, 2011.

32. Interview by author, January 4, 2011.

33. Interview by author, December 17, 2010.

34. Matt Carlson, "Sources as News Producers," in *The SAGE Handbook of Digital Journalism*, ed. Tamara Witschge et al. (Los Angeles: Sage Publications, 2016), 236–49.

35. James W. Carey, "A Cultural Approach to Communication," in *Communication as Culture* (Boston: Unwin Hyman, 1988), 13–36. Laura Grindstaff also makes this point about the motives of people who appear on TV talk shows in *The Money Shot: Trash, Class, and the Making of TV Talk Shows* (Chicago: University of Chicago Press, 2002), 129.

3. THE INTERVIEW STAGE PART 1:
ENCOUNTERING JOURNALISTS

1. Janet Malcolm, *The Journalist and the Murderer* (New York: Vintage, 1990).

2. Ruth A. Palmer, "The Journalist and the Murderer Revisited: What Interviews with Journalism Subjects Reveal About a Modern Classic," *Journalism*, March 11, 2016, 2, doi:10.1177/1464884916636125.

3. This is essentially the characterization of journalistic subjects in Malcolm's book, but a similar, if less hyperbolic, version also emerges in some scholarly examinations of journalists' interpersonal relations with their subjects and sources. See, for example, Isabel Awad, "Journalists and Their Sources," *Journalism Studies* 7, no. 6 (December 1, 2006): 922–39, doi:10.1080/14616700600980702; Sandra L. Borden, "Empathic Listening: The Interviewer's Betrayal," *Journal of Mass Media Ethics* 8, no. 4 (December 1, 1993): 219–26, doi:10.1207/s15327728jmmeo804_3.

4. Although not primarily thought of as a scholar of the mass media, Erving Goffman stands alone among theorists of microsocial interaction for his influence on mass communication and media studies research. His concepts of framing and front- and backstage behaviors in particular have been applied in prominent works in the field, including some concerned specifically with how an individual's normal behavior in face-to-face encounters is altered when transmitted through different media technologies. For examples, see Danah Boyd, "Taken Out of Context: American Teen Sociality in Networked Publics" (Ph.D. diss., University of California, 2008), http://www.danah.org/papers/TakenOutOfContext.pdf; Joshua Meyrowitz, *No Sense of Place* (New York: Oxford University Press, 1985).

5. Erving Goffman, *Interaction Ritual: Essays on Face-to-Face Behavior* (New York: Pantheon Books, 1967). The description of face-work in this chapter comes from the essay "On Face-Work" (5–46), and the description of conversational involvement is from the essay "Alienation from Interaction" (113–36). The theme of maintaining the ceremonial order runs throughout the book but is emphasized in the essay "The Nature of Deference and Demeanor" (47–96).

6. Interview by author, July 28, 2010.

7. Martin Gottlieb, "Dangerous Liaisons: Journalists and Their Sources," *Columbia Journalism Review* 28, no. 2 (July 1989): 31.

8. Melvin Mencher, *Melvin Mencher's News Reporting and Writing*, 10th ed. (Boston: McGraw-Hill, 2006), 293.

9. Ibid., 312.

10. Isabel Wilkerson, "Interviewing Sources," *Nieman Reports* 56, no. 1 (Spring 2002): 1, http://niemanreports.org/articles/interviewing-sources/.

11. Borden, "Empathic Listening."

12. Borden makes this argument in ibid., 220, citing Howell, *The Empathic Communicator* (Prospect Heights, Ill.: Waveland, 1986).

13. Interview by author, October 30, 2009. All quotes from Alegra are from this interview.

14. Malcolm, *The Journalist and the Murderer*, 98–99.

15. Interview by author, February 18, 2010.

16. Interview by author, October 19, 2009.

17. Interview by author, April 28, 2010.
18. Interview by author, December 7, 2010.
19. Interview by author, May 25, 2010. All quotes from Carmen are from this interview.
20. Interview by author, October 14, 2010. All quotes from Deanne are from this interview.
21. Erving Goffman, *Frame Analysis: An Essay on the Organization of Experience* (Cambridge, Mass: Harvard University Press, 1974). Throughout this chapter my description of Goffman's theory of frames comes from this source unless otherwise noted.
22. Ibid., 473.
23. Interview by author, November 16, 2010. Redacted to protect the interviewee's privacy. All quotes from Eve are from this interview.
24. Interview by author, July 30, 2010.
25. Interview by author, November 18, 2010.
26. Interview by author, November 9, 2009.
27. Interview by author, October 14, 2010.
28. Interview by author, March 20, 2010. All quotes from Dudley are from this interview.
29. Interview by author, November 11, 2010. All quotes from Jay are from this interview.
30. Interview by author, August 4, 2010.
31. Interview by author, November 3, 2009. All quotes from Kim are from this interview.
32. Interview by author, March 5, 2010.
33. Interview by author, November 12, 2010.
34. Interview by author, November 5, 2010.
35. Interview by author, March 3, 2010.
36. Interview by author, May 3, 2010.
37. Interview by author, December 5, 2010.
38. Malcolm, *The Journalist and the Murderer*, 4.

4. THE INTERVIEW STAGE PART 2:
FROM INTERACTION TO STORY

1. Interview by author, August 29, 2010. All quotes from Annie are from this interview.
2. Herbert J. Gans, *Deciding What's News: A Study of CBS Evening News, NBC Nightly News, Newsweek, and Time* (New York: Vintage, 1979), 117.
3. Nikki Usher, *Making News at The New York Times* (Ann Arbor: University of Michigan Press, 2014).
4. Todd Gitlin, *Media Unlimited: How the Torrent of Images and Sounds Overwhelms Our Lives* (New York: Metropolitan Books, Henry Holt, 2007), 121.
5. Interview by author, January 8, 2011.
6. Interview by author, March 5, 2010. All quotes from Thomas are from this interview.
7. Interview by author, March 12, 2010. All quotes from Flora are from this interview.
8. Interview by author, February 18, 2010. All quotes from Leyla are from this interview.
9. Interview by author, December 5, 2010. All quotes from Fatima are from this interview.
10. Janet Malcolm, *The Journalist and the Murderer* (New York: Vintage, 1990).
11. Interview by author, March 2, 2010.

12.   Interview by author, February 18, 2010.

13.   Interview by author, November 25, 2009. All quotes from Daniel are from this interview.

14.   Interview by author, November 11, 2009.

15.   Interview by author, August 17, 2010.

16.   Interview by author, November 9, 2009. All quotes from Colleen are from this interview.

17.   Interview by author, November 29, 2010. All quotes from Bella are from this interview.

18.   Interview by author, September 16, 2010.

19.   Interview by author, September 16, 2010. All quotes from Monica are from this interview.

20.   Erving Goffman, *Interaction Ritual: Essays on Face-to-Face Behavior* (New York: Pantheon Books, 1967).

21.   Interview by author, October 14, 2010. All quotes from Deanne are from this interview.

22.   Interview by author, November 11, 2009.

23.   Gans, for example, concluded that powerful sources usually have more power in their tug-of-war with journalists. More recently, Matt Carlson has argued that in the current media environment, powerful subjects with their own resources and audiences can effectively use media tools to bypass journalists altogether. Gans, *Deciding What's News*, 116; Matt Carlson, "Sources as News Producers," in *The SAGE Handbook of Digital Journalism*, ed. Tamara Witschge et al. (Los Angeles: Sage Publications, 2016), 236–49.

5. TRUTH (PERCEPTIONS) AND CONSEQUENCES: HOW NEWS SUBJECTS JUDGE ACCURACY AND ERROR

1.   This chapter is derived, in part, from Ruth Palmer, "Context Matters: What News Subjects Can Tell Us About Accuracy and Error," *Journalism Studies* 13, no. 6 (December 2012): 1–16, doi:10.1080/1461670X.2011.644457.

2.   Interview by author, October 30, 2009. All quotes from Alegra are from this interview.

3.   Scott Maier, "Accuracy Matters: A Cross-Market Assessment of Newspaper Error and Credibility," *Journalism and Mass Communication Quarterly* 82, no. 3 (Autumn 2005): 533–51, doi:10.1177/107769900508200304; Scott Maier, "Setting the Record Straight: When the Press Errs, Do Corrections Follow?," paper presented at the International Communication Association Conference, Dresden, Germany, 2006); Philip Meyer, *The Vanishing Newspaper: Saving Journalism in the Information Age* (Columbia: University of Missouri Press, 2009); David Pritchard, "Why Unhappy Subjects of News Coverage Rarely Complain," in *Holding the Media Accountable*, ed. David Pritchard (Bloomington: Indiana University Press, 2000).

4.   Mitchell Charnley, "A Study of Newspaper Accuracy," *Journalism Quarterly* 13, no. 4 (December 1, 1936): 394.

5.   For example, see Larry L. Burris, "Accuracy of News Magazines as Perceived by News Sources," *Journalism Quarterly* 62 (Winter 1985): 825–27; J. Richard Cote, "A Study of Accuracy of Two Wire Services," *Journalism Quarterly* 47 (Winter 1970): 661–66; Gary Hanson and Stanley T. Wearden, "Measuring Newscast Accuracy: Applying a Newspaper Model to Television," *Journalism and Mass Communication Quarterly* 81, no. 3 (Autumn 2004): 546–58, doi:10.1177/107769900408100306.

6. Charnley, "A Study of Newspaper Accuracy"; Fred Berry, "A Study of Accuracy in Local News Stories of Three Dailies," *Journalism Quarterly* 44 (Autumn 1967): 482–90; William Blankenburg, "News Accuracy: Some Findings on the Meaning of Errors," *Journal of Communication* 20 (December 1970): 375–86; Charles Brown, "Majority of Readers Give Papers an 'A' for Accuracy," *Editor & Publisher* 63 (February 13, 1965); Hal Marshall, "Newspaper Accuracy in Tucson," *Journalism Quarterly* 54, no. 1 (1977): 165–68; Maier, "Accuracy Matters."

7. Fred Berry introduced the objective and subjective categories, which others subsequently adopted. Berry, "A Study of Accuracy in Local News Stories of Three Dailies," 487.

8. William Tillinghast, for example, found that even on factual errors reporters disagreed with subjects half the time, and that they disputed a full 95 percent of subjective errors reported by their subjects. See William A. Tillinghast, "Newspaper Errors: Reporters Dispute Most Source Claims," *Newspaper Research Journal* 3 (Fall 1982): 14–23; See also Scott R. Maier, "How Sources, Reporters View Math Errors in News," *Newspaper Research Journal* 24, no. 4 (2003): 48–63; Philip Meyer, "A Workable Measure of Auditing Accuracy in Newspapers," *Newspaper Research Journal* 10 (Winter 1988): 39–51.

9. William A. Tillinghast, "Source Control and Evaluation of Newspaper Inaccuracies," *Newspaper Research Journal* 3 (Fall 1982): 22.

10. Maier, "Accuracy Matters," 543.

11. On a Likert-like scale from 1 to 7, with 7 considered most severe, the most severe objective errors (incorrect addresses) received only a 3.3, and the most egregious subjective errors, at 4.21, were those in the "other" category, exceeding the next most severe subjective category ("story sensationalized," at 3.22) by almost a full point. Ibid., 541.

12. Blankenburg, "News Accuracy"; Tillinghast, "Source Control and Evaluation of Newspaper Inaccuracies."

13. Pritchard, "Why Unhappy Subjects of News Coverage Rarely Complain."

14. Blankenburg, "News Accuracy," 385.

15. Pritchard, "Why Unhappy Subjects of News Coverage Rarely Complain," 30.

16. Interview by author, November 16, 2009.

17. Interview by author, November 25, 2009. All quotes from Daniel are from this interview.

18. Tillinghast, "Source Control and Evaluation of Newspaper Inaccuracies."

19. Interview by author, November 10, 2009.

20. Interview by author, March 10, 2010.

21. Interview by author, March 2, 2010.

22. Interview by author, October 14, 2010.

23. Interview by author, March 2, 2010.

24. Interview by author, March 23, 2010.

25. Interview by author, March 3, 2010.

26. Interview by author, January 4, 2011. Street names have been changed.

27. Interview by author, September 30, 2010.

28. Interview by author, November 12, 2010.

29. Interview by author, November 24, 2010.

30. Interview by author, November 3, 2009.

31. Interview by author, May 3, 2010. All quotes from Patricia are from this interview.

32. Interview by author, January 8, 2011. All quotes from Michelle are from this interview.

33. Interview by author, May 4, 2010.

34. Interview by author, October 19, 2009. All quotes from Maggie are from this interview.

35. Interview by author, October 26, 2009.

36. This was also the most common explanation Maier found in a pair of surveys about corrections. See Scott Maier, "Getting It Right? Not in 59 Percent of Stories," *Newspaper Research Journal* 23 (Winter 2002): 10–24; Maier, "Setting the Record."

37. Interview by author, January 4, 2011.

38. Interview by author, January 5, 2011.

39. These do occur under extraordinary circumstances in the form of editor's notes, such as the one that appeared in the *New York Times* acknowledging its mishandling of its coverage of accused spy Wen Ho Lee. See "From the Editors; The Times and Wen Ho Lee," *New York Times*, September 26, 2000, http://www.nytimes.com/2000/09/26/us/from-the-editors -the-times-and-wen-ho-lee.html.

40. Christine Urban, "Examining Our Credibility: Perspectives of the Public and the Press" (Washington, D.C.: ASNE, 1999), http://asne.org/kiosk/reports/99reports/1999examinin gourcredibility/; American Society of Newspaper Editors, "Newspaper Credibility: Building Reader Trust" (Washington, D.C.: ASNE, 1984).

41. Interview by author, August 29, 2010.

6. THAT'S ME! . . . BUT IT'S NOT ME: AESTHETIC, EMOTIONAL, AND EXISTENTIAL EFFECTS OF CONFRONTING OUR NEWS SELVES

1. Interview by author, July 28, 2010. All other quotes from Billy are from this interview.

2. Interview by author, November 3, 2009.

3. Erving Goffman, "On Face-Work," in *Interaction Ritual* (New York: Pantheon Books, 1967), 5–45.

4. Christopher Prendergast, *The Triangle of Representation* (New York: Columbia University Press, 2000), 3.

5. Susan Harter, "Developmental Perspectives on the Self-System," in *Handbook of Child Psychology: Socialization, Personality, and Social Development*, ed. E. M. Hetherington, 4th ed., vol. 4 (New York: Wiley, 1983), 279.

6. Roland Barthes, *Camera Lucida: Reflections on Photography* (New York: Hill and Wang, 2010); Susan Sontag, *On Photography* (New York: Picador, 2001).

7. Sontag, *On Photography*, 14.

8. Ibid.

9. Rachel M Calogero, Stacey Tantleff-Dunn, and J. Kevin Thompson, "Objectification Theory: An Introduction," in *Self-Objectification in Women: Causes, Consequences, and Counteractions* (Washington, D.C.: American Psychological Association, 2011).

10. Interview by author, January 4, 2011.

11. Sontag, *On Photography*, 14.

12. Interview by author, November 10, 2009.

13. Erving Goffman, *Interaction Ritual: Essays on Face-to-Face Behavior* (New York: Pantheon Books, 1967).

14. Danah Boyd, "Taken Out of Context: American Teen Sociality in Networked Publics" (Ph.D. diss., University of California, 2008), http://www.danah.org/papers/TakenOutOf-Context.pdf; Alice E. Marwick and Danah Boyd, "I Tweet Honestly, I Tweet Passionately: Twitter Users, Context Collapse, and the Imagined Audience," *New Media & Society*, July 7, 2010, doi:10.1177/1461444810365313.

15. Sigmund Freud, "The 'Uncanny,'" in *The Standard Edition of the Complete Psychological Works of Sigmund Freud, Volume XVII (1917–1919): An Infantile Neurosis and Other Works* (1919), 217–56.

16. Ibid., 217.

17. Interview by author, October 14, 2010.

18. Interview by author, May 6, 2010.

19. Interview by author, July 26, 2010.

20. Interview by author, February 11, 2010.

21. Orville G. Brim, *Look at Me!: The Fame Motive from Childhood to Death* (Ann Arbor: University of Michigan Press, 2009).

22. Interview by author, October 9, 2009.

23. Interview by author, October 18, 2010.

24. Interview by author, October 30, 2009.

25. Their emphasis. Paul F. Lazarsfeld and Robert K. Merton, "Mass Communication, Popular Taste, and Organized Social Action," in *Mass Communication and American Social Thought: Key Texts, 1919–1968*, ed. John Durham Peters and Peter Simons (Lanham, Md.: Rowman & Littlefield, 2004), 233.

26. Peter Simonson, "Mediated Sources of Public Confidence: Lazarsfeld and Merton Revisited," *Journal of Communication* 49, no. 2 (1999): 113, doi:10.1111/j.1460-2466.1999.tb02796.x.

27. Interview by author, March 5, 2010.

28. Interview by author, August 4, 2010.

29. Interview by author, September 16, 2010.

30. Barthes, *Camera Lucida*, 77.

31. Brim, *Look at Me!*, 58.

32. David Giles, *Illusions of Immortality: A Psychology of Fame and Celebrity* (New York: St. Martin's Press, 2000), 44.

33. Interview by author, December 17, 2010.

34. Interview by author, November 16, 2010.

35. Barthes, *Camera Lucida*, 88–89.

36. "Press Widely Criticized, but Trusted More than Other Information Sources," Pew Research Center for the People and the Press, September 22, 2011, http://www.people-press.org/2011/09/22/press-widely-criticized-but-trusted-more-than-other-institutions/.

37. Interview by author, November 5, 2010. All quotes from Keith are from this interview.

38. Interview by author, March 11, 2010.

7. CELEBRATION, CONDEMNATION, REPUTATION: AUDIENCE FEEDBACK AS AN INDICATOR OF STATUS AND STIGMA

1. Interview by author, January 8, 2011.

2. Daniel J. Solove, *The Future of Reputation: Gossip, Rumor, and Privacy on the Internet* (New Haven: Yale University Press, 2007), 31.

3. See Charles Horton Cooley, *Human Nature and the Social Order* (New York: Schocken Books, 1964), 184. Solove points this out as well in his *The Future of Reputation*, 31.

4. Here again I refer to James Carey's well-known dual model of communication, as transmission and as ritual. James W. Carey, "A Cultural Approach to Communication," in *Communication as Culture* (Boston: Unwin Hyman, 1988), 13–36.

5. Many scholars have made the argument that news reinforces social norms. Two of the most well-known examples are James W. Carey and Paul Lazarsfeld and Robert Merton, in their pieces discussed in this chapter. See Carey, "A Cultural Approach to Communication"; Paul F. Lazarsfeld and Robert K. Merton, "Mass Communication, Popular Taste, and Organized Social Action," in *Mass Communication and American Social Thought: Key Texts, 1919–1968*, ed. John Durham Peters and Peter Simons (Lanham, Md.: Rowman & Littlefield, 2004), 230–41.

6. Gaye Tuchman, *Making News: A Study in the Construction of Reality* (New York: Free Press, 1978), 122.

7. Herbert J. Gans, *Deciding What's News: A Study of CBS Evening News, NBC Nightly News, Newsweek, and Time* (New York: Vintage, 1979), 15.

8. Peter Simonson, "Mediated Sources of Public Confidence: Lazarsfeld and Merton Revisited," *Journal of Communication* 49, no. 2 (1999): 113, doi:10.1111/j.1460-2466.1999.tb02796 .x; John Durham Peters, "Historical Tensions in the Concept of Public Opinion," in *Public Opinion and the Communication of Consent*, ed. Theodore Glasser and Charles T. Salmon (New York: Guilford Press, 1995), 7.

9. Lazarsfeld and Merton, "Mass Communication, Popular Taste, and Organized Social Action," 233.

10. James B. Lemert, "Two Studies of Status Conferral," *Journalism and Mass Communication Quarterly* 43 (March 1966): 25–94; James B. Lemert and Karl J. Nestvold, "Television News and Status Conferral," *Journal of Broadcasting* 14, no. 4 (1970): 491–97; Simonson, "Mediated Sources of Public Confidence."

11. Thorstein Veblen, *The Theory of the Leisure Class*, new ed. (New York: Dover Publications, 1994).

12. Alain de Botton, *Status Anxiety* (New York: Pantheon Books, 2004), viii.

13. Since Veblen's classic *The Theory of the Leisure Class* (1899), many scholars have focused on consumer products as forms of status display, including Laurie Simon Bagwell and B. Douglas Bernheim, "Veblen Effects in a Theory of Conspicuous Consumption," *American Economic Review* 86, no. 3 (June 1996): 349, https://www0.gsb.columbia.edu/faculty/lhodrick/veblen%20effects.pdf. Many others have explored how different social practices can communicate status, such as Richard A. Peterson and Roger M. Kern, "Changing Highbrow Taste: From Snob to Omnivore," *American Sociological Review* 61, no. 5 (October 1, 1996): 900–907, https://www.jstor.org/stable/2096460.

14. Lazarsfeld and Merton, "Mass Communication, Popular Taste, and Organized Social Action," 233.

15. Interview by author, November 10, 2009.

16. Simonson, "Mediated Sources of Public Confidence."

17. Interview by author, November 29, 2010.

18. Carey, "A Cultural Approach to Communication."

19. Interview by author, October 18, 2010.

20. Carey, "A Cultural Approach to Communication."

21. Erving Goffman, *Stigma: Notes on the Management of Spoiled Identity* (New York: Simon & Schuster, 1986), 4, 17.

22. Interview by author, November 11, 2009.

23. Edward E. Jones et al., *Social Stigma: The Psychology of Marked Relationships* (New York: W. H. Freeman, 1984), 58.

24. Simonson, in "Mediated Sources of Public Confidence," argues that these factors, along with the copresence of celebrities, likely affect the degree of status conferred.

25. Interview by author, February 18, 2010.

26. Interview by author, November 2, 2009.

27. Jeffrey Rosen, "The Web Means the End of Forgetting," *New York Times Magazine*, July 21, 2010, http://www.nytimes.com/2010/07/25/magazine/25privacy-t2.html.

28. Interview by author, November 16, 2009.

29. Goffman, *Stigma*, 1, 5.

30. Erving Goffman, "Symbols of Class Status," *British Journal of Sociology* 2, no. 4 (December 1, 1951): 4, doi:10.2307/588083.

31. Jones et al., *Social Stigma*.

32. Ibid., 57.

33. Ibid., 44.

34. Ibid., 71; Goffman, *Stigma*, 30.

35. Solove, *The Future of Reputation*, 11.

36. Interviews by author, August 29 and May 4, 2010.

37. Interview by author, January 8, 2011. All quotes from Michelle are from this interview.

38. Jones et al., *Social Stigma*, 5.

39. Interview by author, May 21, 2010. All quotes from Helen are from this interview.

40. Interview by author, March 11, 2010.

41. Interview by author, December 17, 2010. All quotes from Beth are from this interview.

42. Goffman, *Stigma*, 4.

43. Philosopher Martha Nussbaum and legal scholar Daniel Solove make this observation about the disproportionality of shame punishments in general. Jacob Rowbottom makes the same argument specifically about shaming in the news. Martha C. Nussbaum, *Hiding from Humanity: Disgust, Shame, and the Law* (Princeton, N.J.: Princeton University Press, 2004), 234; Solove, *The Future of Reputation*, 95; Jacob Rowbottom, "To Punish, Inform, and Criticise: The Goals of Naming and Shaming," in *Media and Public Shaming*, ed. Julian Petley (London: I. B. Tauris, 2013), 1–18

44. Romayne Smith Fullerton and Maggie Jones Patterson, "Crime News and Privacy: Comparing Crime Reporting in Sweden, The Netherlands, and the United Kingdom," in Petley, *Media and Public Shaming*, 115–43.

45.   Rowbottom, "To Punish, Inform, and Criticise"; Lord Justice Leveson, "Leveson In-
      quiry: Culture, Practice and Ethics of the Press," November 29, 2012, http://www.official
      -documents.gov.uk/document/hc1213/hc07/0780/0780.asp.

46.   Smith Fullerton and Jones Patterson, "Crime News and Privacy."

47.   Jones et al., *Social Stigma*, 57.

8. MAKING THE NEWS IN A DIGITAL WORLD

1.   Interview by author, November 16, 2009.

2.   Danah Boyd, "Taken Out of Context: American Teen Sociality in Networked Publics"
      (Ph.D. diss., University of California, 2008), 27, http://www.danah.org/papers/TakenOu-
      tOfContext.pdf.

3.   On reading rooms, see Andrew Hobbs, "The Reading World of A Provincial Town: Preston,
      Lancashire 1855–1900," in *The History of Reading*, vol. 2: *Evidence from the British Isles,
      c. 1750–1950*, ed. K. Halsey and W. Owens (Basingstoke, England: Palgrave MacMillan, 2011),
      121–38. On mailing newspapers, see Michael Schudson, *The Good Citizen: A History of
      American Civic Life* (New York: Martin Kessler Books, 1999), 68; On sharing newspapers
      on the frontier to alleviate a sense of isolation, see William E. Huntzicker, "Historians and
      the American Frontier Press," *American Journalism* 5, no. 1 (1988): 30.

4.   The increasing importance of news sharing via social networks was already clear in 2011.
      See Kenneth Olmstead, Amy Mitchell, and Tom Rosenstiel, "Facebook Is Becoming In-
      creasingly Important," Pew Research Center Project for Excellence in Journalism, May 9,
      2011, http://www.journalism.org/analysis_report/facebook_becoming_increasingly_im-
      portant; Anne Sophie Kümpel, Veronika Karnowski, and Till Keyling, "News Sharing in
      Social Media: A Review of Current Research on News Sharing Users, Content, and Net-
      works," *Social Media+Society* (December 2015): 1–14, doi:10.1177/2056305115610141.

5.   Interview by author, March 10, 2010.

6.   Interview by author, May 21, 2010. All quotes from Helen are from this interview.

7.   Interview by author, September 20, 2010.

8.   Interview by author, March 5, 2010.

9.   Interview by author, November 12, 2009.

10.   Interview by author, November 9, 2009.

11.   Interview by author, May 3, 2010.

12.   Interview by author, May 3, 2010.

13.   Interview by author, June 18, 2010.

14.   Interview by author, May 25, 2010.

15.   Erving Goffman, *Stigma: Notes on the Management of Spoiled Identity* (New York: Simon &
      Schuster, 1986). Unless otherwise noted, my description of Goffman's conception of stigma
      is from this text.

16.   Ibid., 57.

17.   Here Goffman departs from Durkheim's more famous definition of "social fact" in Emile
      Durkheim, "What Is a Social Fact?," in *The Rules of Sociological Method*, trans. W. D. Halls
      (New York: Cambridge University Press, 1895), 50–84.

18. Interview by author, May 3, 2010.

19. Interview by author, March 10, 2010.

20. Interview by author, April 28, 2010.

21. Interview by author, November 9, 2009.

22. Interview by author, July 28, 2010.

23. Interview by author, November 2, 2009. All quotes from Mike are from this interview.

24. Nick Bilton, "Erasing the Digital Past," *New York Times*, April 1, 2011, http://www.nytimes.com/2011/04/03/fashion/03reputation.html.

25. Interview by author, March 11, 2010.

26. Interview by author, December 17, 2010. All quotes from Beth are from this interview.

27. Interview by author, February 18, 2010.

28. Amanda Lenhart et al., "Online Harassment, Digital Abuse, and Cyberstalking in America," Data and Society Research Institute and Center for Innovative Public Health Research, November 21, 2016, https://www.datasociety.net/pubs/oh/Online_Harassment_2016.pdf.

9. LESSONS FOR SUBJECTS AND JOURNALISTS

1. For example, Isabel Awad, "Journalists and Their Sources," *Journalism Studies* 7, no. 6 (December 1, 2006): 922–39, doi:10.1080/14616700600980702; Sandra L. Borden, "Empathic Listening: The Interviewer's Betrayal," *Journal of Mass Media Ethics* 8, no. 4 (December 1, 1993): 219–26, doi:10.1207/s15327728jmme0804_3; Fred Brown and SPJ Ethics Committee, *Journalism Ethics: A Casebook of Professional Conduct for News Media* (Portland, Ore.: Marion Street Press, 2011).

2. Rasmus Kleis Nielsen, "Folk Theories of Journalism," *Journalism Studies*, April 6, 2016, doi:10.1080/1461670X.2016.1165140.

3. C. W. Anderson, "Between Creative and Quantified Audiences: Web Metrics and Changing Patterns of Newswork in Local US Newsrooms," *Journalism* 12, no. 5 (July 1, 2011): 550–66, doi:10.1177/1464884911402451; Nikki Usher, *Making News at the New York Times* (Ann Arbor: University of Michigan Press, 2014).

4. Janet Malcolm, *The Journalist and the Murderer* (New York: Vintage, 1990).

5. Michael Schudson, "Four Approaches to the Sociology of News," in *Mass Media and Society*, ed. James Curran and Michael Gurevitch (London: Hodder Arnold, 2005), 172–97.

6. Interviews by author, November 5 and November 11, 2010.

7. For example, C. W. Anderson, "Journalism: Expertise, Authority, and Power in Democratic Life," in *The Media and Social Theory*, ed. David Hesmondhalgh and Jason Toynbee (New York: Routledge, 2008), 248–64; Matt Carlson, "Introduction: The Many Boundaries of Journalism," in *Boundaries of Journalism: Professionalism, Practices and Participation*, ed. Matt Carlson and Seth C. Lewis (New York: Routledge, 2015), 1–18.

8. This has been a consistent finding since the 1970s. See the introduction for more detail on this literature. The tug-of-war analogy is from Herbert J. Gans, *Deciding What's News: A Study of CBS Evening News, NBC Nightly News, Newsweek, and Time* (New York: Vintage, 1979), 117.

9. Brown and SPJ Ethics Committee, *Journalism Ethics*, 227.

10. In their work on how public interest groups and other organizations try to influence how crime news is reported, Ericson et al. found the same thing, noting, "As our research documents, from the perspective of sources the news media are very powerful, in possession of key resources that frequently give them the upper hand." Richard Ericson, Patricia M. Baranek, and Janet B. L. Chan, *Negotiating Control: A Study of News Sources* (Toronto: University of Toronto Press, 1989), 378.

11. Art Swift, "Americans' Trust in Mass Media Sinks to New Low," *Gallup.com*, September 14, 2016, http://www.gallup.com/poll/195542/americans-trust-mass-media-sinks-new-low .aspx.

12. Scholars trying to probe the reasons for declining trust usually find they have to go beyond polling. Ladd, for example developed a series of field experiments to probe the issue. See Jonathan M. Ladd, *Why Americans Hate the Media and How It Matters* (Princeton, N.J.: Princeton University Press, 2011). For an example of a qualitative study that takes a constructive approach, see Stephen Coleman, Scott Anthony, and David E. Morrison, "Public Trust in the News" (Oxford: Reuters Institute, 2009), http://reutersinstitute.politics.ox.ac .uk/publication/public-trust-news.

13. Brown and SPJ Ethics Committee, *Journalism Ethics*, 226.

14. Usher, *Making News at the New York Times*.

15. Interview by author, January 3, 2011.

16. Interview by author, January 8, 2011.

17. Jay Rosen, "He Said, She Said Journalism: Lame Formula in the Land of the Active User," *PressThink*, April 12, 2009, http://archive.pressthink.org/2009/04/12/hesaid_shesaid.html; Cristine Russell, "Climate Change: Now What?," *Columbia Journalism Review*, August 2008, http://www.cjr.org/feature/climate_change_now_what.php; Margaret Sullivan, "He Said, She Said, and the Truth," *New York Times*, September 15, 2012, http://www.nytimes.com/2012/09 /16/public-editor/16pubed.html.

18. Arthur S. Brisbane, "Should The Times Be a Truth Vigilante?," *Public Editor's Journal*, January 12, 2002, http://publiceditor.blogs.nytimes.com/2012/01/12/should-the-times-be-a -truth-vigilante/.

19. Michael A. Cohen, "Media Should Stop Treating Clinton and Trump as Equals," *Boston Globe*, September 14, 2016, https://www.bostonglobe.com/opinion/2016/09/14/media -should-stop-treating-clinton-and-trump-equals/e4qMIleYb56VY69T4VYAKL/story .html; Justin Peters, "Does the New York Times Have a False Balance Problem?," *Slate*, September 13, 2016, http://www.slate.com/articles/news_and_politics/culturebox/2016 /09/nyt_public_editor_says_false_balance_isn_t_a_problem_is_also_guilty_of_it.html; Liz Spayd, "The Truth About 'False Balance,'" *New York Times*, September 10, 2016, http: //www.nytimes.com/2016/09/11/public-editor/the-truth-about-false-balance.html.

20. Michael Barthel and Jeffrey Gottfried, "Majority of U.S. Adults Think News Media Should Not Add Interpretation to the Facts," *Pew Research Center*, November 18, 2016, http://www .pewresearch.org/fact-tank/2016/11/18/news-media-interpretation-vs-facts/.

21. Paul F. Lazarsfeld and Robert K. Merton, "Mass Communication, Popular Taste, and Organized Social Action," in *Mass Communication and American Social Thought: Key Texts, 1919–1968*, ed. John Durham Peters and Peter Simons (Lanham, Md.: Rowman & Littlefield, 2004), 230–41; Peter Simonson, "Mediated Sources of Public Confidence: Lazarsfeld

and Merton Revisited," *Journal of Communication* 49, no. 2 (1999): 109–22, doi:10.1111/j.1460 -2466.1999.tb02796.x.

22. Once more, the idea of communication as transmission and as ritual is from James W. Carey, "A Cultural Approach to Communication," in *Communication as Culture* (Boston: Unwin Hyman, 1988), 13–36.

23. Mary Anne Franks, "It's Time for Congress to Protect Intimate Privacy," *Huffington Post*, July 18, 2016, http://www.huffingtonpost.com/mary-anne-franks/revenge-porn-intimate -privacy-protection-act_b_11034998.html.

24. Amanda Lenhart et al., "Online Harassment, Digital Abuse, and Cyberstalking in America," Data and Society Research Institute and Center for Innovative Public Health Research, November 21, 2016, https://www.datasociety.net/pubs/oh/Online_Harassment_2016.pdf.

25. Society of Professional Journalists, "SPJ Code of Ethics," Society of Professional Journalists, 2014, http://www.spj.org/ethicscode.asp.

26. On naming people-of-interest in crimes, see Tom Jackman, "Naming a Murder Suspect Who Hasn't Been Charged: Should the Media Do It? Would You?," *Washington Post*, August 1, 2012, https://www.washingtonpost.com/blogs/the-state-of-nova/post/naming-a -murder-suspect-who-hasnt-been-charged-should-the-media-do-it-would-you/2012/08 /01/gJQAIipUOX_blog.html; Donna Shaw, "Dilemma of Interest," *American Journalism Review* (March 2006), http://ajrarchive.org/Article.asp?id=4042. For examples on controversies over revealing intimate details of private figures' lives, see Jana Kasperkevic, "Gawker's Top Editors Quit in Protest Over Removal of a Controversial Post," *Guardian*, July 20, 2015, sec. Media, http://www.theguardian.com/media/2015/jul/20/gawker-editors -quit-removed-post; Peter Thiel, "Peter Thiel: The Online Privacy Debate Won't End with Gawker," *New York Times*, August 15, 2016, http://www.nytimes.com/2016/08/16/opinion /peter-thiel-the-online-privacy-debate-wont-end-with-gawker.html.

27. Awad, "Journalists and Their Sources."

28. Quoted in Theodore Glasser, "Objectivity and News Bias," in *Philosophical Issues in Journalism*, ed. Elliot D. Cohen (New York: Oxford University Press, 1992), 176–85.

29. Awad, "Journalists and Their Sources"; Borden, "Empathic Listening."

30. Matthias Revers, "Journalistic Professionalism as Performance and Boundary Work: Source Relations at the State House," *Journalism* 15, no. 1 (2014): 37–52, doi:10.1177/1464884913480459.

31. Romayne Smith Fullerton and Maggie Jones Patterson, "Crime News and Privacy: Comparing Crime Reporting in Sweden, The Netherlands, and the United Kingdom," in *Media and Public Shaming*, ed. Julian Petley (London: I. B. Tauris, 2013), 115–43.

32. Stephen Coleman, *How Voters Feel* (Cambridge: Cambridge University Press, 2014), 4.

33. See Ladd for an overview of frequent explanations for anti-media sentiment. His study finds that elite antimedia rhetoric and tabloidization are especially strong contributing factors. Ladd, *Why Americans Hate the Media and How It Matters*.

34. Arlie Russell Hochschild, *Strangers in Their Own Land: Anger and Mourning on the American Right* (New York: New Press, 2016).

35. "In Presidential Contest, Voters Say 'Basic Facts,' Not Just Policies, Are in Dispute," U.S. Politics and Policy, *Pew Research Center*, October 14, 2016, http://www.people-press .org/2016/10/14/in-presidential-contest-voters-say-basic-facts-not-just-policies-are-in -dispute/.

36. Ricardo Bilton, "With Its First Community Reporter, the Texas Tribune Is Turning Texans Themselves Into Its Next Big Beat," *Nieman Lab*, November 28, 2016, http://www .niemanlab.org/2016/11/with-its-first-community-reporter-the-texas-tribune-is-turning -texans-themselves-into-its-next-big-beat/.

NOTE ON METHOD

1. "How News Happens," Pew Research Center's Project for Excellence in Journalism, January 11, 2010, http://www.journalism.org/analysis_report/how_news_happens.
2. Barney Glaser and Anselm Strauss, *The Discovery of Grounded Theory: Strategies for Qualitative Research* (Chicago: Aldine Transaction, 1999).
3. Ibid.
4. Sandra L. Borden, "Empathic Listening: The Interviewer's Betrayal," *Journal of Mass Media Ethics* 8, no. 4 (December 1, 1993): 219–26, doi:10.1207/s15327728jmme0804_3.
5. Martin Gottlieb, "Dangerous Liaisons: Journalists and Their Sources," *Columbia Journalism Review* 28, no. 2 (July 1989): 31.

BIBLIOGRAPHY

American Society of Newspaper Editors. "Newspaper Credibility: Building Reader Trust." Washington, D.C.: ASNE, 1984.

Anderson, C. W. "Between Creative and Quantified Audiences: Web Metrics and Changing Patterns of Newswork in Local US Newsrooms." *Journalism* 12, no. 5 (July 1, 2011): 550–66. doi:10.1177/1464884911402451.

——. "Journalism: Expertise, Authority, and Power in Democratic Life." In *The Media and Social Theory*, ed. David Hesmondhalgh and Jason Toynbee, 248–64. New York: Routledge, 2008.

——. *Rebuilding the News: Metropolitan Journalism in the Digital Age*. Philadelphia: Temple University Press, 2013.

Armstrong, Cory. "Story Genre Influences Whether Women Are Sources." *Newspaper Research Journal* 27, no. 3 (Summer 2006): 66–81.

"The Audience Turn in Journalism (Studies)." Panel presented at the International Communication Association, San Juan, Puerto Rico, May 22, 2015.

Awad, Isabel. "Journalists and Their Sources." *Journalism Studies* 7, no. 6 (December 1, 2006): 922–39. doi:10.1080/14616700600980702.

Bagwell, Laurie Simon, and B. Douglas Bernheim. "Veblen Effects in a Theory of Conspicuous Consumption." *American Economic Review* 86, no. 3 (June 1996): 349.

Barnhurst, Kevin G., and Diana Mutz. "American Journalism and the Decline in Event-Centered Reporting." *Journal of Communication* 47, no. 4 (December 1997): 27–52. doi:10.1111/j.1460-2466.1997.tb02724.x.

Barthel, Michael, and Jeffrey Gottfried. "Majority of U.S. Adults Think News Media Should Not Add Interpretation to the Facts." Pew Research Center, November 18, 2016. http://www.pewresearch.org/fact-tank/2016/11/18/news-media-interpretation-vs-facts/.

Barthes, Roland. *Camera Lucida: Reflections on Photography*. New York: Hill and Wang, 2010.

Berry, Fred. "A Study of Accuracy in Local News Stories of Three Dailies." *Journalism Quarterly* 44 (Autumn 1967): 482–90.

Bilton, Nick. "Erasing the Digital Past." *New York Times*, April 1, 2011. http://www.nytimes.com/2011/04/03/fashion/03reputation.html.

Bilton, Ricardo. "With Its First Community Reporter, the Texas Tribune Is Turning Texans Themselves Into Its Next Big Beat." *Nieman Lab*, November 28, 2016. http://www.nieman-lab.org/2016/11/with-its-first-community-reporter-the-texas-tribune-is-turning-texans-themselves-into-its-next-big-beat/.

Blankenburg, William. "News Accuracy: Some Findings on the Meaning of Errors." *Journal of Communication* 20 (December 1970): 375–86.

Borden, Sandra L. "Empathic Listening: The Interviewer's Betrayal." *Journal of Mass Media Ethics* 8, no. 4 (December 1, 1993): 219–26. doi:10.1207/s15327728jmme0804_3.

Boyd, Danah. "Taken Out of Context: American Teen Sociality in Networked Publics." Ph.D. dissertation, University of California, 2008. http://www.danah.org/papers/TakenOutOf-Context.pdf.

Brim, Orville G. *Look at Me!: The Fame Motive from Childhood to Death*. Ann Arbor: University of Michigan Press, 2009.

Brisbane, Arthur S. "Should the Times Be a Truth Vigilante?" *Public Editor's Journal*, January 12, 2002. http://publiceditor.blogs.nytimes.com/2012/01/12/should-the-times-be-a-truth-vigilante/.

Brown, Charles. "Majority of Readers Give Papers an 'A' for Accuracy." *Editor & Publisher* 63 (February 13, 1965).

Brown, Fred, and SPJ Ethics Committee. *Journalism Ethics: A Casebook of Professional Conduct for News Media*. Portland, Ore.: Marion Street Press, 2011.

Brown, Jane Delano, Carl R. Bybee, Stanley T. Wearden, and Dulcie Murdock Straughan. "Invisible Power: Newspaper News Sources and the Limits of Diversity." *Journalism Quarterly* 64, no. Spring (1987): 45–54. doi:10.1177/107769908706400106.

Burris, Larry L. "Accuracy of News Magazines as Perceived by News Sources." *Journalism Quarterly* 62 (Winter 1985): 825–27.

Calogero, Rachel M, Stacey Tantleff-Dunn, and J. Kevin Thompson. "Objectification Theory: An Introduction." In *Self-Objectification in Women: Causes, Consequences, and Counteractions*. Washington, D.C.: American Psychological Association, 2011.

Carey, James W. "A Cultural Approach to Communication." In *Communication as Culture*, 13–36. Boston: Unwin Hyman, 1988.

Carlson, Matt. "Introduction: The Many Boundaries of Journalism." In *Boundaries of Journalism: Professionalism, Practices and Participation*, ed. Matt Carlson and Seth C. Lewis, 1–18. New York: Routledge, 2015.

——. "Sources as News Producers." In *The SAGE Handbook of Digital Journalism*, ed. Tamara Witschge, C. W. Anderson, David Domingo, and Alfred Hermida, 236–49. Los Angeles: Sage Publications, 2016.

Carlson, Matt, and Seth C. Lewis, eds. *Boundaries of Journalism: Professionalism, Practices and Participation*. New York: Routledge, 2015.

Charnley, Mitchell. "A Study of Newspaper Accuracy." *Journalism Quarterly* 13, no. 4 (December 1, 1936): 394.

Cohen, Michael A. "Media Should Stop Treating Clinton and Trump as Equals." *Boston Globe*, September 14, 2016. https://www.bostonglobe.com/opinion/2016/09/14/media-should-stop-treating-clinton-and-trump-equals/e4qMIleYb56VY69T4VYAKL/story.html.

Coleman, Stephen. *How Voters Feel*. Cambridge: Cambridge University Press, 2014.

Coleman, Stephen, Scott Anthony, and David E. Morrison. *Public Trust in the News*. Oxford: Reuters Institute, 2009. https://reutersinstitute.politics.ox.ac.uk/sites/default/files/Public%20Trust%20in%20the%20News%20A%20Constructivist%20Study%20of%20the%20Social%20Life%20of%20the%20News_0.pdf.

Cooley, Charles Horton. *Human Nature and the Social Order*. New York: Schocken Books, 1964.

Costera Meijer, Irene. "Practicing Audience-Centred Journalism Research." In *The SAGE Handbook of Digital Journalism*, ed. Tamara Witschge, C. W. Anderson, David Domingo, and Alfred Hermida, 546–61. Los Angeles: Sage Publications, 2016.

Cote, J. Richard. "A Study of Accuracy of Two Wire Services." *Journalism Quarterly* 47 (Winter 1970): 661–66.

De Botton, Alain. *Status Anxiety*. New York: Pantheon Books, 2004.

Detel, Hanne. "Disclosure and Public Shaming in the Age of New Visibility." In *Media and Public Shaming*, ed. Julian Petley, 77–96. London: I. B. Tauris, 2013.

Durkheim, Emile. "What Is a Social Fact?" In *The Rules of Sociological Method*, trans. W. D. Halls, 50–84. New York: Cambridge University Press, 1895.

Ericson, Richard, Patricia M. Baranek, and Janet B. L. Chan. *Negotiating Control: A Study of News Sources*. Toronto: University of Toronto Press, 1989.

Featherstone, Mike. *Consumer Culture and Postmodernism*. Newbury Park, Calif.: Sage, 1991.

Fishman, Mark. *Manufacturing the News*. Austin: University of Texas Press, 1988.

Forde, Kathy Roberts. "Discovering the Explanatory Report in American Newspapers." *Journalism Practice* 1, no. 2 (June 2007): 227–44. doi:10.1080/17512780701275531.

Franks, Mary Anne. "It's Time for Congress to Protect Intimate Privacy." *Huffington Post*, July 18, 2016. http://www.huffingtonpost.com/mary-anne-franks/revenge-porn-intimate-privacy-protection-act_b_11034998.html.

Freud, Sigmund. "The 'Uncanny.'" In *The Standard Edition of the Complete Psychological Works of Sigmund Freud, Volume XVII (1917–1919): An Infantile Neurosis and Other Works*, 217–56, 1919.

"From the Editors; the Times and Wen Ho Lee." *New York Times*, September 26, 2000. http://www.nytimes.com/2000/09/26/us/from-the-editors-the-times-and-wen-ho-lee.html.

Furnham, Adrian. *Lay Theories: Everyday Understanding of Problems in the Social Sciences*, ed. Michael Argyle. Oxford: Pergamon, 1988.

Gamson, Joshua. *Freaks Talk Back: Tabloid Talk Shows and Sexual Nonconformity*. Chicago: University of Chicago Press, 1998.

Gans, Herbert J. *Deciding What's News: A Study of CBS Evening News, NBC Nightly News, Newsweek, and Time*. New York: Vintage Books, 1979.

Giles, David. *Illusions of Immortality: A Psychology of Fame and Celebrity*. New York: St. Martin's Press, 2000.

Gitlin, Todd. *Media Unlimited: How the Torrent of Images and Sounds Overwhelms Our Lives*. New York: Henry Holt, 2007.

——. *The Whole World Is Watching: Mass Media in the Making & Unmaking of the New Left*. Berkeley: University of California Press, 1980.

Glaser, Barney, and Anselm Strauss. *The Discovery of Grounded Theory: Strategies for Qualitative Research*. Chicago: Aldine Transaction, 1999.

Glasser, Theodore. "Objectivity and News Bias." In *Philosophical Issues in Journalism*, ed. Elliot D. Cohen, 176–85. New York: Oxford University Press, 1992.

Goffman, Erving. *Frame Analysis: An Essay on the Organization of Experience*. Cambridge, Mass: Harvard University Press, 1974.

——. *Interaction Ritual: Essays on Face-to-Face Behavior*. New York: Pantheon Books, 1967.

——. "On Face-Work." In *Interaction Ritual*, 5–45. New York: Pantheon Books, 1967.

——. *Stigma: Notes on the Management of Spoiled Identity*. New York: Simon & Schuster, 1986.

——. "Symbols of Class Status." *British Journal of Sociology* 2, no. 4 (December 1, 1951): 294–304. doi:10.2307/588083.

Gottlieb, Martin. "Dangerous Liaisons: Journalists and Their Sources." *Columbia Journalism Review* 28, no. 2 (July 1989): 21–35.

Grindstaff, Laura. *The Money Shot: Trash, Class, and the Making of TV Talk Shows*. Chicago: University of Chicago Press, 2002. http://www.press.uchicago.edu/ucp/books/book/chicago/M/bo3630693.html.

——. "Self-Serve Celebrity: The Production of Ordinariness and the Ordinariness of Production in Reality Television." In *Production Studies: Cultural Studies of Media Industries*, ed. Vicki Mayer, Miranda Banks, and John Thornton Caldwell, 71–86. New York: Routledge, 2009.

Hallin, Daniel C. "Soundbite News: Television Coverage of Elections, 1968–88." In *We Keep America on Top of the World*, 133–52. New York: Routledge, 1993.

——. *The Uncensored War: The Media and Vietnam*. Berkeley: University of California Press, 1989.

Hallin, Daniel C., Robert Karl Manoff, and Judy K. Weddle. "Sourcing Patterns of National Security Reporters." *Journalism Quarterly* 70, no. 4 (Winter 1993): 753–66. doi:10.1177/107769909307000402.

Hanson, Gary, and Stanley T. Wearden. "Measuring Newscast Accuracy: Applying a Newspaper Model to Television." *Journalism and Mass Communication Quarterly* 81, no. 3 (Autumn 2004): 546–58. doi:10.1177/107769900408100306.

Harter, Susan. "Developmental Perspectives on the Self-System." In *Handbook of Child Psychology: Socialization, Personality, and Social Development*, ed. E. M. Hetherington, 4th ed., 4:278–385. New York: Wiley, 1983.

Herbst, Susan. *Reading Public Opinion: How Political Actors View the Democratic Process*. Chicago: University of Chicago Press, 1998.

Hess, Stephen. "Washington Reporters." *Society* 184 (1981): 55–66.

Hobbs, Andrew. "The Reading Life of a Provincial Town: Preston, Lancashire 1855–1900." In *The History of Reading*, Volume 2: *Evidence from the British Isles, c.1750–1950*, ed. K. Halsey and W. Owens, 121–38. Basingstoke, England: Palgrave Macmillan, 2011.

Hochschild, Arlie Russell. *Strangers in Their Own Land: Anger and Mourning on the American Right*. New York: New Press, 2016.

"How News Happens." Pew Research Center's Project for Excellence in Journalism, January 11, 2010. http://www.journalism.org/analysis_report/how_news_happens.

Howell, William Smilley. *The Empathic Communicator*. Prospect Heights, Ill.: Waveland Press, 1986.

Huntzicker, William E. "Historians and the American Frontier Press." *American Journalism* 5, no. 1 (1988): 28–45.

"In Presidential Contest, Voters Say 'Basic Facts,' Not Just Policies, Are in Dispute." U.S. Politics and Policy. Pew Research Center, October 14, 2016. http://www.people-press.org /2016/10/14/in-presidential-contest-voters-say-basic-facts-not-just-policies-are-in -dispute/.

Jackman, Tom. "Naming a Murder Suspect Who Hasn't Been Charged: Should the Media Do It? Would You?" *Washington Post*, August 1, 2012. https://www.washingtonpost.com/blogs /the-state-of-nova/post/naming-a-murder-suspect-who-hasnt-been-charged-should-the -media-do-it-would-you/2012/08/01/gJQAIipUOX_blog.html.

Jones, Edward E., Amerigo Farina, Albert H. Hastorf, Hazel Markus, Dale T. Miller, and Robert A. Scott. *Social Stigma: The Psychology of Marked Relationships*. New York: W. H. Freeman, 1984.

Kasperkevic, Jana. "Gawker's Top Editors Quit in Protest over Removal of a Controversial Post." *Guardian*, July 20, 2015, sec. Media. http://www.theguardian.com/media/2015/jul/20 /gawker-editors-quit-removed-post.

Kinsley, Michael. "Speaking Candidly, Journalists Are Truly Snakes." *Bloomberg*, November 4, 2011. http://www.bloomberg.com/news/2011-11-04/speaking-candidly-journalists-are-truly -snakes-michael-kinsley.html.

Kümpel, Anne Sophie, Veronika Karnowski, and Till Keyling. "News Sharing in Social Media: A Review of Current Research on News Sharing Users, Content, and Networks." *Social Media+Society*, December 2015, 1–14. doi:10.1177/2056305115610141.

Ladd, Jonathan M. *Why Americans Hate the Media and How It Matters*. Princeton, N.J.: Princeton University Press, 2011.

Lazarsfeld, Paul F., and Robert K. Merton. "Mass Communication, Popular Taste, and Organized Social Action." In *Mass Communication and American Social Thought: Key Texts, 1919–1968*, ed. John Durham Peters and Peter Simons, 230–41. Lanham, Md.: Rowman & Littlefield, 2004.

Lemert, James B. "Two Studies of Status Conferral." *Journalism and Mass Communication Quarterly* 43 (March 1966): 25–94.

Lemert, James B., and Karl J. Nestvold. "Television News and Status Conferral." *Journal of Broadcasting* 14, no. 4 (1970): 491–97.

Lenhart, Amanda, Michele Ybarra, Kathryn Zickuhr, and Myeshia Price-Feeney. "Online Harassment, Digital Abuse, and Cyberstalking in America." Data and Society Research Institute and Center for Innovative Public Health Research, November 21, 2016. https://www. datasociety.net/pubs/oh/Online_Harassment_2016.pdf.

Leveson, Lord Justice. "Leveson Inquiry: Culture, Practice and Ethics of the Press." London: United Kingdom, November 29, 2012. http://www.official-documents.gov.uk/document /hc1213/hc07/0780/0780.asp.

Lopez, German. "The Daily Beast Tried to Prove Olympians Like Sex, but Instead May Have Outed Gay Athletes." *Vox*, August 12, 2016. http://www.vox.com/2016/8/11/12440186/daily -beast-olympics-gay.

Luker, Kristin. *Salsa Dancing Into the Social Sciences*. Cambridge, Mass.: Harvard University Press, 2010.

Luljak, Tom. "The Routine Nature of Journalistic Deception." In *Holding the Media Accountable*, ed. David Pritchard, 11–26. Bloomington: Indiana University Press, 2000.

Madianou, Mirca. "Audience Reception and News in Everyday Life." In *The Handbook of Journalism Studies*, ed. Karin Wahl-Jorgensenn and Thomas Hanitzsch, 325–37. New York: Routledge, 2008.

Maier, Scott. "Accuracy Matters: A Cross-Market Assessment of Newspaper Error and Credibility." *Journalism and Mass Communication Quarterly* 82, no. 3 (Autumn 2005): 533–51. doi:10.1177/107769900508200304.

——. "Getting It Right? Not in 59 Percent of Stories." *Newspaper Research Journal* 23 (Winter 2002): 10–24.

——. "How Sources, Reporters View Math Errors in News." *Newspaper Research Journal* 24, no. 4 (2003): 48–63.

——. "Setting the Record Straight: When the Press Errs, Do Corrections Follow?" Paper presented at the International Communication Association Conference, Dresden, Germany, 2006.

Malcolm, Janet. *The Journalist and the Murderer*. New York: Vintage Books, 1990.

Marshall, Hal. "Newspaper Accuracy in Tucson." *Journalism Quarterly* 54, no. 1 (1977): 165–68.

Marwick, Alice E., and Danah Boyd. "I Tweet Honestly, I Tweet Passionately: Twitter Users, Context Collapse, and the Imagined Audience." *New Media & Society*, July 7, 2010. doi:10.1177/1461444810365313.

Mencher, Melvin. *Melvin Mencher's News Reporting and Writing*. 10th ed. Boston: McGraw-Hill, 2006.

Meyer, Philip. "A Workable Measure of Auditing Accuracy in Newspapers." *Newspaper Research Journal* 10 (Winter 1988): 39–51.

——. *The Vanishing Newspaper: Saving Journalism in the Information Age*. Columbia: University of Missouri Press, 2009.

Meyrowitz, Joshua. *No Sense of Place*. New York: Oxford University Press, 1985.

Nielsen, Rasmus Kleis. "Folk Theories of Journalism." *Journalism Studies*, April 6, 2016. doi:10.1080/1461670X.2016.1165140.

Nord, David Paul. *Communities of Journalism: A History of American Newspapers and Their Readers*. Urbana: University of Illinois Press, 2006.

Nussbaum, Martha C. *Hiding from Humanity: Disgust, Shame, and the Law*. Princeton, N.J.: Princeton University Press, 2004.

Olmstead, Kenneth, Amy Mitchell, and Tom Rosenstiel. "Facebook Is Becoming Increasingly Important." Pew Research Center Project for Excellence in Journalism, May 9, 2011. http://www.journalism.org/analysis_report/facebook_becoming_increasingly_important.

Palmer, Ruth. "Context Matters: What News Subjects Can Tell Us About Accuracy and Error." *Journalism Studies* 13, no. 6 (December 2012): 1–16. doi:10.1080/1461670X.2011.644457.

——. "The Journalist and the Murderer Revisited: What Interviews with Journalism Subjects Reveal About a Modern Classic." *Journalism*, March 11, 2016. doi:10.1177/1464884916636125.

Peters, John Durham. "Historical Tensions in the Concept of Public Opinion." In *Public Opinion and the Communication of Consent*, ed. Theodore Glasser and Charles T. Salmon, 3–32. New York: Guilford Press, 1995.

Peters, Justin. "Does the New York Times Have a False Balance Problem?" *Slate*, September 13, 2016. http://www.slate.com/articles/news_and_politics/culturebox/2016/09/nyt_public_ed itor_says_false_balance_isn_t_a_problem_is_also_guilty_of_it.html.

Peterson, Richard A., and Roger M. Kern. "Changing Highbrow Taste: From Snob to Omnivore." *American Sociological Review* 61, no. 5 (October 1, 1996): 900–907.

Petley, Julian. *Media and Public Shaming: Drawing the Boundaries of Disclosure*. London: I. B. Tauris, 2013. http://reutersinstitute.politics.ox.ac.uk/publication/media-and-public-shaming.

Prendergast, Christopher. *The Triangle of Representation*. New York: Columbia University Press, 2000.

"Press Widely Criticized, but Trusted More than Other Information Sources." Pew Research Center for the People and the Press, September 22, 2011. http://www.people-press.org/2011/09/22/press-widely-criticized-but-trusted-more-than-other-institutions/.

Pritchard, David. "Why Unhappy Subjects of News Coverage Rarely Complain." In *Holding the Media Accountable*, ed. David Pritchard. Bloomington: Indiana University Press, 2000.

Revers, Matthias. "Journalistic Professionalism as Performance and Boundary Work: Source Relations at the State House." *Journalism* 15, no. 1 (2014): 37–52. doi:10.1177/1464884913480459.

Rosen, Jay. "He Said, She Said Journalism: Lame Formula in the Land of the Active User." *PressThink*, April 12, 2009. http://archive.pressthink.org/2009/04/12/hesaid_shesaid.html.

——. "The People Formerly Known as the Audience." *Pressthink*, June 27, 2006. http://archive.pressthink.org/2006/06/27/ppl_frmr.html.

Rosen, Jeffrey. "The Web Means the End of Forgetting." *New York Times*, July 21, 2010. http://www.nytimes.com/2010/07/25/magazine/25privacy-t2.html.

Rosenberg, Alyssa. "Gawker's Relaunch and the Role of Niceness in Journalism." *Washington Post*, July 27, 2015. https://www.washingtonpost.com/news/act-four/wp/2015/07/27/gawkers-relaunch-and-the-role-of-niceness-in-journalism/.

Rowbottom, Jacob. "To Punish, Inform, and Criticise: The Goals of Naming and Shaming." In *Media and Public Shaming*, ed. Julian Petley, 1–18. London: I. B. Tauris, 2013.

Russell, Cristine. "Climate Change: Now What?" *Columbia Journalism Review*, August 2008. http://www.cjr.org/feature/climate_change_now_what.php.

Ryfe, David M. *Can Journalism Survive?: An Inside Look at American Newsrooms*. Cambridge: Polity, 2012.

Schudson, Michael. "Four Approaches to the Sociology of News." In *Mass Media and Society*, ed. James Curran and Michael Gurevitch, 172–97. London: Hodder Arnold, 2005.

——. *The Good Citizen: A History of American Civic Life*. New York: Martin Kessler Books, 1999.

Schudson, Michael, and Katherine Fink. "The Rise of Contextual Journalism, 1950s–2000s." *Journalism* 15, no. 1 (2014): 3–20. doi:10.1177/1464884913479015.

Shafer, Jack. "Unsolicited Advice for Future Subjects of Magazine Profiles." *Slate*, June 23, 2010. http://www.slate.com/articles/news_and_politics/press_box/2010/06/unsolicited_advice_for_future_subjects_of_magazine_profiles.html.

Shaw, Donna. "Dilemma of Interest." *American Journalism Review*, March 2006. http://ajrarchive.org/Article.asp?id=4042.

Sigal, Leon V. *Reporters and Officials: The Organization and Politics of Newsmaking*. Lexington, Mass: D. C. Heath, 1973.

Simonson, Peter. "Mediated Sources of Public Confidence: Lazarsfeld and Merton Revisited." *Journal of Communication* 49, no. 2 (1999): 109–22. doi:10.1111/j.1460-2466.1999.tb02796.x.

Smith Fullerton, Romayne, and Maggie Jones Patterson. "Crime News and Privacy: Comparing Crime Reporting in Sweden, the Netherlands, and the United Kingdom." In *Media and Public Shaming*, ed. Julian Petley, 115–43. London: I. B. Tauris, 2013.

Society of Professional Journalists. "SPJ Code of Ethics." Society of Professional Journalists, 2014. http://www.spj.org/ethicscode.asp.

Solove, Daniel J. *The Future of Reputation: Gossip, Rumor, and Privacy on the Internet*. New Haven, Conn: Yale University Press, 2007.

Sontag, Susan. *On Photography*. New York: Picador, 2001.

Spayd, Liz. "The Truth About 'False Balance.'" *New York Times*, September 10, 2016. http://www.nytimes.com/2016/09/11/public-editor/the-truth-about-false-balance.html.

Sullivan, Margaret. "He Said, She Said, and the Truth." *New York Times*, September 15, 2012. http://www.nytimes.com/2012/09/16/public-editor/16pubed.html.

Swidler, Ann. *Talk of Love: How Culture Matters*. Chicago: University of Chicago Press, 2001.

Swift, Art. "Americans' Trust in Mass Media Sinks to New Low." *Gallup.com*, September 14, 2016. http://www.gallup.com/poll/195542/americans-trust-mass-media-sinks-new-low.aspx.

Thiel, Peter. "Peter Thiel: The Online Privacy Debate Won't End with Gawker." *New York Times*, August 15, 2016. http://www.nytimes.com/2016/08/16/opinion/peter-thiel-the-online-privacy-debate-wont-end-with-gawker.html.

Tillinghast, William A. "Newspaper Errors: Reporters Dispute Most Source Claims." *Newspaper Research Journal* 3 (Fall 1982): 14–23.

——. "Source Control and Evaluation of Newspaper Inaccuracies." *Newspaper Research Journal* 3 (Fall 1982): 14–23.

Tuchman, Gaye. *Making News: A Study in the Construction of Reality*. New York: Free Press, 1978.

Turow, Joseph. "Audience Construction and Culture Production: Marketing Surveillance in the Digital Age." *ANNALS of the American Academy of Political and Social Science* 597, no. 1 (January 1, 2005): 103–21. doi:10.1177/0002716204270469.

Urban, Christine. "Examining Our Credibility: Perspectives of the Public and the Press." Washington: ASNE, 1999. http://asne.org/kiosk/reports/99reports/1999examiningour-credibility/.

Usher, Nikki. *Making News at the New York Times*. Ann Arbor: University of Michigan Press, 2014.

Veblen, Thorstein. *The Theory of the Leisure Class*. Reprints of Economic Classics. New York: A. M. Kelley, 1975.

——. *The Theory of the Leisure Class*. New edition. Dover Publications, 1994.

Wilkerson, Isabel. "Interviewing Sources." *Nieman Reports* 56, no. 1 (Spring 2002): 16.

Wouters, Cas. "Etiquette Books and Emotion Management of in the 20th Century: Part One: The Integration of Social Classes." *Journal of Social History* 29, no. 1 (1995): 107–24.

Zoch, Lynn, and Judy Turk. "Women Making News: Gender as a Variable in Source Selection and Use." *Journalism and Mass Communication Quarterly* 75, no. 4 (Winter 1998): 762. doi:10.1177/107769909807500410.

INDEX

abuse: cyber-, 14–17, 149, 212; journalist's potential for, 21, 103–4, 201–3, 214; news production potential for, 213; protection from abusive comments, 180

accuracy assessment: context of, 108–9; criteria for, 105; expectations affecting, 111–12; feedback affecting, 112 14; holistic accuracy and, 211–12; interviewees' versus news industry's perception of, 114–15; quantifying errors to understand, 106–8; triggers and goals affecting, 28, 58, 109–11. *See also* error perception; inaccuracy, news story

activist, 177, 179; highly invested in news article, 204–5; on mission to inform public, 29–30; wary of story framing, 63–64, 73–74

ad hominem attacks, 16–17

antimedia rhetoric, 213–15, 241*n*33

audience: blogs' limited, 9, 30; conferring status or stigma, 149–50; creating, sharing, and commenting, 15–16, 173–74, 178–82, 238*n*4; email feedback from, 113–14, 154; Facebook, 138, 153–54, 164–65, 173–75, 177, 186; -focused community outreach, 216–17; news subject's goals and, 149; shaming, terrorizing by, 16–17, 169–71, 237*n*43; social media, 173–75; strangers as, 175–77; studies on, 3, 15–16, 195, 219–20, 221–23; targeted, 187–89; turn, 15; Twitter, 134, 173–74, 182; unrestrained personal attacks from, 177. *See also* harassment

audience studies, 3, 15–16, 219–20; sample biases and lacunae in, 195, 221–23

audience turn, 15

Barthes, Roland, 19, 129–31, 143

behavioral cues, journalist's, 5, 80

behavioral deviance: media's role in amplifying stigma, 150–52; as newsworthy, 16; nuanced reporting about, 170–71; stigma conferral and, 161–63, 166–69, 191; stigma conferral examples, 166–69

betrayal: con artist metaphor for, 49, 73; as exception not rule, 102–3, 203; *The Journalist and the Murderer* on, 1, 12, 49, 76, 90–92, 103, 196, 203; of news subject's expectations, 91–93; as perceived by interviewee, 19; timing and intent as key to, 202–4